Also by Carlean Johnson

Six Ingredients or Less **Chicken**

Six Ingredients or Less **Families on the Go**

Six Ingredients or Less **Light & Healthy**

Six Ingredients or Less **Pasta & Casseroles**

Six Ingredients or Less **Slow Cooker**

Also by Linda Hazen and Carlean Johnson

Six Ingredients or Less **Low-Carb**

Six Ingredients or Less **Diabetic**

Hazen & Johnson

Six
ingredients
or less®

Linda Hazen

Carlean Johnson

CJ
Books
Washington

Six Ingredients or Less, 4th Edition

Original cover design: CarrotStick Marketing

Original interior layout design: JAE Design

Edition graphics and interior layout: Night Owl Graphics

Printed in the United States of America

Library of Congress Catalog Card Number: 2011907021
ISBN 978-0-942878-10-3

CJ Books
PO Box 339
Moyie Springs, ID 83845

www.sixingredientsorless.com
facebook/sixingredientsorless
email: info@sixingredientsorless.com

Dedication

This book is dedicated to my husband Joe. When it comes to
writing cookbooks and carrying the torch my mother held so well,
he is my personal cheerleader, confidant, supporter, encourager
and beloved. Thank you, Joe, for your gentle nudges.
Linda

Acknowledgments

After almost 30 years, and millions of Six Ingredients or Less books sold, I am honored to thank so many people along the way that have brought us to this fourth edition of the original Six Ingredients or Less.

First, and foremost, my mother Carlean Johnson, who worked tirelessly since 1980 developing the Six Ingredients or Less series. She was a pioneer and the very first person to come up with the "less ingredients" concept. She always strove to develop quick, delicious recipes with ingredients you'll have on-hand. I hope to carry her torch well.

I also want to continually thank my dear friend and assistant Deepa Paranjapye for her diligence to work, learn and be available when I could not. Deepa is truly my right hand.

To Wendy Amundson who came on at the last minute to quickly design the interior and tweak the exterior. She has been a life saver.

And last, but not least, to my family who anxiously awaits each new book and hopefully asks "are you testing recipes today?"

Linda Hazen, 2011

Table of Contents

Introduction

This is the cookbook for the cook who never has enough time. Time or lack of it, is a problem for many of us. Yet there is a concern about feeding our family well and selecting foods that are quick and nutritious as well as pleasing to everyone. This is a collection of recipes designed for the busy person who wants to serve tasty dishes with a minimum of time and effort. Included are basic recipes for everyday cooking as well as those for special occasions and holiday entertaining. Not only will these recipes save you time, but hopefully money as well.

With our ever-changing lifestyles, we do not have time to spend long hours in the kitchen planning meals from lengthy and complicated recipes. You need to get in and out of the kitchen fast and yet have recipes than can be a gourmet's delight or just a simple everyday meal. Our recipes use basic foods you normally have on hand. You don't have a lot of time to spend in the kitchen. SIX INGREDIENTS OR LESS is a one of a kind cookbook that you will enjoy even if you are not in a hurry.

We are proud to introduce the 4th edition of SIX INGREDIENTS OR LESS. Recipes have been updated. Favorite time-tested recipes have remained and new recipes have been added. Every kitchen needs a book that belongs out on the counter where it can become worn with frequent use. This is that type of cookbook. It was written to be used daily for most of your cooking needs. Add your own personal touches and who would guess you hadn't spent all day in the kitchen. Cooking needn't be a chore and can be fun. Let others help in the preparation and time in the kitchen can be kept to a minimum.

These recipes are enjoyed in my kitchen and they can be enjoyed in yours.

Happy Cooking!
Carlean Johnson
Linda Hazen
Gig Harbor, Washington.

appetizers & beverages

Savory Italian Hot Poppers

24 servings

A quick disappearing appetizer that can be made ahead, refrigerated and broiled or grilled just before serving.

20	to 24 jalapeño peppers
1	pound ground chicken
1	(0.7-oz) package Italian seasoning mix
1	(8-oz) package cream cheese
20	to 24 slices (approx. 1-lb) bacon

Wear gloves. Wash peppers, remove stems and slice along one side from stem end to tip. Remove seeds and membranes.

In a medium skillet, brown chicken until done. Remove from heat. Add seasoning mix and cream cheese; mix thoroughly. Spoon a small amount of mixture into each pepper. Wrap each pepper with a slice of bacon and place on sprayed broiling pan with bacon ends on bottom.

Broil about 5 minutes, turning ¼ turn and broil another 5 minutes. Continue turning and broiling until all sides of bacon are crisp.

Per pepper: Cal 100, Carb 1g, Fib 0g, Pro 6g, Fat 8g, Sod 242mg, Sug 0g

Spanakopitta

15 servings

½	cup chopped onion
1	(10-oz) package frozen spinach
1	large egg
½	cup cream
2	cups (8-oz) crumbled Feta cheese
1	(16-oz) package phyllo dough

Preheat oven to 350°F. In a sprayed skillet, sauté onions until soft. Add spinach, cook for about 10 minutes; cool.

In a bowl, mix together spinach mixture, egg, cream, Feta cheese and salt and pepper to taste. In a sprayed 13x9-inch baking dish, lay a sheet of phyllo dough, spray with cooking spray. Repeat layering 5 more sheets and spraying each one.

Spread half the filling evenly over phyllo. Repeat with 6 more layers of phyllo, then filling, then 6 more layers of phyllo, spraying each layer. With sharp knife cut into squares. Bake for 50 to 55 minutes or until top is golden brown.

note: For a richer pie, use butter instead of cooking spray.

Per serving: Cal 139, Carb 13g, Fib 1g, Pro 5g, Fat 8g, Sod 288mg, Sug 1g

Sweet & Spicy Chicken Meatballs 16 servings

These meatballs are delicious on their own, but if desired, you can serve with a bowl of chili sauce for dipping.

- 1 **pound ground chicken**
- 1 **cup dried breadcrumbs**
- ½ **cup finely diced green onion**
- ½ **cup finely diced cilantro**
- 5 **tablespoons sweet chili sauce**
- 2 **tablespoons lemon juice**

In a large bowl, mix together all ingredients. Add salt and pepper to taste. Form mixture into evenly shaped balls.

In a large skillet (using butter, oil or spray) panfry meatballs in batches until well browned all over and cooked thoroughly. Serve warm with toothpicks.

note: To help prevent mixture from sticking to hand when making burgers or meatballs, first dampen hands with water.

Per meatball: Cal 139, Carb 3g, Fib 0g, Pro 3g, Fat 1g, Sod 95mg, Sug 1g

Chicken Kabobs 6 servings

No need to go to a restaurant to enjoy this dish- you can easily make it yourself.

- 2 **to 3 chicken breasts, skinned, boned**
- 1 **teaspoon lemon juice**
- ⅓ **cup grated onion**
- 1 **teaspoon paprika**
- 1 **teaspoon curry powder**

Cut chicken into 1-inch cubes. Combine remaining ingredients in a bowl. Add salt and pepper to taste. Toss chicken in the mixture and marinate at least 2 hours. Place chicken on skewers and broil or grill for 7 to 10 minutes or until done, turning once.

Serve with peanut dipping sauce on page 304.

Per Serving Cal 87, Carb 1g, Fib 0g, Pro 15g, Fat 2g, Sod 85mg, Sug 0g

Sweet and Sour Wrap-Ups   about 4 dozen

These go fast. You can prepare the bacon and water chestnuts ahead; cover and refrigerate. Mix sauce, cover, and set aside. Canned water chestnuts seem to be getting smaller. You may want to open the cans ahead and check, especially if you are serving a crowd.

- **1   pound lean bacon**
- **2   (8-oz each) cans water chestnuts**
- **1½   cups ketchup**
- **⅔   cup sugar**
- **¼   cup fresh lemon juice**

Preheat Oven to 375°F. Cut bacon crosswise into thirds. Cut small water chestnuts in half or larger ones into thirds. Wrap 1 piece of bacon around each water chestnut. Secure with wooden toothpicks. Place in 13x9-inch baking dish and bake 30 minutes or until bacon is crisp. Drain off fat.

Combine remaining ingredients; pour over bacon. Reduce heat to 325° and bake 20 to 30 minutes, basting once or twice. Serve hot.

Per wrap: Cal 29, Carb 3g, Fib 0g, Pro 1g, Fat 1g, Sod 114mg, Sug 2g

Teriyaki Chicken Wings   8 servings of 2 each

A richly glazed appetizer that can also be served as a main dish. I like to marinate meat & poultry in a large zip type bag. This way, you can simply flip the bag over a few times instead of having to turn each piece.

- **16   chicken drumettes (meaty leg portion)**
- **¼   cup light soy sauce**
- **¾   cup firmly packed brown sugar**
- **1   tablespoon honey**
- **4   thin slices fresh ginger**
- **1   green onion, cut into 1-inch pieces**

Preheat oven to 350°F. Rinse drumettes and pat dry. In a medium bowl, combine remaining ingredients, stirring to dissolve the sugar. Add chicken; cover and chill at least 3 hours, turning occasionally.

Place chicken, in one layer, on a foil-lined shallow baking pan. Bake 30 to 35 minutes, or until cooked through, basting frequently.

Per 2 wings: Cal 394, Carb 11g, Fib 0g, Pro 29g, Fat 25g, Sod 343mg, Sug 11g

Tortilla Appetizers

40 appetizers

A nice make-ahead appetizer.

- **2** **(8-oz) packages cream cheese**
- **1** **(1-oz) package Ranch dressing mix**
- **¼** **cup chopped green onions**
- **½** **cup finely chopped red peppers**
- **½** **cup chopped black olives**
- **4** **(10-inch) tortillas**

Beat cream cheese until light. Add dressing mix and beat until blended. Add remaining ingredients and spread on the tortillas. Roll up tightly and wrap in wax paper, twisting ends. Chill at least 2 hours. Cut into 1-inch slices.

Per Serving: Cal 67, Carb 4g, Fib 1g, Pro 2g, Fat 5g, Sod 94mg, Sug 0g

Tomato Basil Flatbread

20 servings

Always devoured quickly in our home.

- **1** **(11-oz) tube refrigerated Pizza crust**
- **1** **cup mayonnaise**
- **1** **cup Parmesan cheese, grated**
- **1** **small bunch fresh basil, chopped**
- **2** **cloves garlic, crushed**
- **2** **to 4 Roma tomatoes, sliced**

Preheat oven to 425°F. Cover a large baking sheet with parchment paper (or spray well). Roll out pizza dough to approximately 11x 14-inches. Place in oven and bake for 8 minutes.

Meanwhile, combine mayonnaise, parmesan cheese, basil and garlic.

Remove pizza dough from oven, spread cheese mixture over dough, distribute tomato slices over top and return to oven for 6-10 minutes or until crust is done and mixture is bubbling.

Per serving: Cal 131, Carb 8g, Fib 0g, Pro 2g, Fat 10g, Sod 201mg, Sug 1g

Sausage Stuffed Mushrooms

Allow 2 to 3 mushrooms per person

Large mushrooms
Italian sausage
Grated Parmesan cheese

Preheat oven to 350°F. Wipe mushrooms with damp cloth or clean with mushroom brush. Remove stems and center, making room for sausage.

Fill each mushroom with sausage until mounded and rather compact. Place on baking sheet and sprinkle lightly with Parmesan cheese. Bake 25 to 30 minutes or until sausage is cooked through. Serve hot.

Per serving: Cal 57, Carb 2g, Fib 0g, Pro 3g, Fat 4g, Sod 182mg, Sug 0g

Stuffed Pepper Shells

These stuffed peppers make a colorful side dish with assorted menus and pasta dishes. It also makes a nice addition to a vegetable tray served with a salad and your favorite hot bread.

Small red peppers, halved and seeded
Mozzarella cheese, shredded
Pesto

Preheat oven to 375°F. Fill each pepper half with cheese. You will want to mound slightly because the cheese will compact as it melts. Drizzle with 1 to 2 teaspoons pesto. Place on a baking sheet and bake 10 to 12 minutes or until cheese is melted. Serve hot.

variation: Use firm, but ripe, plum tomatoes. Cut tomatoes in half and remove flesh and seeds to form a bowl. Continue as above. You can omit the pesto and substitute Monterey Jack cheese with peppers for the Mozzarella cheese.

microwave: Place on microwave dish and cook 1½ to 2 minutes or just until cheese has melted.

Per ½ pepper: Cal 168, Carb 3g, Fib 1g, Pro 9g, Fat 14g, Sod 328mg, Sug 0.2g

Little Tomatoes with Cheese
1 serving

These are those beautiful little tomatoes that are still attached to the vine.

- **1   small red tomato, about 1½-inches**
- **1   tablespoon Pepper Jack cheese, shredded**
- **½   teaspoon sliced almonds, coarsely crumbled**
- **Chopped parsley**

Preheat oven to 350°F. Remove a ¼-inch slice from the rounded part of the tomatoes (opposite the stem). Remove pulp and place up-side-down on paper towels to drain.

Form cheese into a sort of ball and fill tomato. There should be a slight mound above the tomato. Sprinkle with almonds and parsley. Bake 5 minutes to melt cheese. Don't overcook or the tomatoes will be too soft.

Per Tomato: Cal 45, Carb 4g, Fib 1g, Pro 2g, Fat 2g, Sod 43mg, Sug 2g

Herbed Tomato Crostini
18 appetizers

Crostinis have become very popular during the last few years. Serve with your favorite cold drink or as an accompaniment to salad or soup.

- **1   French bread baguette**
- **¼   cup herb or other flavored olive oil**
- **½   teaspoon minced fresh garlic**
- **18   thin slices Mozzarella cheese (to fit bread)**
- **4   medium Plum tomatoes, thinly sliced**
- **Chopped parsley or fresh basil leaves**

Preheat oven to 350°F. Cut bread diagonally into ½-inch slices; place on a baking sheet. Combine oil and garlic. Brush on bread slices. Bake 6 to 8 minutes or until lightly toasted.

Top each with a slice of cheese and tomato. Lightly brush with remaining oil. Sprinkle with parsley or basil. Return to oven for just a minute to slightly soften the cheese.

Per appetizer: Cal 125, Carb 8g, Fib 1g, Pro 7g, Fat 7g, Sod 210mg, Sug 1g

Apricot Almond Brie

Favorite appetizer and definitely the one I use most often. Serve with a glass of white wine and your guests will never know it took you less than 10 minutes to put together.

- **1 (8 to 10-oz) wedge Brie cheese**
- **½ cup apricot preserves**
- **1 tablespoon Grand Marnier liqueur**
- **1 tablespoon toasted sliced almonds**

Remove top rind from cheese. Place cheese on serving plate. In a small saucepan, combine preserves and liqueur and heat through, but do not boil.

Spoon some of the sauce over cheese (save remainder for later). Sprinkle almonds over top. Serve with butter crackers.

Per 1oz serving: Cal 138, Carb 10g, Fib 0g, Pro 6g, Fat 8g, Sod 178mg, Sug 8g

Pineapple Cheese Balls   2 cheese balls

Serve this most requested recipe to friends the next time you feel like entertaining. If desired, you can place the mixture in a small serving dish rather than rolling in the nuts. This eliminates the second cup of nuts, making the recipe somewhat less expensive.

- **2 (8-oz each) packages cream cheese, softened**
- **1 (8-oz) can crushed pineapple, drained**
- **2 cups finely chopped pecans or walnuts, divided**
- **¼ cup finely chopped green pepper**
- **2 tablespoons finely chopped onion**
- **1 tablespoon seasoned salt**

In mixer bowl, beat cream cheese until smooth. Add crushed pineapple, 1 cup of the nuts, green pepper, onion and salt; mix well. Cover and chill.

Divide mixture in half; shape into balls and roll in nuts. Cover and chill several hours or overnight. Serve with crackers. This is especially good with Wheat Thins®.

Per tbsp: Cal 65, Carb 2g, Fib 1g, Pro 1g, Fat 6g, Sod 160mg, Sug 1g

Hot Artichoke Dip

1   (9-oz) can artichoke hearts, drained, coarsely chopped
1   (4-oz) can chopped green chilies
1   cup mayonnaise
1   cup grated Parmesan cheese

Combine ingredients in medium saucepan; heat through. Serve warm with chips, crackers, or bread cubes.

variation: Add ½ cup smoked salmon, crab, bacon, or chopped water chestnuts. This is a 4th of July must for our family and friends.

Per tbsp: Cal 24 Carb 3g,Fib 0g, Pro 0g, Fat 1g, Sod 33mg, Sug 2g

Dill Dip   1⅓ cups

An oldie, but still a favorite. Serve with chilled vegetables such as carrot sticks, cherry tomatoes, raw cauliflower, celery, cucumber rounds, and green pepper.

⅔   cup mayonnaise
⅔   cup sour cream
1   teaspoon dry minced onion
1   teaspoon dill weed
1   teaspoon Beau Monde seasoning

Combine ingredients until well mixed. Cover and chill several hours or overnight to blend flavors. Remove from refrigerator just prior to serving.

Per 2 tbsp: Cal 65, Carb 0g, Fib 0g, Pro 0g, Fat 7g, Sod 49mg, Sug 0g

Heavenly Fruit Dip   about 3 cups

It takes about 3 minutes to mix this and have it chilling in the refrigerator. Serve as a dip with fresh fruit or as a dressing over fruit salad. Yum!

1   (3.4-oz) box instant vanilla pudding mix
2½ cups Half and Half
1   tablespoon sugar
½   teaspoon rum extract
½   teaspoon vanilla extract

Combine ingredients in small mixing bowl; beat with rotary beater or lowest speed of mixer for about 2 minutes. Cover and chill several hours or overnight.

Per tbsp: Cal 24 Carb 3g, Fib 0g, Pro 0g, Fat 1g, Sod 33mg, Sug 2g

Humus   2 cups

A Classic.

- **1   (15-oz) can garbanzo beans (chick peas)**
- **1   garlic clove, peeled, minced**
- **6   tablespoons Tahini (sesame seed paste)**
- **⅓   cup lemon juice**
- **½   teaspoon ground cumin**
- **2   teaspoons olive oil**

Place garbanzo beans in colander, rinse under cold water and drain well.

In a food processor, add first five ingredients and puree until smooth. Place in a serving bowl and top with olive oil. Serve with pita chips.

Per 2 tbsp: Cal 63, Carb 6g, Fib 1g, Pro 2g, Fat 4g, Sod 31mg, Sug 0g

Linda's Guacamole   about 2 cups

To prevent mixture from turning brown, cover with a layer of mayonnaise, spreading completely to the edge. Cover and store in refrigerator. When ready to serve, simply stir in the mayonnaise. Serve with nachos, quesadillas or fajitas.

- **2   ripe avocados**
- **1   clove garlic, minced**
-     **Juice of ½ lime**
-     **Dash hot pepper sauce**
- **1   small tomato, diced**
-     **Salt and pepper to taste**

Peel and slice avocados. In a small bowl, combine avocado slices, garlic, lime juice, and pepper sauce; mash with fork until blended. Add tomato, salt and pepper to taste.

Per tbsp: Cal 22 Carb 2g, Fib 1g, Pro 0g, Fat 2g, Sod 11mg, Sug 0g

Pineapple-Strawberry Fruit Salsa   1¾ cups

First we had tomato based salsas. Then we started adding corn, black beans and olives. Now we have fruit based salsas which are wonderful served with flank steak, chicken, turkey, ham or tortillas.

- **1 (8-oz) can pineapple tidbits or ¾ cup**
- **¾ cup chopped fresh strawberries**
- **2 tablespoons finely chopped green pepper**
- **1 tablespoon fresh lime juice**
- **1 tablespoon apricot preserves**

Combine ingredients; cover and chill until ready to serve.

Per 2 tbsp: Cal 14, Carb 4g, Fib 0.g, Pro 0g, Fat 0g, Sod 1mg, Sug 3g

Easy Salsa   about 3½ cups

Serve as a dip or as a topping for meats, salads, and hamburgers.

- **3 cups chopped Plum tomatoes**
- **¼ cup chopped onion**
- **1 (4-oz) can chopped green chilies**
- **1 tablespoon apple cider vinegar**
- **¾ teaspoon salt**

Combine ingredients; cover and chill several hours to blend flavors.

Per 2 tbsp: Cal 7, Carb 2g, Fib 0g, Pro 0g, Fat 0g, Sod 117mg, Sug 1g

Corn-Tomato Salsa   2¼ cups

This salsa has a tasty southwestern kick to it.

- **1 cup fresh or frozen corn**
- **1 cup chopped tomatoes (seeds removed)**
- **¼ cup sliced green onions**
- **1 small fresh jalapeño pepper, seeded and finely chopped**
- **1 tablespoon chopped cilantro**
- **1 tablespoon white wine vinegar**

In a medium bowl, combine all the ingredients. Cover and chill until ready to serve.

Per 2 tbsp: Cal 10, Carb 2g, Fib 0g, Pro 0g, Fat 0g, Sod 2mg, Sug 1g

Sugar Coated Peanut Snacks

about 4½ cups

Loved by all ages, these peanuts don't stay around very long. Very easy.

- 2 **cups sugar**
- 1 **tablespoon packed light brown sugar**
- 1½ **teaspoons vanilla extract**
- 4 **cups raw peanuts**

Preheat oven to 200°F. Combine both sugars and vanilla in a large heavy saucepan along with 1 cup water. Stir until well mixed and cook over medium heat until most of the sugar has dissolved. Add peanuts. Bring mixture to a boil and cook, stirring frequently, until syrup has cooked away and peanuts are coated. This happens very quickly at the end, so watch carefully.

Spread on a sprayed 15x10-inch jelly roll pan. Bake 60 minutes, stirring every 15 minutes.

Per 2 tbsp: Cal 240, Carb 22g, Fib 3g, Pro 8g, Fat 16g, Sod 6mg, Sug 18g

Holiday Glazed Nuts

about 6 cups

This tasty treat has become a Christmas tradition in our family. Best if not made on a rainy day.

- 6 **cups mixed nuts**
- 1 **cup sugar**
- ½ **cup light corn syrup**
- ½ **cup butter**
- 1 **teaspoon vanilla extract**
- 1 **teaspoon baking soda**

Preheat oven to 200°F. Arrange nuts evenly in a 15x10-inch jelly roll pan.

Combine sugar, corn syrup and butter in a heavy medium saucepan. Cook over medium heat, until sugar melts, stirring frequently. Bring to a boil and cook, but do not stir, 5 minutes. Remove from heat. Carefully stir in vanilla extract and baking soda.

Pour mixture over nuts and stir well to coat. Separate nuts as best you can. Bake 60 minutes, stirring every 15 minutes. Carefully spread on foil. Using two forks quickly separate the nuts and let cool.

Per ¼ cup: Cal 277, Carb 20g, Fib 3g, Pro 6g, Fat 21g, Sod 267mg, Sug 13g

Lime Spritzer

Good Wine Choices: Chardonnay, Chablis, Riesling, etc.

- ½ **cup white wine**
- 1 **lime (1 tablespoon juice and 1 slice)**
- ½ **cup lemon-lime soda, or to taste**

Combine wine, lime juice, and soda. Pour over ice. Garnish with a lime slice.

Per Serving: Cal 134, Carb 15g, Fib 0g, Pro 0g, Fat 0g, Sod 25mg, Sug 13g

White Grape Juice Spritzer   1 Serving

This nonalcoholic drink is very refreshing. It can also be made in a pitcher using equal quantities or to taste.

- ¾ **cup white grape juice, chilled**
- ¾ **cup lemon-lime soda pop, chilled**
- **Lime slices, cut in half**

Combine ingredients. Pour into an attractive serving glass with ice. Add a lime slice and serve.

Per serving: Cal 205, Carb 53g, Fib 2g, Pro 1g, Fat 0g, Sod 38mg, Sug 44g

Diablo Drink

A refreshing party drink on a hot summer day or evening. The crushed pineapple adds that extra something.

- 1 **(12-oz) can limeade concentrate**
- 1 **juice can white rum**
- 1 **(2-litre) bottle lemon-lime soda pop, chilled**
- **Crushed pineapple, drained**
- **Ice cubes**

In pitcher, combine limeade concentrate and rum. Add pop to taste. To each glass, add a little pineapple and ice cubes. Pour limeade mixture on top.

Per 8 oz: Cal 21, Carb 35g, Fib 0g, Pro 0g, Fat 0g, Sod 29mg, Sug 32g

Vanilla-Raspberry Treat   1 serving

If desired, top with whipped cream or chocolate sprinkles

½   cup vanilla ice cream

½   cup diet or regular raspberry soda, chilled

Place ice cream in a 12-oz glass and pour raspberry soda over top.

Paulina's Italian Cream Soda

If desired, garnish with a dollop of whipped cream and a strawberry slice.

2   tablespoons strawberry syrup, or to taste

1   cup chilled club soda

1   tablespoon heavy cream

Pour syrup into a glass filled with ice cubes. Add club soda. Stir in the cream.

Per Serving: Cal 112, Carb 16g, Fib 0g, Pro 0g, Fat 6g, Sod 29mg, Sug 15g

Easy Party Punch   50 punch cup servings

Kind to your budget. Great for picnics, weddings, showers, parties, etc.

1   (.14-oz) package cherry Kool-Aid®

1   (.14-oz) package raspberry Kool-Aid®

2   cups sugar

2   quarts water

1   (46-oz) can unsweetened pineapple juice

2   quarts ginger ale (or to taste)

Combine first 5 ingredients, chill. When ready to serve, stir in ginger ale.

Per Cup: Cal 78, Carb 21g, Fib 0g, Pro 0g, Fat 0g, Sod 10mg, Sug 21g

Cranberry Punch

40 punch cup servings

- **2** **(46-oz each) cans unsweetened pineapple juice**
- **½** **cup fresh lemon juice**
- **2** **cups cranberry juice**
- **1** **cup sugar**
- **2** **quarts ginger ale**

Combine first 4 ingredients and chill. When ready to serve, stir in ginger ale.

Per ½ cup: Cal 53, Carb 14g, Fib 0g, Pro 0g, Fat 0g, Sod 6mg, Sug 14g

Holiday Eggnog Punch

about 4 quarts

This is a large recipe that will serve at least 12 to 14 people. If you have a small group, make half the recipe.

- **2** **quarts purchased eggnog**
- **1** **quart vanilla ice cream, softened**
- **1** **(2-liter) bottle lemon-lime soda pop, chilled**

Combine eggnog and ice cream in a large punch bowl. Gently stir in the pop.

Per ½ cup: Cal 145, Carb 20g, Fib 0g, Pro 3g, Fat 6g, Sod 57mg, Sug 16g

Strawberry Smoothie

3 to 4 servings

- **1** **(6-oz) can frozen lemon juice concentrate**
- **2** **cups sliced strawberries**
- **1** **cup milk**
- **½** **cup sugar**
- **6** **ice cubes**

Place ingredients in blender along with 1 cup water and blend until thoroughly mixed and ice is crushed. Serve right away.

Per serving: Cal 121, Carb 29g, Fib 2.g, Pro 2g, Fat 1g, Sod 35mg, Sug 25g

breads

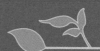

Yeast is a living substance that causes the bread to rise. Granulated yeast is probably the most popular form of yeast used and is readily available and can be purchased in small ¼-ounce packages, in 4-ounce jars and sometimes in bulk packages. Yeast will expire so be sure to check the date on the package.

Active dry yeast can be regular yeast or the rapid rise. Both must be activated with a warm liquid (between 105°F-115°F). For best results, rapid rise yeast should be used in recipes calling for that particular typr of yeast.

There are also special yeasts for bread machines. Experiment and see what works best for you.

Quick Focaccia Bread   8 servings.

A nice crisp bread to serve with soups or salads.

- **1   (10-oz) can refrigerated breadsticks**
- **1   teaspoon olive oil**
- **½   teaspoon basil**
- **½   teaspoon rosemary**
- **½   teaspoon garlic powder**

Preheat oven to 350°F. Separate bread sticks, but do not unroll. Place on a sprayed baking sheet and press into 4-inch circles. Brush lightly with olive oil. Combine remaining ingredients; sprinkle over dough. Bake 12 to 15 minutes or until lightly browned.

Per Serving: Cal 106, Carb 17g, Fib 1g, Pro 3g, Fat 2g, Sod 263mg, Sug 2g

Supper Cheese Bread

6 servings

A definite cheese flavor. Best served fresh from the oven, but can be reheated.

- 1½ **cups baking mix**
- 1 **large egg**
- ¼ **cup milk**
- 1 **cup (4-oz) Cheddar cheese, shredded, divided**
- 1 **teaspoon poppy seeds**
- 2 **tablespoons butter, melted**

Preheat oven to 400°F. Combine baking mix, egg, milk, and ½ cup of the cheese; stir just until moistened. The dough will be stiff, but sticky. Pat dough evenly onto bottom of a sprayed 9-inch pie pan. Sprinkle with remaining cheese and poppy seeds; pour butter over top. Bake 20 to 25 minutes or until lightly browned. Cut into wedges and serve hot.

Per wedge: Cal 201, Carb 23g, Fib 2g, Pro 8g, Fat 9g, Sod 361mg, Sug 3g

Herb Cheese Bread

10 to 12 servings

This bread packs an impressive amount of flavor. Serve with barbecued ribs or grilled chicken. Add potato salad and corn on the cob and you have a full meal everyone will enjoy.

- 1 **loaf French bread, halved lengthwise**
- ⅓ **cup olive oil**
- ½ **teaspoon dried oregano, crushed**
- 2 **teaspoons dried basil, crushed**
- 1 **cup (4-oz) Monterey Jack cheese, shredded**
- 1 **cup (4-oz) Cheddar cheese, shredded**

Preheat oven to 350°F. Combine oil, oregano, and basil. Spread on cut sides of bread. Combine cheese and sprinkle on bottom half of bread, using all the cheese. Top with second half of bread. Press slightly; making sure all of the cheese is inside the bread. Wrap in foil. Bake 10 to 15 minutes or until hot. Cut into 1½-inch slices.

Per serving: Cal 180, Carb 10g, Fib 1g, Pro 6.g, Fat 12g, Sod 239mg, Sug 1g

Garlic Cheese Bread
10 to 12 servings

The garlic spread can be prepared up to an hour before ready to use.

- **1 loaf French bread**
- **1 large garlic clove**
- **½ cup butter, sliced**
- **2 tablespoons shredded Cheddar cheese**
- **2 tablespoons grated Parmesan cheese**

Preheat oven to 450°F. Slice bread lengthwise and place on a baking sheet. Place garlic in a small food processor or blender and process to mince.

Add butter, Cheddar and Parmesan and process just until blended and smooth. Spread evenly on the bread and bake 4 to 5 minutes or until heated through and just beginning to crisp. Cut into diagonal slices and serve.

Per Slice: Cal 83, Carb 9g, Fib 0g, Pro 2g, Fat 4.25g, Sod 148.72mg, Sug 0.48g

Poppy Seed French Bread
25 servings

I wouldn't plan on leftovers with this recipe. You can reheat bread in the oven, but it doesn't work well in the microwave.

- **1 large loaf unsliced French bread**
- **¾ cup butter, melted**
- **1 teaspoon poppy seeds**
- **¼ teaspoon garlic powder**
- **½ teaspoon paprika**

Preheat oven to 400°F. Remove crust from top and sides of loaf. Slice lengthwise down the center, being careful to cut down to the bottom crust, but not through it. Then cut bread in ½-inch slices, again being careful not to cut through the bottom crust.

Combine remaining ingredients. Brush mixture over top and sides of bread and between the slices (you may not need all of the mixture, depending on the size of the bread). Wrap bread in foil and set aside until just before serving.

When ready to bake, fold foil down on all sides; place on baking sheet. Bake 12 to 15 minutes or until golden brown. Serve on plate or in basket and have guests pull off pieces of bread to eat.

Per slice: Cal 96, Carb 9g, Fib 0g, Pro 1g, Fat 6g, Sod 155mg, Sug 1g

The Basic Muffin
12 muffins

- 2 **cups flour**
- ½ **cup sugar**
- 1 **tablespoon baking powder**
- 5 **tablespoons oil**
- 1 **egg**
- ¾ **cup milk**

Preheat oven to 400°F. Combine first 3 ingredients in a mixing bowl.

Combine remaining ingredients and add to dry mixture, stirring just until lightly moistened. Spoon into a sprayed muffin tin, filling ⅔ full. Bake 18 to 20 minutes or until lightly browned and center tests done.

variations: Add one or two of the following ingredients.
1 cup blueberries
½ cup dried cranberries
½ cup dried nuts
1 tablespoon freshly grated lemon or orange peel

Per muffin: Cal 160, Carb 23g, Fib 1g, Pro 3g, Fat 7g, Sod 149mg, Sug 7g

Jalapeno Corn Muffins
6 muffins

- 1 **(8½-oz) box corn muffin mix**
- 1 **large egg, lightly beaten**
- ⅓ **cup milk**
- ¾ **cup (3-oz) Monterey Jack cheese with peppers**

Preheat oven to 375°F. Combine corn muffin mix, egg, and milk in a medium bowl, mixing just until moistened. Spoon into a sprayed muffin tin.

Cut cheese into 6 cubes. Place one in each muffin cup, pressing down with a spoon and making sure each is covered with batter. Bake 10 to 12 minutes or until golden and firm to the touch. Remove and serve hot.

Per muffin: Cal 224, Carb 30g, Fib 1g, Pro 7g, Fat 9g, Sod 476mg, Sug 8g

Really Quick Muffins

With most muffin recipes, you can save time by combining the dry ingredients in one bowl and the liquid ingredients in another bowl. Lightly spray muffin tins and set aside. When ready to bake, combine the ingredients and bake. You can also mix the dry ingredients in a resealable bag and store in pantry until ready to use.

Bacon & Corn Muffins   9 to 12 muffins

These cornbread muffins have a flavorful hint of onion, bacon and cheese.
I find it really hard to eat just one.

- **1** **(8½-oz) box corn muffin mix**
- **⅓** **cup milk**
- **1** **large egg**
- **6** **slices bacon, cooked and crumbled**
- **⅓** **cup finely chopped onion**
- **¼** **cup (1-oz) Cheddar cheese, shredded**

Preheat oven to 400°F. Place corn muffin mix in small mixing bowl. Add milk and egg; stir mixture just enough to moisten. Gently fold in the bacon, onion and cheese. Spoon into a sprayed muffin tin. Bake 10 to 15 minutes or until golden and cooked through.

note: If using the older smaller muffin tins, this recipe will make 12 muffins. If using a larger size most commonly used today, it will make 9 muffins.

Per muffin: Cal 113, Carb 15g, Fib 0g, Pro 4g, Fat 4g, Sod 278mg, Sug 4g

Cheesy Muffins   12 muffins

A biscuit-like muffin with crunchy sides on top. Best eaten hot from the oven.
If using a dark pan, reduce heat to 400°F.

- **2** **cups flour**
- **1** **tablespoon, plus 1 teaspoon baking powder**
- **¾** **teaspoon salt**
- **2** **tablespoons butter, chilled**
- **1** **cup (4-oz) sharp Cheddar cheese, shredded**
- **1** **cup milk**

Preheat oven to 425°F. Combine flour, baking powder and salt in medium mixing bowl. Cut in butter with a fork or pastry blender. Stir in cheese until coated with flour mixture. Add milk and stir just until flour mixture is moistened.

Spoon into 12 sprayed muffin cups. Bake 12 to 15 minutes or until tester inserted in center comes out clean.

Per muffin: Cal 140, Carb 18g, Fib 1g, Pro 5g, Fat 6g, Sod 411mg, Sug 2g

Bran Muffins
12 large muffins

- **2**   **cups milk**
- **2**   **cups All-Bran® cereal**
- **¼**   **cup butter, softened**
- **2**   **large eggs**
- **5**   **teaspoons baking powder**
- **2**   **cups flour**

Preheat oven to 375°F. Pour milk over cereal. Let stand until soft (about 5 minutes).

Cream butter in mixer bowl. Add eggs and beat until smooth. Add bran mixture. Combine baking powder and flour. Add to bran mixture, stirring just enough to moisten the flour. Spoon into sprayed muffin cups, filling almost full. Bake 25 to 30 minutes or until tester inserted in center comes out clean.

note: **Recipe does not require sugar.**

Per muffin: Cal 169, Carb 26g, Fib 4g, Pro 6g, Fat 6g, Sod 310mg, Sug 4g

Sally Lunn Muffins
12 large muffins

A wonderfully light, not too sweet muffin

- **½**   **cup butter, softened**
- **⅓**   **cup sugar**
- **1**   **large egg**
- **3**   **teaspoons baking powder**
- **1½**   **cups flour**
- **¾**   **cup milk**

Preheat oven to 400°F. In a mixer bowl, cream butter and sugar until thoroughly blended. Add egg and mix well. Combine baking powder and flour. Add to the creamed mixture alternately with the milk, starting and ending with flour.

Spoon into a sprayed muffin tin, filling ¾ full. Bake 18 to 20 minutes or until tester inserted in center comes out clean. Remove and place on rack. Best served right away.

Per muffin: Cal 151, Carb 17g, Fib 1g, Pro 3g, Fat 8g, Sod 206mg, Sug 5g

Sour Cream Muffins

12 muffins

This simple muffin recipe is easy to make and is great anytime. Serve for breakfast along with sausages and fresh

- ½   cups sugar
- 3   teaspoons baking powder
- 2   cups flour
- ½   cup chilled butter, sliced
- 2   large eggs, lightly beaten
- ½   cup sour cream

Preheat oven to 400°F. In medium mixing bowl, combine sugar, baking powder and flour. Cut butter into flour mixture, using a pastry blender or two knives, until mixture resembles small peas.

Add eggs and sour cream; stir until all the flour is moistened (batter will be quite stiff). Spoon into a sprayed muffin tin, filling about 2/3 full. Bake 18 to 20 minutes or until golden and tester inserted in center comes out clean.

Per muffin: Cal 195, Carb 22g, Fib 1g, Pro 3g, Fat 10g, Sod 210mg, Sug7g

Whole Wheat Muffins

12 muffins

- 2   cups whole wheat flour
- ½   cup sugar
- 3½   teaspoons baking powder
- 1   large egg, lightly beaten
- 3   tablespoons butter, melted
- 1½   cups milk

Preheat oven to 375°F. In large mixing bowl, combine first 3 ingredients. Combine remaining ingredients and add to dry mixture, stirring just until flour is moistened. Spoon into a sprayed muffin tin, filling ¾ full. Bake 25 to 30 minutes or until tester inserted in center comes out clean.

tip: To prevent muffin tins from warping, fill any empty cups with water.

Per muffin: Cal 149, Carb 24g, Fib 3g, Pro 5g, Fat 4g, Sod 200mg, Sug 8g

tip

For a longer storage life, keep whole wheat flour in the freezer. Then remove amount needed and let come to room temperature before using.

Lemon Poppy Seed Muffins

12 muffins

- 1 (16-oz) package Pound Cake mix
- 1 cup sour cream
- 2 large eggs
- 1 tablespoon poppy seeds
- 1 tablespoon freshly grated lemon zest
- 1 teaspoon lemon extract

Preheat oven to 325°F. Combine all the ingredients in a mixer bowl. Beat on medium speed about 2 minutes or until well blended and smooth. Spoon into 12 sprayed muffin cups, filling a little more than half full. Bake for 20 to 30 minutes or until tester inserted in center comes out clean. Carefully remove from pan and let cool or serve warm.

Per muffin: Cal 228, Carb 28g, Fib 0g, Pro 3g, Fat 10g, Sod 222mg, Sug 16g

Quick & Easy Blueberry Muffins

12 muffins

A baking mix comes in handy for these quick easy muffins. Serve with Roasted Chicken, Garlic Mashed Potatoes and fresh broccoli or asparagus.

- 2 cups baking mix
- ¼ cups sugar
- 1 cup sour cream
- 2 large eggs, lightly beaten
- ½ cup chopped walnuts or pecans
- 1 cup blueberries

Preheat oven to 425°F. In medium bowl, combine baking mix and sugar. Combine sour cream and eggs and add to flour mixture, stirring just enough to moisten. Gently fold in nuts and blueberries. Spoon into sprayed muffin cups filling ¾ full. Bake 20 to 25 minutes or until tester inserted in center comes out clean. Remove from pan and place on rack to cool.

Per muffin: Cal 195, Carb 26g, Fib 2g, Pro 6g, Fat 8g, Sod 235mg, Sug 7g

Indian Fry Bread

6 large fry breads

Fry Bread reminds me a little bit of elephant ears, but in my opinion, is better and more versatile. Some recipes call for yeast, but this baking powder dough is much easier to make.

2¼ cups flour

2 teaspoons baking powder

1 teaspoon salt

2 tablespoons shortening, divided
(melt 1 tablespoon and set aside to cool)

Oil for frying

Cinnamon sugar

Combine flour, baking powder and salt. Add 1 tablespoon shortening and cut in with a fork. Add about ¾ cup warm water, a little at a time, until dough can be formed into a ball. Place on a lightly floured surface and knead briefly until smooth. Divide into 6 pieces and roll into balls. Brush all over with the melted shortening and let stand 45 minutes.

Roll each ball into a 5 inch circle or oval. Cut a 1½-inch slit in the middle. Cook in about ¼ to ½ inch of oil heated to 360°F in a deep skillet or pot, cooking one at a time. Cook until golden, about 1 minute per side. Remove and drain on paper towels. Sprinkle immediately with cinnamon sugar. Enjoy!

variation: You can play around with this recipe and make it the way you want it. The 5 inch circles will make rounds that are nice and crisp. If you want yours more "bready", roll out thicker and smaller circles or ovals. Serve with jam or spread with butter as a bread course. You can also top the rounds with a taco salad or with hot chili and cheese.

Per Fry bread: Cal 344, Carb 39g, Fib 2g, Pro 5g, Fat 19g, Sod 571mg, Sug 2g

Easy Cheese Rolls   15 rolls

A rather sharp tangy flavor of cheddar cheese is enclosed in one of the lightest rolls ever. The dough cycle of the bread machine makes this recipe a dream for the busy cook. These also freeze beautifully. Don't use this recipe unless your machine will hold 4 cups flour on the dough cycle-the dough will rise quite high and could overflow the machine.

1½ **cups milk (115° F)**
1 **cup (4-oz) Cheddar cheese, shredded**
1 **tablespoon sugar**
1 **teaspoon salt**
4 **cups flour**
1 **package dry yeast**

Preheat oven to 400°F. Combine ingredients in mixer bowl in order given. Mix thoroughly, adding a small amount of water or flour if needed to make a nice dough that isn't sticky or dry. Cover and let rise until double in size.

Remove from pan and punch down. Divide into 15 pieces (about golf ball size). Form each into a smooth ball and place in greased muffin cups. Cover with towel or waxed paper and let rise until doubled in size, about 45 to 60 minutes. Bake 12 to 14 minutes or until golden. Remove and serve or let cool.

tip: If shiny tops are desired, brush hot rolls with a little melted butter.

Per roll: Cal 163, Carb 26g, Fib 1g, Pro 6g, Fat 4g, Sod 212mg, Sug 3g

Easy Pecan Rolls   12 rolls

Occasionally, we just must have something to satisfy our sweet tooth. I like to make these on a lazy Saturday morning when I can linger over a cup of hot coffee and enjoy a roll or two.

½ **cup firmly packed brown sugar**
½ **cup butter, melted**
36 **to 48 pecan halves, depending on size**
Cinnamon
2 **cups baking mix**

Preheat Oven to 450°F. Place 2 teaspoons brown sugar and 2 teaspoons melted butter in each of 12 muffin cups; stir to blend. Place 3 to 4 pecan halves in each cup. Sprinkle lightly with cinnamon.

Combine baking mix and ½ cup water until a soft dough forms; beat about 20 strokes. Spoon into muffin cups. Bake 8 to 10 minutes; watch carefully so they don't burn. Invert pan on waxed paper, leaving pan over rolls for about a minute.

Per roll: Cal 229, Carb 29g, Fib 2g, Pro 4g, Fat 12g, Sod 270mg, Sug 10g

Banana Bread   2 loaves

An old favorite. Serve hot with plenty of honey and butter. This continues to be one of my customer's favorite recipes.

1	cup butter, softened
1¾	cups sugar
2	cups mashed very ripe bananas
4	large eggs, well beaten
2	teaspoons baking soda
2¼	cups flour

Preheat oven to 350°F. In a large mixer bowl, cream butter and sugar. Add bananas and eggs. Combine baking soda and flour. Add to banana mixture; stirring by hand, until flour is moistened.

Pour batter into two sprayed 9x5x3-inch loaf pans. Bake 50 to 55 minutes or until tester inserted in center comes out clean. Run knife around edge and turn out immediately. Cool on rack.

Per slice: Cal 128, Carb 17g, Fib 1g, Pro 2g, Fat 6g, Sod 51mg, Sug 10g

Herb Popovers   9 popovers

A delightful crunchy outside with an out-of-this world flavor! Time the popovers so they can be served immediately.

2	large eggs
1	cup flour
½	teaspoon salt
1	cup milk
4½	teaspoons butter
1	(4-oz) container Garlic with Herb cheese, softened

Preheat oven to 425°F. In a mixer bowl, combine eggs, flour, salt and milk. Beat until well blended (may still be a little lumpy). Put ½ teaspoon butter in each of nine 2½-inch muffin tins. Place in oven to melt butter. Remove from oven and brush inside of tins with the butter to coat. Fill one-third full with batter. Top with 1 teaspoon of the cheese. Pour remaining batter over top, filling about two-thirds full. Bake for 25 to 30 minutes or until puffed and golden brown. Serve immediately.

tip: Leftover herb cheese can be served with crackers as a snack or for additional popovers.

Per popover: Cal 136, Carb 12g, Fib 0g, Pro 4g, Fat 8g, Sod 245mg, Sug 2g

Blueberry Drop Biscuits   12 biscuits

Serve these easy to make biscuits anytime. If desired, substitute dried cranberries for the blueberries.

- **1   cup flour**
- **½   teaspoon salt**
- **1½   teaspoons baking powder**
- **1   tablespoon butter, chilled**
- **½   cup milk**
- **½   cup fresh blueberries**

Preheat oven to 375°F. Combine flour, salt, and baking powder in a mixing bowl. Cut in butter with two knives or a pastry blender. Add milk, stirring just enough to moisten. Carefully fold in blueberries. Drop by tablespoon onto a sprayed baking sheet. Bake 12 to 14 minutes or until lightly browned.

Per biscuit: Cal 63,Carb 9g, Fib 0g, Pro 1g, Fat 2g,Sod 184mg, Sug 1g

Sour Cream Drop Biscuits   8 biscuits

Easy, quick and amazingly very good.

- **1   cup self-rising flour**
- **¼   cup butter, cut into small pieces**
- **½   cup sour cream**

Preheat oven to 450°F. Place flour and butter in a food processor. Process quickly 3 to 4 times until mixture is crumbly. Add sour cream and process just until mixture is moistened. Gently form into 8 balls and place on a baking sheet. Bake 12 to 15 minutes or until lightly browned and cooked through.

note: If not using a food processor, cut butter into flour until mixture is crumbly or butter pieces are smaller than a pea. Add sour cream and mix until all the flour is stirred into the dough. You may need to mix with your hands.

Per biscuit: Cal 135, Carb 12g, Fib 0g, Pro2g, Fat 8g, Sod 240mg,Sug 1g

Biscuit Dough

Should be rolled or patted out evenly. If using a biscuit or cookie cutter, always press straight down. This makes for a better looking biscuit, scone or cookie.

You don't have a cookie cutter? Pat the dough into a square and cut into small squares with a knife. Dough placed with edges touching will have a softer crust. Those placed slightly apart will be more brown and have more crust.

Baking Powder Biscuits   12 biscuits

- 2 **cups flour**
- 3 **teaspoons baking powder**
- 1 **teaspoon salt**
- ¼ **cup shortening**
- ¾ **cup milk**

Preheat oven to 450°F. Combine flour, baking powder and salt in a mixing bowl. Cut in shortening with two knives or a pastry blender. Add milk and stir until flour is moistened.

Turn out on lightly floured board and knead about 20 times. Roll out or pat to ½-inch thickness. Cut with biscuit cutter and place on ungreased baking sheet. Bake 8 to 10 minutes or until lightly browned.

Per biscuit: Cal 121, Carb 17g, Fib 1g, Pro 3g, Fat 5g, Sod 337mg, Sug 1g

Kristina Kringler   about 12 servings

Have some friends over and serve fresh fruit with Heavenly Fruit Dip and Kristina Kringler. They'll love it and you won't have spent all day in the kitchen.

- 1 **cup chilled butter, plus 2 tablespoons melted**
- 2 **cups flour, divided**
- 2 **teaspoons almond extract, divided**
- 3 **large eggs**
- 1½ **cups sifted powdered sugar**
- **Chopped walnuts or pecans**

Preheat oven to350°F. With 2 knives or a pastry blender, cut ½ cup of the butter into 1 cup of the flour. Sprinkle 2 tablespoons water over mixture; lightly mix with a fork. Form into a ball; divide in half. On ungreased baking sheet pat each half into a strip 12x3-inches, allowing about 3 inches between the strips.

In medium saucepan, bring ½ cup butter and 1 cup water to a full boil. Remove from heat; quickly stir in 1 teaspoon almond extract and the remaining 1 cup flour. Return pan, over low heat, and stir until mixture forms a ball; this takes about a minute. Remove from heat. Add eggs; beat vigorously until smooth. Spread half of mixture evenly over each strip completely covering the dough. Bake 35 to 45 minutes or until lightly browned. Remove from baking sheet and cool on rack.

Combine remaining 2 tablespoons butter with powdered sugar, 1 teaspoon almond extract and 1 tablespoon water. Beat until smooth. It may be necessary to add more powdered sugar or water to make a nice consistency for spreading. Spread strips with frosting and sprinkle with nuts.

Per serving: Cal 188, Carb 21g, Fib 1g, Pro 2g, Fat 11g, Sod 78mg, Sug 11g

Cream Puffs

10 to 12 large or 35 to 40 small cream puffs.

Leave cream puffs whole and frost with powdered sugar glaze. Or fill with whipped cream, pudding or ice cream. Tiny cream puffs can also be filled with assorted meat fillings and served as appetizers.

- ½ **cup butter**
- 1 **cup water**
- 1 **cup flour**
- 4 **large eggs**

Preheat oven to 400°F. In medium saucepan, bring butter and water to a rolling boil. Add flour and stir vigorously over low heat until mixture forms a ball, about 1 minute. Remove from heat.

Add eggs, one at a time, beating thoroughly. Drop from spoon onto ungreased baking sheet, about 3-inches apart, making desired size cream puffs. Bake 45 to 50 minutes for large and 30 minutes for small cream puffs, or until lightly browned and dry. Allow to cool. Cut off tops; remove soft dough and fill with desired filling.

Per puff: Cal 38,Carb 2g, Fib 0g, Pro 1g,Fat 3g, Sod 24mg, Sug 0g

Basic Crepes

about 16 crepes

This versatile crepe is good for many things, such as pancakes, main dishes, and desserts. The best thing about crepes is that they can be made ahead and frozen.

- 3 **large eggs, well beaten**
- 1 **cup milk**
- 1 **tablespoon sugar**
- ¼ **teaspoon salt**
- ¾ **cup flour**

Beat together the eggs and milk in a mixer bowl. Add remaining ingredients and beat with mixer until smooth.

Pour about 2 tablespoons batter into a buttered 8-inch skillet that has been preheated. Working quickly, rotate pan to spread batter evenly over the bottom. When cooked (this takes just a minute) turn crepe and cook other side.

Turn out on dish and leave flat or roll up. Repeat, lightly buttering pan for each crepe.

Per serving: Cal 188, Carb 21g,Fib 1g, Pro 2g, Fat 11g,Sod 79mg, Sug 11g

Scones   8 scones

You really can't beat a basic hot scone filled with butter and your favorite jam, but if you want, you can add any of the following ingredients for a different tasty treat: fresh lemon or orange peel, chopped nuts, chocolate or white chocolate chips, dried apricots, raisins, dried or fresh blueberries or dried cranberries.

2	cups flour
¼	cup sugar
1	tablespoon baking powder
½	teaspoon salt
½	cup chilled butter, cut up
¾	cup milk

Preheat oven to 400°F. In a medium mixing bowl, combine flour, sugar, baking powder and salt. Add butter and cut in with two knives or a pastry blender, until mixture resembles small crumbs. (This could also be done in a food processor.)

Add milk and mix just until combined; mixture will be sticky. Place on a sprayed baking sheet. Flatten the dough into about a ¾-inch thick round. Cut into 8 wedges, but do not separate. If desired, sprinkle lightly with sugar. Bake 15 to 18 minutes or until lightly browned and cooked through.

Per scone: Cal 236, Carb 29g, Fib 1g, Pro 4g, Fat 12g, Sod 239mg, Sug 7g

Cinnamon Rolls   12 rolls

1	package dry yeast
2	tablespoons sugar
2½	to 2¾ cups baking mix
⅓	cup cinnamon sugar
2	tablespoons butter, melted
2	cups powdered sugar

Preheat oven to 350°F. Dissolve yeast in ¾ cup warm water (110-115°F); pour into mixing bowl. Add sugar and baking mix; stir until well mixed, but slightly sticky.

Turn out onto a lightly floured surface and knead 4 to 5 minutes or until smooth. Roll into a 14x12-inch rectangle. Brush with melted butter. Sprinkle with cinnamon sugar. Roll up, starting with the long side; pinch dough to seal. Cut roll into 12 equal sections. Place in a sprayed muffin tin or on baking sheet and flatten to about a 3-inch circle. Bake 12 to 15 minutes or until lightly browned. Remove and place on cooling rack.

Combine powdered sugar with just enough water to make a thick glaze. Drizzle over warm rolls.

Per roll: Cal 160, Carb 37g, Fib 1g, Pro 1g, Fat 2g, Sod 65mg, Sug 31g

Easy Dinner Rolls   15 to 18 rolls

My mother told me about this recipe. Different, delicious, and very easy to prepare. My daughter likes to add 1 teaspoons fresh orange peel for a delicious citrus flavor.

- 1   (8½-oz) box yellow or white cake mix
- 1   package dry yeast
- ½   teaspoon salt
- 1¼ cups hot tap water
- 2½ to 3 cups flour

Preheat oven to 400°F. Combine cake mix, yeast, and salt in a large bowl. Add water and flour to make soft dough. (Dough will be quite sticky.) Cover; let rise until doubled, 1 to 1½ hours.

Stir down dough; spoon onto a well floured surface. Gently turn dough a couple of times to lightly coat with flour. Shape into desired size rolls and place on sprayed baking sheets. Or shape into balls and place in sprayed muffin tins. Cover and let rise until double, about 1 hour. Bake 10 to 15 minutes or until golden.

Per roll: Cal 124, Carb 24g, Fib 1g, Pro 3g, Fat 2g, Sod 167mg, Sug 6g

Refrigerator Rolls   about 18 to 20 rolls

- 2   packages dry yeast
- 3   large eggs, beaten
- ½   cup shortening
- ½   cup sugar
- 1½ teaspoons salt
- 4½ cups flour

Dissolve yeast in ¼ cup water (105° to 115°F). Set aside for 10 minutes.

Combine yeast mixture, eggs, shortening, sugar, salt and 2½ cups flour with 1 cup water. Beat by hand or with mixer until smooth. Add enough remaining flour to make a soft dough. Cover; let rise until doubled, about 1 to 1½ hours.

Preheat oven to 400°F. Punch dough down. (At this point you can shape into rolls, let rise and then bake or you can refrigerate dough.) If refrigerated, remove about 3 hours before baking. Shape into desired size rolls. Place on baking sheet and let rise until doubled, about 2 hours. Bake 12 to 15 minutes or until lightly browned.

Per roll: Cal 169, Carb 25g, Fib 1g, Pro 4g.Fat 6g, Sod 185mg, Sug 5g

Focaccia   10 servings

Sit back and enjoy the compliments when you serve your own, hot from the oven Focaccia. Makes delicious bread for sandwiches and a good base for a pizza. This recipe works well in my bread machine using the dough cycle.

1	**package dry yeast**
2	**to 2½ cups flour**
1	**teaspoon sugar**
½	**teaspoon salt**
1	**tablespoon, plus 1 teaspoon olive oil**
	Garlic salt or grated Parmesan cheese

Preheat oven to 425°F. In a large mixer bowl, combine yeast, 1½ cups of the flour, sugar and salt. Add ¾ cup hot tap water and the 1 tablespoon olive oil. Beat until smooth. By hand, stir in enough of the remaining flour to make a soft, but not sticky dough. Place on a lightly floured surface and knead about 5 minutes. Place in a lightly greased bowl. Cover and set in warm place until doubled, about 60 minutes.

Lightly spray a 12-inch pizza pan or large baking sheet with nonstick spray. With fingers, flatten dough into an 11-inch circle. Prick surface of dough with a fork. Brush with remaining 1 teaspoon olive oil. Sprinkle lightly with garlic salt or Parmesan cheese. Let rise in warm place 30 minutes. Bake 18 to 20 minutes or until golden. Best served warm.

variation: Brush with oil. Top with 2/3 cup narrow strips of red and green peppers. Sprinkle with ¼ cup (1-ounce) Mozzarella cheese, shredded. Or omit oil and spread lightly with 2 to 3 tablespoons pesto. Top with ¼ cup chopped oil-packed sun-dried tomatoes

Per slice: Cal 122, Carb 21g, Fib 1g, Pro 3g, Fat 2g, Sod 125mg, Sug 1g

Testing for Doneness

Always check breads just before the minimum baking time. Yeast type breads should be nicely browned. Carefully turn out bread and tap the bottom with your fingers. If it sounds hollow, it should be done. If not, return to pan and bake a few minutes longer. Quick breads should be dry when a tester inserted in center comes out clean.

Pizza Dough

Pizza dough mixed in a bread machine is a breeze to make and so much better and economical than purchased crusts. Your bread machine must be able to hold 4 cups flour on the dough cycle. This recipe has an added bonus of being very low in fat, only 4 grams for the entire recipe.

1½	cups water (115°F)
3¼	to 4 cups flour
½	teaspoon salt
1	package dry yeast

Combine ingredients in mixer bowl in order given. Mix thoroughly, adding a small amount of water or flour if needed to make a smooth dough. Cover and let rise until double in size.

Preheat oven to 425°F. Remove from bowl and punch down. Press dough into desired pans; add toppings and bake until cooked through and cheese is melted.

tip: Thin crust: two 16-inch pizzas
Thick crust: two 12-inch pizzas
Individual: five 9-inch pizzas

Per slice: Cal 102, Carb 21g, Fib 1.g, Pro 3g, Fat 0g, Sod 73mg, Sug 1g

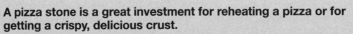

A pizza stone is a great investment for reheating a pizza or for getting a crispy, delicious crust.

Roll the pizza dough to desired thinness and carefully lay on the hot pizza stone. Top with desired toppings, bake.

cakes, desserts & pies

Butter

All is not created equal

In testing recipes and in day-to-day cooking, we have experienced quite different results between brands of butter. We noticed that most of the quality butters contain 8 grams of saturated fat per tablespoon and the cheaper brands contain only 7 grams. This difference can have quite a dramatic result in some recipes.

The recipes most affected are candies, cakes, cookies and muffins. The higher fat content always produced the best results, and in some instances, the lower fat content butter caused the recipe to fail completely. To make things even more confusing, we did find one 7 gram brand that worked as well as the 8 gram.

I like to use the less expensive butter for table or non-baking use and save the more expensive butter for baking.

Tiramisu Layer Cake 12 servings

My family loves Tiramisu and this is a great alternative to the traditional dessert. They ask for this cake time and time again.

- **1 (18.25-oz) package white cake mix**
- **3 large eggs**
- **⅓ cup oil**
- **2 teaspoons instant coffee crystals**
- **¼ cup coffee (brewed or made from instant coffee crystals)**
- **6 tablespoons coffee liqueur**

Preheat oven to 350°F. Grease and flour three 9-inch cake pans. In a mixer bowl, combine cake mix, eggs, oil and 1 cup water. Beat on medium speed for 2 minutes.

Pour ⅓ of the batter into first pan, and ⅓ into second pan. Stir instant coffee crystals into remaining batter; pour into last pan. Bake all three for 10-12 minutes or until tester inserted in the center comes out clean. Let cool in pan for 5 minutes. Remove from pan; cool on rack.

In a cup, combine coffee and coffee liqueur. Using a skewer, poke holes in cake about 1-inch apart. Spoon coffee mixture evenly among 3 cakes.

When ready to assemble, frost each layer with Amazing Mascarpone Frosting on page 61, stacking cakes with coffee layer in the center. Finish frosting the entire cake. Refrigerate. Even better made day ahead for flavor to blend and mellow.

Per slice: Cal 282, Carb 35g, Fib 0g, Pro 4g, Fat 12g, Sod 322mg, Sug 22g

Kahlúa® Cake 16 servings

My family requests this cake again and again. I'm thankful it couldn't be easier-no frosting necessary!

- **1 (18.25-oz) box Devil's Food Cake mix**
- **1 (3.9-oz) box instant chocolate pudding mix**
- **1 (16-oz) container light sour cream**
- **4 large eggs**
- **1 cup Kahlúa® or coffee liqueur**

Preheat oven to 350°F. In a mixer bowl combine all ingredients and beat on medium speed until smooth, about 2 minutes. Pour batter into well greased and floured Bundt pan.

Bake 45 to 50 minutes or until top springs back when lightly pressed with finger. Cool 10 minutes in pan. Remove from pan; cool on rack. If desired, dust cake with powdered sugar. For special occasion, serve with whipped cream or vanilla ice cream.

note: Do not substitute regular sour cream for the light. The cake will be too heavy and not rise or cook through without burning on the outside.

Per Slice: Cal 274, Carb 37g, Fib 0g, Pro 6g, Fat 8g, Sod 374mg, Sug 27g

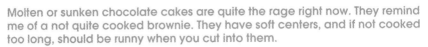

Little Molten Cakes 6 servings

Molten or sunken chocolate cakes are quite the rage right now. They remind me of a not quite cooked brownie. They have soft centers, and if not cooked too long, should be runny when you cut into them.

- ½ **cup butter**
- 1 **(4-oz) bar bittersweet chocolate**
- 3 **large eggs**
- ½ **cup sugar**
- ⅓ **cup flour**
- **Vanilla, coffee or chocolate chip ice cream**

Preheat oven to 450°F. Melt butter and chocolate in a small saucepan or in the microwave oven. Stir to blend. Set aside.

In mixer bowl, beat eggs and sugar at medium speed, until thickened and light in color. Add flour and beat to blend. Stir in chocolate mixture. Pour into six lightly buttered 6-ounce ramekins, dividing batter evenly. Place in a shallow baking pan and bake 12 minutes, or until tops are somewhat dry and start to crack in the middle.

At this point, you can unmold cakes or serve in ramekins. To unmold, let stand 2 to 3 minutes, run a knife around edge and remove. Serve topped with ice cream.

Per cake w/o Ice cream: Cal 328, Carb 27g, Fib 2g, Pro 5g, Fat 25g, Sod 148, Sug 19g

Triple Fudge Cake 12 servings

This is a heavy spongy type cake, and is great for eating out of hand and for sack lunches.

- 1 **(3-oz) box regular chocolate pudding mix**
- 2 **cups milk**
- 1 **(18.25-oz) box Devils food cake mix**
- ½ **cup semi-sweet chocolate chips**
- ½ **cup chopped walnuts**

Preheat oven to 350°F. Prepare pudding mix with milk as directed on box. Remove from heat; stir dry cake mix into hot pudding. Mixture will be quite thick and spongy.

Pour into a sprayed 13x9-inch pan. Sprinkle with chocolate chips and nuts and bake 30 to 35 minutes or until tester inserted in center comes out clean.

Per Slice: Cal 190, Carb 28g, Fib 1g, Pro 3g, Fat 7g, Sod 224mg, Sug 18g

Chocolate Chocolate Cake   12 servings

An intensely dark chocolate cake with a dark chocolate frosting. It is a restaurant favorite changed somewhat to make it easier for the home cook.

- **2   (18.25-oz each) boxes Dark Chocolate Fudge cake mix**
- **3   large eggs**
- **¾   cup mayonnaise**
- **¾   cup brewed coffee**
- **1½ cups Coca Cola®**
- **Family Favorite Chocolate frosting on page 62 or purchased chocolate frosting**

Preheat oven to 350°F. In mixer bowl, add 1 box cake mix and only 1½ cups of the second box of cake mix.

Combine eggs, mayonnaise, coffee and Coca Cola® beating until well-mixed. Add to cake mix and beat on low about 1 minute to combine ingredients. Beat on medium speed about 2 minutes until smooth. Pour into a sprayed 13x9-inch baking pan and bake 35 to 45 minutes or until a tester inserted in center comes out clean. Allow to cool before frosting.

Per slice w/o frosting: Cal 314, Carb 37g, Fib 1g, Pro 3g, Fat 16g, Sod 365mg, Sug 23g

Pineapple Upside-Down Cake   10 to 12 servings

Want a dessert, but don't have a lot of time? This cake can be mixed and ready for the oven in less than 10 minutes.

- **1   (18-oz) box white cake mix**
- **⅓   cup vegetable oil**
- **3   large eggs**
- **6   canned pineapple rings, drained (two 8-oz cans)**
- **6   maraschino cherries, drained**
- **1   cup chopped pecans or walnuts, divided**

Preheat oven to 350°F. In mixer bowl, combine the cake mix, oil, eggs and the amount of water called for in the mix. Beat 30 seconds to mix; then beat on medium-high for 2 minutes.

Meanwhile, arrange pineapples in bottom of a sprayed 10-inch springform pan. (Spray bottom only.) Place a cherry in center of each. Sprinkle with ½ cup of the nuts. Pour batter over top. Sprinkle remaining ½ cup nuts over batter. Bake 40 to 45 minutes or until a tester inserted in center comes out clean. Let cool 10 minutes before turning out on rack to cool.

note: The yellow cake mixes have changed over the last few years. So I prefer using white mix with whole eggs rather than egg whites.

Per Slice: Cal 355, Carb 41g, Fib 2g, Pro 5g, Fat 20g, Sod 326mg, Sug 27g

Blueberry Coffee Cake   12 to 16 servings

This cake is best served same day made.

- 2 **cups flour**
- 1 **teaspoon baking powder**
- 4 **large eggs, lightly beaten**
- 1 **cup vegetable oil**
- 1 **cup sugar**
- 1 **(21-oz) can blueberry pie filling**

Preheat oven to 350°F. Combine flour and baking powder in a mixer bowl. Add next 3 ingredients and mix until smooth. Spread half the batter in a sprayed 13x9-inch baking pan; the layer will be thin. Spoon pie filling evenly over top. Pour remaining batter over top and gently spread to cover the filling. Bake 35 to 45 minutes or until a tester inserted in center comes out clean. Serve warm.

Per Slice: Cal 312, Carb 40g, Fib 2g, Pro 3g, Fat 17g, Sod 57mg, Sug 25g

Banana Cake   12 to 16 servings

You really don't need a frosting with this cake, but for those die-hard frosting lovers, try the Cream Cheese Frosting on page 62

- 1 **(18.25-oz) box yellow cake mix**
- ¼ **cup vegetable oil**
- 4 **large eggs**
- 1½ **cups mashed very ripe bananas, about 3 large**
- ¾ **cup chopped walnuts**

Preheat oven to 350°F. In a mixer bowl, combine cake mix, oil, eggs and 1 cup water. Beat until well mixed, about 2 to 3 minutes. Stir in the bananas and nuts. Pour into a sprayed 13x9-inch baking pan and bake 25 to 30 minutes or until a cake tester inserted in center comes out clean. Place on rack and cool.

Per Slice: Cal 248, Carb 34g, Fib 1g, Pro 4g Fat 12g, Sod 233mg, Sug 20g

Eggnog Cake   10 to 12 servings

A very good light-textured cake made even better with a scoop of vanilla ice cream. Purchase a cake mix without the pudding added. If the cake is for company, lightly dust the top with powdered sugar or garnish with fresh fruit.

- 1 **(18.25-oz) box yellow cake mix**
- ¼ **teaspoon nutmeg**
- ¼ **cup butter, melted**
- 1½ **cups purchased eggnog**
- 2 **large eggs**
- ½ **teaspoon rum extract**

Preheat oven to 350ºF. Brush a 10-inch tube cake pan or Bundt pan with shortening. Sprinkle with flour; shake off excess. Combine all the ingredients in a mixer bowl and beat until blended. Then beat on medium speed until batter is smooth, about 2 minutes.

Pour batter into prepared pan and bake 45 to 55 minutes or until tester inserted in center comes out clean. Cool in pan 10 minutes. Remove from pan; cool on rack.

Per Slice: Cal 275, Carb 37g, Fib 0g, Pro 5g, Fat 12g, Sod 390mg, Sug 22g

Chocolate Cake   12 servings

This popular moist chocolate cake is perfect for a picnic or potluck dinner. The mayonnaise takes the place of the eggs and the oil in the recipe.

- 2 **cups flour**
- 1 **cup sugar**
- ¼ **cup cocoa**
- 2 **teaspoons baking soda**
- 1 **cup mayonnaise**
- 1 **teaspoon vanilla extract**

Preheat oven to 350ºF. In mixer bowl, combine the flour, sugar, cocoa, and baking soda. Add mayonnaise, vanilla and 1½ cups water. Beat on medium speed about one minute or until well mixed and smooth. Pour into a sprayed 13x9-inch baking pan. Bake 25 to 30 minutes or until a tester inserted in center comes out clean.

note: Frost with one of your favorite frostings.

Per Slice: Cal 202, Carb 23g, Fib 1g, Pro 2g, Fat 12g, Sod 96mg, Sug 10g

Cherry Cake Squares

20 servings

1 cup butter, softened

1½ cups sugar

4 large eggs

1 teaspoon lemon extract

2 cups flour

1 (21-oz) can cherry or blueberry pie filling

Preheat oven to 350°F. Cream butter and sugar in large mixer bowl until light and fluffy. Add eggs, one at a time, beating after each addition. Add lemon extract. Stir in flour. Pour batter into a sprayed 15x10x1-inch jelly roll pan.

Mark off 20 squares. Put 1 tablespoon pie filling in center of each square. Bake 45 minutes or until tester inserted in center comes out clean. Cool and cut into squares. If desired, sprinkle with powdered sugar before serving.

variation: For a quick and easy coffee cake, prepare the cake batter and pour half of the batter into a greased Bundt cake pan. Sprinkle with ¼ cup cinnamon sugar. Pour remaining batter over top. You may have to increase baking time. Or, place paper liners in muffin cups and fill a little over half full. Make a slight indentation in center and fill with cherry pie filling. Bake 30 to 35 minutes. Cool and drizzle with powdered sugar glaze.

Per square: Cal 229, Carb 33g, Fib 1g, Pro 3g, Fat 10g, Sod 86mg, Sug 23g

Coconut Snack Cake

9 servings

I love those little boxes of cake mixes. They are so convenient to have on hand when you don't really want a large cake or dessert.

1 (9-oz) box yellow cake mix

1 large egg

1½ cups flaked coconut

½ cup packed light brown sugar

1 teaspoon vanilla extract

5 tablespoons heavy cream or evaporated milk

Preheat oven to 350°F. Combine cake mix with the egg and ½ cup water as directed on box. Pour into a sprayed 8x8-inch baking dish and bake 18 to 20 minutes or until tester inserted in center comes out clean. Place on a rack and allow to cool 10 minutes.

Combine remaining ingredients and carefully spread over cake. Place under broiler and broil about 2 minutes or until lightly browned (watch carefully, it can burn very quickly). Let cool.

Per Slice: Cal 292, Carb 53g, Fib 2g, Pro 4g, Fat 13g, Sod 273mg, Sug 30g

Cranberry-Nut Cake 6 to 8 servings

A quick cake that can be prepared in less than 10 minutes.

- **1 cup, plus 1 tablespoon sugar**
- **1 cup flour**
- **⅔ cup coarsely chopped pecans**
- **2 cups cranberries**
- **2 large eggs, lightly beaten**
- **½ cup butter, melted**

Preheat oven to 350°F. In a mixing bowl, combine the 1 cup sugar and flour. Add pecans and cranberries, tossing to coat. Add eggs and butter and stir until thoroughly mixed.

Pour into a sprayed 8x8-inch baking dish. Sprinkle the 1 tablespoon sugar evenly over the top. Bake 30 to 35 minutes or until tester inserted in center comes out clean. Serve warm or room temperature.

Per Slice: Cal 268, Carb 36g, Fib 2g, Pro 3g, Fat 14g, Sod 102mg, Sug 22g

Coconut Pecan Cake 12 to 16 servings

Serve with scrambled eggs, ham slices and sliced tomatoes or cantaloupe.

- **4 large eggs**
- **1 (16-oz) box light brown sugar**
- **½ cup vegetable oil**
- **2 cups baking mix**
- **1 (7-oz) package flaked coconut**
- **1 cup chopped pecans or walnuts**

Preheat oven to 350°F. In a mixer bowl, lightly beat the eggs. Add brown sugar and mix well. Stir in the oil. Add the baking mix, a small amount at a time and mix well. Stir in the coconut and nuts. Pour into an ungreased 13x9-inch baking pan and bake 35 to 45 minutes or until a tester inserted in center comes out clean. Let cool slightly, cut into squares.

Per Slice: Cal 378, Carb 49g, Fib 3g, Pro 6g, Fat 20g, Sod 163mg, Sug 37g

Mom's Orange Cake

12 to 16 servings

My brothers and I loved it when Mom made this cake. We always knew we were in for a special treat.

- 1 **(18.25-oz) box white cake mix with pudding**
- 1 **(3-oz) box lemon gelatin**
- 4 **large eggs**
- ¾ **cup vegetable oil**
- 3½ **cups sifted powdered sugar**
- 1 **(6-oz) can frozen orange juice concentrate, thawed**

Preheat oven to 325ºF. In a mixer bowl, combine the cake mix, gelatin, eggs, oil and ¾ cup water. Beat about 2 minutes or until smooth and thoroughly mixed. Pour into a sprayed deep 13x9-inch baking pan. Bake for 30 to 40 minutes or until a tester inserted in the center comes out clean. Let cool on rack 10 minutes.

Meanwhile, combine powdered sugar and orange juice and beat until smooth. When cake has cooled slightly, poke holes all the way to the bottom, using a kitchen fork or a skewer. Pour glaze over cake and spread to cover. Let cool.

tip: For easier mixing, make sure the orange juice concentrate has thoroughly thawed, and is at room temperature.

Per Slice: Cal 435, Carb 70g, Fib 0g, Pro 4g, Fat 17g, Sod 282mg, Sug 56g

Date Nut Cake

9 servings

A wonderfully moist date cake. Serve plain, with ice cream or frosted with a buttercream or cream cheese frosting.

- 8 **ounces dates, finely chopped, about one cup**
- ½ **cup butter**
- 1 **cup firmly packed light brown sugar**
- 1 **teaspoon baking soda**
- 1½ **cups flour**
- 1 **cup chopped walnuts**

Preheat oven to 375ºF. Combine dates and butter with ¾ cup hot water. Let stand 10 minutes.

Meanwhile, combine sugar, baking soda and flour in a mixing bowl. Add to date mixture. Stir in walnuts. Pour into sprayed 8x8-inch baking pan. Bake 30 to 40 minutes or until tester inserted in center comes out clean. Let cool on rack.

Per Slice: Cal 494, Carb 42g, Fib 3g, Pro 8g, Fat 35g, Sod 76mg, Sug 23g

Special Lunch Box Cake

12 servings

Wrap individual slices in foil and freeze until ready to use.

- **2 cups sugar, divided**
- **2 teaspoons baking soda**
- **2 cups flour**
- **2 large eggs, lightly beaten**
- **1 (17-oz) can fruit cocktail, undrained**
- **¾ cup coarsely chopped walnuts**

Preheat oven to 350°F. In mixing bowl, combine 1½ cups of the sugar, baking soda and flour. Add eggs and fruit cocktail. Mix well and pour into a sprayed 13x9-inch baking pan. Sprinkle remaining ½ cup sugar evenly over top. Sprinkle with nuts. Bake 60 minutes or until a tester inserted in center comes out clean.

Per Slice: Cal 234, Carb 47g, Fib 2g, Pro 4.g, Fat 7g, Sod 13mg, Sug 29g

Raisin Walnut Cake

12 servings

Don't be put off by the 1 cup mayonnaise. It actually takes the place of eggs and fat in the recipe and makes for a wonderfully moist cake that requires no frosting.

- **1 cup raisins**
- **1 cup chopped walnuts**
- **2 teaspoons baking soda**
- **1 cup sugar**
- **1 cup mayonnaise**
- **2 cups flour**

Preheat oven to 350°F. Combine raisins, walnuts and baking soda in a large mixing bowl. Add 1 cup hot water and set aside while measuring remaining ingredients.

Add sugar to raisin-nut mixture. Then stir in mayonnaise until blended. Stir in flour just until smooth. Pour into a lightly sprayed 13x9-inch baking dish. Bake 25 to 30 minutes or until a tester inserted in center comes out clean.

variation: Substitute 1 cup chopped dates for the raisins. For chocolate cake add 6 tablespoons (1½-oz) grated unsweetened chocolate.

Per Slice: Cal 283, Carb 31g, Fib 2g, Pro 3g, Fat 17g, Sod 97mg, Sug 18g

Blueberry Orange Cake 12 servings

So moist you don't need frosting or ice cream. Perfect with a cup of coffee.

- 2 **oranges**
- 1 **(18.25-oz) box lemon cake mix**
- ⅓ **cup vegetable oil**
- 3 **large eggs**
- 1½ **cups fresh or frozen blueberries**

Preheat oven to 350ºF. Wash oranges and grate 1 tablespoon peel. Squeeze oranges to make ½ cup juice. Place orange peel and juice in a large mixer bowl.

Add cake mix, oil, eggs and ½ cup water. Beat on low about 1 minute to combine ingredients. Beat on medium speed for 2 minutes. By hand, carefully fold in the blueberries. Pour into a sprayed 13x9-inch baking dish. Bake 30 to 40 minutes or until a tester inserted in center comes out clean. Place on rack to cool.

Per Slice: Cal 276, Carb 37g, Fib 1g, Pro 5g, Fat 12g, Sod 330mg, Sug23g

Gooey Butter Cake 9 servings

I lived in St. Louis for a number of years and this was a favorite bakery creation. It is more like a dessert recipe than a traditional cake. If desired, sprinkle with powdered sugar and garnish with fresh sliced strawberries or assorted fresh fruit.

- 2 **cups flour, divided**
- 3 **tablespoons plus 1¼ cups sugar**
- ⅓ **cup, plus ¾ cup butter**
- 1 **large egg, lightly beaten**
- ¼ **cup light corn syrup**
- ⅔ **cup canned evaporated milk**

Preheat oven to 325ºF. In a mixing bowl, combine 1 cup of the flour and the 3 tablespoons sugar. Cut the ⅓ cup butter into the flour-sugar mixture until it resembles fine crumbs. Pat into the bottom of an ungreased 8x8-inch baking dish.

For filling, beat remaining ¾ cup butter until soft. Add remaining 1¼ cups sugar and beat until well mixed.

Combine egg and corn syrup; add to mixture and beat until just combined. Add the remaining 1 cup flour and milk alternately to the filling, mixing until just combined. Pour over crust and bake 40 to 50 minutes or until cake is firm. Place on rack to cool.

Per slice: Cal 424, Carb 52g, Fib 1g, Pro 5g, Fat 23g, Sod 199mg, Sug 33g

Pound Cake   10 to 12 servings

Of all the pound cake recipes I have tried, this one seems to be a favorite.

- **1 pound butter, softened**
- **1 (16-oz) box powdered sugar, sifted**
- **6 large eggs**
- **1½ teaspoons vanilla extract**
- **3 cups sifted cake flour**

Preheat oven to 350°F. Cream butter and powdered sugar in large mixer bowl. Add eggs, one at a time, and beat well. Stir in vanilla extract and flour. Pour into a sprayed angel food cake pan. Bake about 1¼ hours or until tester inserted in center comes out clean. Cool. (While still slightly warm, sift additional powdered sugar over top.)

Per slice: Cal 551, Carb 61g, Fib 1g, Pro 5g, Fat 33g, Sod 265mg, Sug 36g

Dutch Cake   8 to 10 servings

Each serving can be garnished with sliced almonds, or my favorite, assorted fresh fruit.

- **½ cup butter, softened**
- **1 cup sugar**
- **1 large egg**
- **½ cup almond paste**
- **1 cup flour**

Preheat oven to 325°F. In mixer bowl, cream the butter and sugar until light and fluffy. Add egg and mix until blended. Add almond paste until blended. Slowly beat in flour. Spread in sprayed 9-inch pie dish. Bake 40 to 50 minutes or until golden. Serve warm or at room temperature.

Per slice: Cal 231, Carb 29g, Fib 1g, Pro 3g, Fat 13g, Sod 76mg, Sug 19g

Cream Cheese Cupcakes

24 cupcakes

The amount of vanilla extract is correct, but if using a good brand of pure vanilla you may wish to decrease this amount.

3	(8-oz each) packages cream cheese, softened
1¼	cups sugar, divided
5	large eggs
3	tablespoons vanilla extract, divided
1	(21-oz) can cherry or blueberry pie filling
1	cup sour cream

Preheat oven to 300°F. In mixer bowl, combine cream cheese and 1 cup of the sugar. Add eggs and 2 tablespoons of the vanilla extract. Beat until thoroughly mixed, 3 to 4 minutes. Line muffin tins with paper cupcake liners. Fill ¾ full and bake for 30 to 40 minutes. Remove from oven and let cool 5 minutes (centers will drop while cooling).

Combine sour cream, the remaining ¼ cup sugar and remaining 1 tablespoon vanilla extract. Fill center of cupcakes with 1 tablespoon sour cream mixture. Spoon a dollop of pie filling on top. Return to oven and bake 5 minutes. Let cool in refrigerator.

Per cupcake: Cal 186, Carb 16g, Fib 0g, Pro 3g, Fat 12g, Sod 101mg, Sug 8g

Brownie Cupcakes

16 cupcakes

Brownie fans will enjoy these. For variety, add 1 cups coarsely chopped walnuts to the batter or sprinkle the top of each cupcake with walnuts before baking.

1	cup butter, softened
⅔	cup semi-sweet chocolate chips
1¾	cups sugar
4	large eggs
1	teaspoon vanilla extract
1	cup flour

Preheat oven to 350°F. Melt butter and chocolate chips in a medium saucepan over low heat. Stir in sugar; mix well. Add eggs, vanilla and flour. Stir until blended and smooth. Pour into cupcake liners, filling ¾ full. Bake 25 to 30 minutes or until tester inserted in center is just slightly moist.

Per Cupcake: Cal 232, Carb 26g, Fib 1g, Pro 3g, Fat 14g, Sod 103mg, Sug 20g

Amazing Mascarpone Frosting   5 cups

I came up with this recipe to be a quick, easy fix compared to separate filling and frosting recipes - which have too many ingredients and are time consuming. It is perfect for the Tiramisu Cake on Page 49

- **1   (8-oz) package Mascarpone cheese, room temperature**
- **2   tablespoons coffee liqueur**
- **2   cups heavy cream, chilled**
- **¾   cup powdered sugar**

In a medium bowl, using a hand mixer beat mascarpone cheese and coffee liqueur until well combined; set aside.In a large mixer bowl, whip cream and powdered sugar until stiff. Gently fold cheese mixture into whipped cream.

Makes enough frosting to fill and frost a three layer cake.

note: To garnish Tiramisu Cake sift cocoa powder over top of cake using a small sieve.

Per 2 tbsp: Cal 78, Carb 3g, Fib 0g, Pro 1g, Fat 7g, Sod 8mg, Sug 3g

Whipped Butter Frosting   3½ cups

This is one of my favorite frostings. The flavor is unique and delicious. It is the traditional frosting for Red Velvet Cake (more than six ingredients) but is equally as good on chocolate cake. It must be kept refrigerated. If you have problems and the mixture looks curdled no matter what you do, switch your brand of butter. That is usually the culprit. Look for butter that has 8 grams of saturated fat per tablespoon.

- **5   tablespoons flour**
- **1   cup milk**
- **1   cup sugar**
- **1   cup butter, softened**
- **1   teaspoon vanilla extract**

Combine flour and milk in small saucepan (do not use aluminum). Cook over low heat until quite thick, stirring constantly. Remove from heat; cool completely.

Cream together sugar, butter and vanilla. Add cooled mixture and beat, beat, beat. When finished, frosting looks like thick whipped cream.

Per 2 tbsp: Cal 84, Carb 7g, Fib 0g, Pro 0g, Fat 6g, Sod 52mg, Sug 6g

Powdered Sugar Glaze   ½ cup

- **1   cup sifted powdered sugar**
- **1   tablespoon hot water**
- **1½   teaspoons light corn syrup**
- **¼   teaspoon vanilla extract**

Combine ingredients in small mixing bowl; stir until smooth.

Family Favorite
Chocolate Frosting 1½ cups

My absolute favorite chocolate frosting. Don't add too much powdered sugar, because the frosting will thicken as it cools. Makes enough frosting for a 13x9-inch cake.

- ¼ **cup milk**
- ¼ **cup butter**
- 1 **cup semi-sweet chocolate chips**
- 1 **teaspoon vanilla extract**
- 2½ **cups sifted powdered sugar**

Combine milk and butter in a small saucepan. Bring to a boil; remove from heat. Add chocolate chips and stir until smooth. Place chocolate mixture, vanilla extract and powdered sugar in a mixer bowl. Beat until spreading consistency. If necessary, thin with a few drops of milk.

Per 2 tbsp Cal 189, Carb 34g, Fib 1g, Pro 1g, Fat 7g, Sod 27mg, Sug 31g

Buttercream Frosting 1½ cups

The frosting can be changed by substituting different liquids for the milk such as lemon or orange juice, coffee, chocolate, etc.

- ¼ **cup butter, softened**
- 3 **cups sifted powdered sugar**
- 1 **teaspoon vanilla extract**
- 3 **to 4 tablespoons milk**

In a small mixer bowl, cream the butter until smooth. Add sugar, vanilla and 3 tablespoons milk. Beat until creamy and thick enough to spread. It may be necessary to add more milk or powdered sugar to get the desired consistency. Makes enough frosting for a 13x9-inch cake.

Per 2 tbsp: Cal 202, Carb 423g, Fib 0g, Pro 0g, Fat 4g, Sod 35mg, Sug 39g

Cream Cheese Frosting about 3 cups

This is a delicious frosting for carrot or lemon cake. Because of the cream cheese, it must be kept refrigerated.

- 1 **(8-oz) package cream cheese, softened**
- ½ **cup butter, softened**
- 1 **teaspoon vanilla extract**
- 1 **(16-oz) box of powdered sugar**

In mixer bowl, beat cream cheese until smooth. Add butter and vanilla and beat until mixed. Add powdered sugar, beating until smooth.

Per 2 tbsp: Cal 123, Carb 17g, Fib 0g, Pro 1g, Fat 6.g, Sod 50mg, Sug 15g

Pineapple Bread Pudding

8 servings

Whether serving family or friends, be prepared for people to ask for seconds.

1	(16-oz) loaf French bread, cut into 1-inch slices
¾	cup butter
6	large eggs
2	(20-oz) cans crushed pineapple, drained
1	cup brown sugar
1	cup flaked coconut

Preheat oven to 375°F. Place bread slices on baking sheet. Bake 4 minutes on each side or until golden brown. Cut toasted slices into 1-inch cubes. Toss with melted butter, set aside.

In a large bowl, beat eggs until thick and lemon colored. Add remaining ingredients; mix well. Fold in bread cubes. Pour into well buttered or sprayed 11x7-inch baking dish; bake 25 to 30 minutes. Serve with whipping cream.

variation: Add currants or chopped nuts.

Per serving: Cal 602, Carb 81g, Fib 4g, Pro 11g, Fat 27g, Sod 578mg, Sug 51g

Croissant Bread Pudding

6 servings

A friend made this recipe for her husband and he ate the whole thing. (Not in one sitting, of course.)

2½	cups Half and Half
6	large eggs, lightly beaten
¾	cup sugar, divided
½	teaspoon cinnamon
8	croissants (day old works best)
¾	cup raisins

Preheat oven to 350°F. Combine Half and Half with the eggs. Combine ½ cup of the sugar with the cinnamon; add to egg mixture. Pour into a sprayed 11x7-inch baking dish.

Tear croissants into bite-size pieces. You should have about 7 cups. Add to custard, pressing down to cover. Sprinkle raisins over top. Sprinkle remaining ¼ cup sugar over raisins. Bake 40 to 50 minutes or until set. Serve warm with a little additional cream.

Per serving: Cal 505, Carb 57g, Fib 1g, Pro 13g, Fat 28g, Sod 385mg, Sug 25g

Devonshire Cream and Berries   1½ cups

- 1 (8-oz) package cream cheese, softened
- ½ cup sifted powdered sugar
- ⅓ cup whipping cream
- 1 teaspoon vanilla extract
- 1½ teaspoons Grand Marnier liqueur
  Fresh strawberries

In mixer bowl, whip cream cheese and powdered sugar until thoroughly blended and smooth. Add whipping cream, vanilla, and Grand Marnier; whip until light. Serve with berries. If not using right away, cover and chill.

Per tbsp: Cal 59, Carb 4g, Fib 0g, Pro 1g, Fat 5g, Sod 29mg, Sug 3g

Cherries Jubilee   4 servings

This is an old recipe, but still a popular one. When you want to serve something spectacular, flame the cherries at the table and impress your guests. I usually double the recipe if serving 4 to 6 people.

- 1 tablespoon sugar
- 1 tablespoon cornstarch
- 1 (16-oz) can Bing cherries, pitted, save juice
- 4 strips orange peel
- ½ teaspoon lemon juice
- ¼ cup warm brandy

Combine sugar and cornstarch in chafing dish or saucepan. Slowly add liquid from canned cherries and blend. Cook over low heat until thickened, stirring constantly. Add cherries, orange peel and lemon juice; heat through.

Pour brandy over top and ignite. Serve over ice cream.

Per serving: Cal 132, Carb 23g, Fib 1g, Pro 1g, Fat 0g, Sod 5mg, Sug 20g

Baklava   35 pieces

The first recipe I used to make Baklava was two pages long. This one is easier and just as moist and delicious. As you can see, it makes a lot, but it can be frozen.

4½   **cups walnuts, finely ground**

3   **cups sugar, divided**

½   **teaspoon cinnamon**

1   **(16-oz) box Phyllo, thawed, at room temperature**

1   **pound butter, melted**

1   **tablespoon lemon juice**

Preheat oven to 300°F. Combine walnuts, 1½ cups of the sugar and cinnamon. Set aside.

Butter a 15x10-inch jellyroll pan. Unroll Phyllo and place on flat surface. Cover with waxed paper or plastic wrap. Then cover with a slightly damp towel. (Phyllo must be kept covered at all times as it dries out quickly.) Lay 1 sheet of Phyllo in pan. You may have to fold one end over to fit pan. Brush with melted butter. Repeat layering until half of the Phyllo has been used.

Spread nut mixture evenly over top. Repeat layering with remaining Phyllo continuing to butter each layer.

With a sharp knife, cut through layers of Phyllo, cutting in a diamond shaped pattern, making cuts about 1½ inches apart. Bake 70 to 80 minutes or until golden brown.

Meanwhile, in medium saucepan, combine 1½ cups water with the remaining 1½ cups sugar and the lemon juice. Bring to a boil, stirring frequently to dissolve sugar. Lower heat and simmer 20 minutes. Let cool slightly. Spoon syrup over Baklava. Let stand 3 to 4 hours to absorb syrup.

note: It's important to measure the walnuts first, then grind them.

Per serving: Cal 240, Carb 21g, Fib 1g, Pro 2g, Fat 18g, Sod 141mg, Sug 13g

Fantastic Cheesecake

12 servings

At first I wasn't going to put this recipe in the cookbook, mainly because of the problems I have been having with several brands of cream cheese. If you have problems with cheesecakes, especially if it is a recipe that has worked in the past, try using a different brand of cream cheese.

⅓ cup graham cracker crumbs

3 (8-oz each) packages cream cheese, softened

4 large eggs

1¾ cups sour cream, divided

1¼ cups sugar, divided

4 tablespoons fresh lemon juice, divided

Preheat oven to 350°F. Butter a 9-inch spring form pan. Add graham cracker crumbs to pan and rotate to cover bottom and sides. Discard loose crumbs.

In mixer bowl, beat the cream cheese until smooth. Add eggs, one at a time, and mix well. Add ¾ cup of the sour cream, 1 cup of sugar and 2 tablespoons of the lemon juice. Mix until blended and smooth. Pour into spring form pan. Bake 35 to 40 minutes or until just firm (do not over bake, the center should still jiggle just a little).

Meanwhile, combine the 1 cup sour cream, ¼ cup sugar, and 2 tablespoons lemon juice. When done, remove cheesecake from oven and carefully spoon sour cream mixture over top. Return to oven and bake 5 minutes. Let cool on rack. Chill.

Per serving: Cal 370, Carb 23g, Fib 0g, Pro 8g, Fat 28g, Sod 256mg, Sug 17g

Quick Cheesecake Toppings

A purchased cheesecake served with your choice of toppings is a lifesaver for the busy host or hostess.

Whole berry cooked blueberry sauce

Whole or chopped assorted fresh fruit

Chocolate sauce sprinkled with sliced almonds

Orange marmalade with Grand Marnier to taste

Melted seedless raspberry or blackberry jam

Caramel sauce

Shaved white chocolate

Hawaiian Delight Cheesecake

8 to 10 servings

You will love the convenience of no-bake cheesecakes. To prevent tiny lumps, make sure the cream cheese is quite soft; then beat thoroughly before adding the pineapple.

- **2 (3-oz) packages soft ladyfingers**
- **2 (8-oz) packages cream cheese, softened**
- **½ cup sugar**
- **1 (20-oz) can crushed pineapple, well drained**
- **1 (8-oz) container frozen whipped topping, thawed**
- **½ cup flaked coconut, toasted**

Place ladyfingers, rounded-side out, around the sides and bottom of a 9-inch springform pan. Fill in with smaller pieces where needed; you will have a few of the ladyfingers left over.

Beat cream cheese until soft. Gradually add the sugar and beat until fluffy. Stir in pineapple and fold in whipped topping. Pour into pan and spread the top until smooth. Sprinkle with coconut. Cover with plastic wrap. Chill overnight or at least several hours.

tip: If you can't find a small 8-oz container of whipped topping, or if you already have a larger container on hand, measure 3 cups for this recipe.

Per Serving: Cal 337, Carb 29g, Fib 1g, Pro 5g, Fat 23g, Sod 162mg, Sug 22g

Lemon Cheesecake

12 servings

This is good. Creamy with a light touch of lemon. Garnish with whipped cream and thin strands of lemon peel.

- **1 (3-oz) box lemon gelatin**
- **2 (8-oz) packages cream cheese, softened**
- **½ cup sugar**
- **½ cup sour cream**
- **¼ cup heavy cream**
- **1 graham cracker pie crust**

Thoroughly mix the lemon gelatin with ¼ cup boiling water, stirring until dissolved.

In mixer bowl, combine remaining ingredients and beat until smooth and light. Add gelatin and beat until smooth. Pour into pie crust. Chill 3 to 4 hours or until set.

Per Serving: Cal 313, Carb 26g, Fib 0g, Pro 5g, Fat 22g, Sod 257mg, Sug 20g

Lemony Berry Bake   4 servings

This is one of my favorite summer dessert recipes.

1	(8-oz) package Neufchatel cream cheese, room temperature
½	cup sour cream
½	cup lemon curd
½	teaspoon lemon zest (optional)
4	cups mixed fresh berries
½	cup light brown sugar

Place oven rack to top position and preheat broiler.

In a bowl, blend cream cheese, sour cream, lemon curd and zest until smooth. Scatter berries in 12" tart pan. Spread mixture over berries to completely cover. Sprinkle with brown sugar.

Place in oven and broil until sugar is bubbly and caramelized, 2 to 4 minutes. Serve warm.

Per serving: Cal 412, Carb 46g, Fib 8g, Pro 6g, Fat 25g, Sod 186mg, Sug 28g

Coconut Custard   6 servings

A nice creamy custard and a great make ahead dessert.

4	large eggs, lightly beaten
⅓	cup sugar
½	teaspoon vanilla extract
1	cup heavy cream
¼	cup flaked coconut
	Nutmeg

Preheat oven to 325°F. Combine eggs, sugar, and vanilla. Mix cream with 2 cups water and gradually add to egg mixture. Stir in coconut. Place 6 ungreased 10-oz ramekins in a 13x9-inch baking dish. Fill ramekins. Sprinkle lightly with nutmeg.

Fill baking dish with 1-inch of boiling water. Carefully place dish in oven. Bake 30 to 40 minutes or until center is just set (still some jiggle left). Let cool on rack. Cover with plastic wrap and chill in refrigerator.

Per Serving: Cal 232, Carb 11g, Fib 0g, Pro 5g, Fat 19g, Sod 64mg, Sug 9g

Strawberry Shortcake   5 servings

This is a wonderfully delicious way to use up those biscuits before the expiration date.

- **1   (10.2-oz) can Grands® biscuits**
- **¼   cup butter, melted**
- **¼   cup sugar**
- **1   tablespoon sliced almonds (optional)**
- **Fresh strawberries, sliced, sweetened**

Preheat oven to 375ºF. Dip each biscuit in melted butter and then into sugar to coat. Place on ungreased baking sheet. Sprinkle a few almonds over each biscuit. Bake 15 to 18 minutes or until cooked through and golden. Serve warm topped with strawberries.

Per Serving: Cal 360, Carb 42g, Fib 3g, Pro 5g, Fat 20g, Sod 691mg, Sug 20g

Apple Raspberry Crisp   8 servings

The raspberries add a nice touch of color and taste. If you want a really scrumptious dessert, top with a scoop of vanilla ice cream or frozen yogurt.

- **8   cups peeled, sliced apples (4 to 5 large)**
- **1   cup fresh or frozen raspberries**
- **½   teaspoon cinnamon**
- **¾   cup flour**
- **1   cup sugar**
- **⅓   cup cold butter**

Preheat oven to 350ºF. Place apple slices in a sprayed 11x7-inch baking dish. Distribute raspberries over top. Sprinkle 3 tablespoons water over fruit. Sprinkle with cinnamon.

In a small mixing bowl, combine the cinnamon, flour, and sugar. Cut in butter with a pastry blender or two knives. Sprinkle over fruit. Bake 50 to 55 minutes or until light golden and apples are cooked through.

variation: Use blueberries, pears, or dried cranberries in place of the raspberries. Or omit the raspberries and use just the apples.

Per Serving: Cal 226, Carb 43g, Fib 3g, Pro 2g, Fat 7.g, Sod 56mg, Sug 29g

Deep Dish Fruit Cobbler

6 servings

This recipe has been in our family for more years than I remember, but at least two generations. It is still one of our favorite desserts. Serve it warm with vanilla ice cream.

- ½   **cup butter, melted**
- 1   **cup baking mix**
- 1   **cup sugar**
- 1   **cup milk**
- 1   **quart fruit, drained (peaches, blackberries, etc.)**

Preheat oven to 375°F. Pour butter into an 11x7-inch baking dish. Stir in baking mix, sugar, and milk. Pour fruit over top. Bake 35 to 40 minutes or until golden brown.

Per Serving: Cal 278, Carb 43g, Fib 2g, Pro 4g, Fat 12g, Sod 257mg, Sug 28g

Apple Peach Cobbler

6 servings

I hope you enjoy this cobbler type dessert. It takes less than 5 minutes to assemble and have ready for the oven.

- 1   **(21-oz) can apple pie filling**
- 1   **(29-oz) can sliced peaches, drained**
- 1   **(9-oz) box yellow cake mix**
- ¼   **cup butter, cut into small thin pieces**

Preheat oven to 350°F. Spoon pie filling into a sprayed 8x8-inch baking dish. Add peaches and stir to mix. Sprinkle cake mix evenly over the top and dot with the butter. Bake 40 to 50 minutes or until the topping is golden.

tip: Don't substitute more peaches for the pie filling since the pie filling acts as the thickener for the cobbler.

Per Serving: Cal 453, Carb 85g, Fib 4g, Pro 3g, Fat 13g, Sod 433mg, Sug 63g

Lovely Lemon Puffs 24 servings

These are so delicious that I had one guest eat three!

- **2** **sheets puff pastry**
- **1** **(10-oz) Jar lemon curd**
- **1**   **(8-oz) container Mascarpone cheese, softened**
- **1½** **teaspoons vanilla, divided**
- **2** **cups whipping cream**
-    **Garnish: mint leaves or sliced strawberries**

Preheat oven to 400° F. Place a piece of parchment paper on a large baking sheet and place sheet of puff pastry on top of parchment. With a knife or pizza wheel, cut pastry into 12 squares. Bake in oven for 12-15 minutes or until lightly browned. Cool.

In the meantime, cream together lemon curd and mascarpone cheese along with ¾ teaspoon vanilla. In a separate bowl, whip cream along with remaining vanilla.

When ready to serve, cut pastry in half horizontally and place bottom piece onto serving plate. Top with 2 tablespoons lemon mixture, top with other half of pastry, top with a spoonful of whipped cream and garnish with a mint leave or strawberry slices. Repeat with remaining pastries.

note: Pastries, filling and whipped cream can be made several hours ahead. Assemble when ready to serve.

Per puff: Cal 168, Carb 11g, Fib 0g, Pro 2g, Fat 13g, Sod 34mg, Sug 8g

Pistachio Dessert

10 to 12 servings

- **50** **Ritz® crackers, crushed**
- **½** **cup butter, melted**
- **1** **quart vanilla ice cream, softened**
- **1** **cup milk**
- **1** **(3.4-oz) package instant pistachio pudding mix**
- **1** **(8-oz) container frozen whipped topping, thawed**

Preheat oven to 350°F. Combine cracker crumbs and butter. Pat evenly into a sprayed 13x9-inch baking dish. Bake 10 to 15 minutes. Remove from oven and let cool.

In mixer bowl, blend ice cream, milk and pudding mix. Pour over crust. Spread whipped topping over top. Chill several hours or overnight.

Per serving: Cal 351, Carb 40g, Fib 1g, Pro 4g, Fat 20g, Sod 440mg, Sug 15g

Vanilla Sherbet Dessert

6 servings

- **1** **pint vanilla ice cream, softened slightly**
- **1** **pint pineapple sherbet**
- **2** **teaspoons fresh orange zest**
- **1½** **tablespoons Grand Marnier liqueur**
- **⅓** **cup toasted flaked coconut**

In a large mixer bowl, combine the first four ingredients; beat just until smooth and blended. Spoon into parfait or wine glasses. Sprinkle with toasted coconut.

tip: Leftover mixture can be frozen. It will be firmer, but is equally as delicious. Make the dessert just before serving, but toast the coconut ahead of time.

Per Serving: Cal 215, Carb 31g, Fib 3g, Pro 3g, Fat 9g, Sod 88mg, Sug 26g

Family Favorite Toffee Delight
12 to 14 servings

When in their teens, this is the dessert my children wanted for their birthday cake. In fact, they still do. Just add candles. My favorite dessert? If I had to choose one, this would be it.

1½ **packages soft-type Ladyfingers, split**
1 **to 1½ quarts chocolate ice cream, softened**
1 **to 1½ quarts vanilla ice cream, softened**
10 **Heath® bars, coarsely crushed**

Line sides and bottom of Angel food cake pan (with removable bottom) with Ladyfingers, rounded side out. Half fill pan with chocolate ice cream. Sprinkle half of the crushed candy over top. Add vanilla ice cream; sprinkle with remaining candy.

Cover with foil and freeze.

note: If you wish to make a smaller dessert, use half the ingredients and a 9x5-inch loaf pan lined with foil (for easy removal).

Per Serving: Cal 561, Carb 59g, Fib 2g, Pro 9g, Fat 32g, Sod 229mg, Sug 51g

Rice Chex® Dessert
12 to 15 servings

This recipe is worth the price of the cookbook. If strawberries are in season, it looks pretty to top each serving with a strawberry and a mint leaf.

2½ **cups crushed Rice Chex cereal**
1 **cup firmly packed light brown sugar**
1 **cup cashews, split**
½ **cup butter, melted**
1 **cup flaked coconut**
½ **gallon vanilla ice cream, softened**

Combine first 5 ingredients; mix thoroughly. Spread half of mixture evenly in buttered 13x9-inch baking dish; pat down. Spread ice cream evenly over top. Sprinkle remaining cereal mixture over ice cream; pat lightly.

Cover and freeze. When ready to serve, remove from freezer and cut into squares.

Per serving: Cal 379, Carb 41g, Fib 2g, Pro 6g, Fat 23g, Sod 166mg, Sug 31g

Upside Down Apple Tart

An old fashioned dessert sure to impress the eye and the pallet.

5   **to 6 golden delicious apples cored and thinly sliced**
1   **lemon (juice & zest)**
1½   **cups sugar, divided**
6   **tablespoons unsalted butter**
1   **sheet refrigerated pie crust**

Preheat oven to 425°F. In a large bowl, toss apples with lemon juice, zest and ½ cup sugar; marinate for 20 minutes, drain.

Meanwhile, in a 10-inch oven proof skillet melt butter. Add remaining sugar and cook over medium heat; stirring with wooden spoon until syrup begins turning caramel brown. Remove from heat and arrange apple slices in bottom of skillet starting on the outside edge and fanning them in a circle towards the center.

Place skillet on stove and cook over medium heat, pressing apples down and basting them as they soften. Once apples begin to soften, about 5 minutes, cover and cook 10 minutes more, basting frequently until juices are thick and syrupy. Remove from heat and let cool slightly.

Unroll pie crust over the apples and press edges of the dough between apples and inside of the skillet. Bake about 20 minutes or until pie crust is golden brown and crisp. Remove from oven.

Select a serving dish a few inches larger than skillet. Place the serving dish over skillet, holding tightly with two hot pads, carefully invert to unmold. Rearrange apple slices if necessary.

Delicious served alone and even more special with lightly sweetened whipped cream, or a scoop of vanilla ice cream.

Per Serving: Cal 263, Carb 41, Fib 2g, Pro 1g, Fat 13g, Sod 151mg, Sug 30g

Pretzel Pie Crust   1 crust

This makes a great crust for ice cream or the Key Lime Pie.

¾   **cup butter, melted**
2⅔ **cups crushed pretzels**
3   **tablespoons sugar**

Preheat oven to 350°F. Combine ingredients and pat into two
9-inch pie pans or one 13x9-inch pan. Bake 10 minutes. Cool.

Per 1/8 piece: Cal 262, Carb 24g, Fib 1g, Pro 2g, Fat 17g, Sod 583mg, Sug 3g

Graham Cracker Crust   1 crust

I know it is more convenient to buy a graham cracker crust, but if time
permits, do try this recipe. You will be surprised at how much better it is and
how much money you will save.

1¼   **cups graham cracker crumbs**
¼   **cup sugar**
⅓   **cup butter, melted**

Preheat oven to 350°F. Combine ingredients and press into bottom and sides of
9-inch pie pan. Bake 10 minutes. Cool.

Per 1/8 piece: Cal 136.52, Carb 14.58g, Fib 0.37g, Pro 0.91g, Fat 8.59g, Sod 135.51mg, Sug 8.58g

Pie Crust   2 single crusts

2½   **cups flour**
½   **teaspoon salt**
¾   **cup shortening**
6   **to 7 tablespoons ice water**

Combine flour and salt in a mixing bowl. With two knives or a pastry blender,
cut in shortening until uniform, about the size of peas. Sprinkle with water, a
tablespoon at a time, and toss with fork. Stir gently, just until dough forms a
ball. Divide into 2 equal parts; place on lightly floured surface and roll to ⅛-inch
thickness. Gently ease into pan to avoid stretching.

Per 1/8 piece: Cal 153, Carb 14g, Fib 1g, Pro 2g, Fat 10g, Sod 73mg, Sug 1g

Steve's Perfect Pie Crust   5 single crusts

This really is a reliable recipe. The dough can be refrigerated up to 3 days or can be frozen. Steve was a lifesaver one Thanksgiving when he made the pumpkin pies for me. The crust turned out flaky and the filling was delicious. You may not always need this large a recipe, but any left over could be formed into balls and frozen or even better yet, roll out to desired size, place on a baking sheet and freeze. Then wrap and freeze until ready to use. If freezing more than one, they can be layered with parchment paper between each layer.

- **4   cups flour**
- **1   tablespoon sugar**
- **2   teaspoons salt**
- **1¾ cups shortening (do not substitute)**
- **1   tablespoon cider or white vinegar**
- **1   large egg**

Combine flour, sugar and salt in a mixing bowl. Cut in shortening with two knives or a pastry blender. Combine vinegar and egg with ½ cup cold water; add to flour mixture. Stir until moistened and dough is formed. Divide dough into 5 equal parts; shape each into a round flat patty ready for rolling. Wrap in waxed paper; chill at least 30 minutes.

When ready to use, place on lightly floured board; roll 1/8-inch thick and 2 inches larger than inverted pie pan.

Per 1/8 piece: Cal 125, Carb 9.g, Fib 0g, Pro 1g, Fat 9g, Sod 118mg, Sug 1g

 an apple a day   You may have additional varieties in your area, but this is a good starting point.

Braeburn	Excellent all purpose apple. Good for eating out of hand or for cooking and baking. Also keeps well.
Cortland	A slightly tart versatile apple. Good for baking.
Elstar	A Sweet-tart flavor; versatile. Good for snacks, salad and baking.
Empire	Best for snacks and salads than for cooking.
Fuji	Good eating apple; sweet, crunchy and flavorful. A good choice for pies.
Gala	Good eating and baking apple.
Golden Delicious	Good eating apple. Perfect for sautéing and baking in casseroles. Great for applesauce and pies.
Granny Smith	Tart and firm apple. A favorite for pies.
Jonagold	Good all around eating, cooking and baking apple.
Jonathon	All-purpose. Good for cooking and baking. Really a good versatile apple.
McIntosh	Sweet-tart flavor. A favorite for snacking. Good for sauces, but not for pies because it loses its shape once cooked.
Red Delicious	A good eating apple, nice for salads.
Rome	Not a favorite for eating. Good for pies, breads, sauce, bread pudding and baking whole.

Pecan Crunch Pie   6 servings

Very good served with vanilla ice cream or whipped cream.

- 3   large egg whites
- 1   cup sugar
- 1   teaspoon baking powder
- 1   teaspoon vanilla extract
- 1   cup crushed graham cracker crumbs
- 1   cup chopped pecans

Preheat oven to 350°F. Beat egg whites until stiff. Combine sugar and baking powder; beat into egg whites. Add vanilla. Fold in graham cracker crumbs, then pecans. Pour into buttered 9-inch pie plate. Bake 30 minutes or until cooked through. Cool.

Per slice: Cal 216, Carb 28g, Fib 2g, Pro 3g, Fat 12g, Sod 153mg, Sug 22g

Daiquiri Pies   2 pies

My daughter made these for Mother's Day one year. They make a delicious, not too heavy dessert. If you don't want to fool with a pie crust, just pour the filling into dessert dishes and top with whipped cream and toasted coconut.

- 2   (9-inch) baked pretzel pie crusts, see page
- 1   (8-oz) package cream cheese, softened
- 1   (14-oz) can sweetened condensed milk
- 1   (6-oz) can limeade concentrate, thawed
- ⅓   cup light rum
- 1   (4-oz) container frozen whipped topping, thawed

In mixer bowl, beat cream cheese until light and fluffy. Add condensed milk and limeade, mix well. Add rum. Fold in whipped topping. Pour into pie crusts. Chill at least 4 hours.

Per slice: Cal 451, Carb 46g, Fib 1g, Pro 6g, Fat 26g, Sod 657mg, Sug 24g

Busy Day Pumpkin Pie   6 servings

This is one of those recipes that is even better the second day.

- 1   (9-inch) unbaked pie crust
- 1   (16-oz) can pumpkin (not pie filling)
- 1   (14-oz) can sweetened condensed milk
- 1   large egg
- 1   teaspoon pumpkin pie spice
- 1   teaspoon cinnamon

Preheat oven to 375°F. Combine first 5 ingredients and blend well. Pour into pie crust. Bake 50 to 55 minutes or until knife inserted just off center comes out clean. Let cool, then place in refrigerator until ready to serve.

Per slice: Cal 313, Carb 44g, Fib 3g, Pro 7g, Fat 12g, Sod 187mg, Sug 31g

Strawberry Margarita Pie

6 servings

A quick, yummy dessert that's quite addictive.

2 ²/₃ cups Angel flake coconut, toasted
½ cup butter, melted
1 (10-oz) package frozen strawberries in syrup, thawed
1 (14-oz) can sweetened condensed milk
½ cup frozen margarita concentrate mix, thawed
2 cups (8-oz container) frozen whipped topping, thawed

In a medium mixing bowl, combine toasted coconut and butter until thoroughly mixed. Press on bottom and sides of a 9-inch pie dish (do not cover the rim of the dish).

Combine strawberries (and juice), condensed milk and margarita mix in a medium bowl; stir until well mixed. Fold in the whipped topping. Pour into pie crust. Freeze pie. If not using right away, cover with plastic wrap to seal.

Per slice: Cal 573, Carb 63g, Fib 3g, Pro 7g, Fat 33g, Sod 317.mg, Sug 60g

To Toast Coconut

Spread coconut in a single layer on a 15x10-inch jelly roll pan. Bake at 325°F for 10 to 15 minutes, stirring frequently, when it starts to brown around the edges. Bake until light golden in color.

Peanut Butter Pie

6 to 8 servings

A graham cracker crust can be substituted for the traditional pie crust. If desired, drizzle each serving with melted chocolate. "Very rich."

1 (9-inch) baked pie crust
1 (8-oz) package cream cheese, softened
1 cup creamy peanut butter
1 cup sugar
2 tablespoons butter, melted
1 cup whipping cream

In mixer bowl, beat the cream cheese until smooth. Add peanut butter, sugar and butter; beat until smooth. Whip the cream and add to peanut butter mixture; mix well. Pour into pie crust. Chill until firm.

Per slice: Cal 593, Carb 36g, Fib 2g, Pro 12g, Fat 48g, Sod 385mg, Sug 21g

Fresh Strawberry Pie

6 servings

Try to make the pie when local berries are available. They are more uniform in size and much more flavorful.

- 1 (9-inch) baked pie shell
- 1 cup sugar
- 1 cup water, divided
- 3 tablespoons cornstarch
- 3 tablespoons strawberry gelatin
- 3 to 4 cups fresh whole small strawberries

Place sugar in a small saucepan. In a small bowl, combine ¼ cup of the water with the cornstarch, stirring until smooth. Add to saucepan along with the remaining ¾ cup water; mix well. Cook over medium-low heat until thickened, stirring frequently. Stir in the gelatin.

Line pie shell with strawberries, pointed end up. Fill in where necessary with smaller berries. Pour sauce over top. Chill until set.

Per slice: Cal 232, Carb 42g, Fib 2g, Pro 2g, Fat 8g, Sod 135mg, Sug 26g

Sour Cream Apple Pie

6 servings

Apple pie is always a favorite and this one is just a little bit different.

- ¾ cup sugar, plus 2 tablespoons
- 3 tablespoons flour
- 1 cup sour cream
- 3 cups coarsely chopped apples (3 medium)
- 1 (9-inch) unbaked pie shell
- 1 teaspoon cinnamon

Preheat oven to 400°F. Combine the ¾ cup sugar, flour and sour cream; mix well. Add chopped apples. Pour into pie crust. Mix the remaining 2 tablespoons sugar with the cinnamon. Sprinkle evenly over apple mixture. Bake 15 minutes. Reduce heat to 350°F and bake 25 to 30 minutes or until apples are tender. Cool.

Per slice: Cal 262, Carb 36g, Fib 2g, Pro 3g, Fat 13g, Sod 132mg, Sug 22g

Apple Crumb Pie   6 servings

Although not a tart apple, the Golden Delicious makes a very good pie. Romes are probably my favorite. For another great apple filling, try a mixture of Golden Delicious, Granny Smith and Fuji apples.

- 1 **(9-inch) unbaked pie crust**
- 6 **to 7 tart apples, peeled and sliced**
- 1 **cup sugar, divided**
- 1 **teaspoon cinnamon**
- ¾ **cup flour**
- ⅓ **cup butter**

Preheat oven to 400°F. Arrange apple slices in pie shell. Combine ½ cup sugar and cinnamon; sprinkle over apples.

Combine remaining sugar and flour in a small bowl. With two knives or a pastry blender, cut in butter until crumbly. Sprinkle over apples. Cover pie with foil and bake 30 minutes. Uncover and bake 10 minutes or until apples are tender.

Per slice: Cal 335, Carb 52g, Fib 4g, Pro 3g, Fat 15g, Sod 174mg, Sug 31g

Quick Lemon Pie   6 to 8 servings

If you like key lime pie, you will enjoy this recipe. I had an abundance of lemons, so I substituted lemons for the limes. When ready to serve, top with the sweetened whipped cream and garnish with fresh lemon peel or fresh berries, if desired.

- 1 **(9-inch) baked pie crust**
- 5 **large egg yolks**
- 1 **(14-oz) can sweetened condensed milk**
- 6 **tablespoons fresh lemon juice**
- 1 **cup heavy cream, whipped with sugar to taste**

Preheat oven to 350°F. Beat egg yolks lightly with a whisk. Gradually stir in the condensed milk, beating until smooth. Whisk in the lemon juice. Pour into pie shell. Cover pie with foil (this prevents crust from over browning) and bake for 10 minutes. Remove foil and bake 5 to 6 minutes. The filling should be set. Cool on rack. Chill until ready to serve. Serve each slice with a dollop of whipped cream.

Per Slice: Cal 432, Carb 42g, Fib 0g, Pro 8g, Fat 26g, Sod 196mg, Sug 29g

Amazing Coconut Pie

6 to 8 servings

This is a very rich dessert and should be cut into smaller slices.

3	large eggs
¼	cup butter
1½	teaspoons vanilla extract
1	(14-oz) can sweetened condensed milk
½	cup baking mix
1	cup flaked coconut

Preheat oven to 350°F. In blender or mixer, combine first 5 ingredients along with 1½ cups water; mix well. Pour into a sprayed deep-dish 10-inch pie plate. Sprinkle coconut over top. Bake 40 to 45 minutes or until mixture is set and knife inserted just off center comes out clean. Chill.

Per slice: Cal 354, Carb 42g, Fib 2g, Pro 9g, Fat 16g, Sod 252mg, Sug 35g

Rustic Pear Pie

6 servings

1	(10-inch) unbaked pie crust
4	medium fairly ripe pears, peeled, cored, sliced
½	cup sugar
3	tablespoons flour
1	tablespoon sliced almonds

Preheat oven to 350°F. Place pie crust loosely in a deep 10-inch pie dish.

In a mixing bowl, toss the pears with the sugar and flour. Spoon into the center of the pie crust, mounding the pears and leaving about a 1-inch border from the edge of the dish. Bring the crust up and over the pears, crimping the folds lightly. Not all the pears will be covered. Cover with foil and bake 15 to 20 minutes or until pears are tender. Remove foil and sprinkle with almonds the last 5 minutes of baking time. Serve warm or room temperature.

variation: Substitute apples or peaches for the pears.

Per Slice: Cal 242, Carb 38g, Fib 3g, Pro 2g, Fat 10g, Sod 141mg, Sug 17g

Almond Cream Cheese Pie
8 servings

No crust – just light and delicious!

- **2 (8-oz each) packages cream cheese, softened**
- **⅔ cup plus 2 tablespoons sugar**
- **3 large eggs**
- **1½ teaspoons almond extract, divided**
- **1 cup sour cream**
- **1 (20-oz) can blueberry or cherry pie filling, chilled**

Preheat oven to 350ºF. Beat cream cheese in large mixer bowl until light and smooth. Add ⅔ cup of the sugar and beat until well mixed. Add eggs, one at a time, beating well after each addition. Add 1 teaspoon almond extract and continue beating a couple of minutes to make sure there aren't any lumps. Pour mixture into a sprayed 10-inch deep pie dish. Bake 25 minutes. Remove from oven and let cool 10 minutes.

Meanwhile, combine sour cream, the remaining 2 tablespoons sugar and ½ teaspoon almond extract. Carefully pour over cheesecake, spreading to ¼ inch from edge. Bake 10 minutes. Let cool; cover with plastic wrap and chill. Serve with a dollop of pie filling.

Per slice: Cal 359, Carb 23g, Fib 0g, Pro 8g, Fat 27g, Sod 213mg, Sug 15g

Banana Split Pie
6 servings

- **1 (9-inch) baked pie crust**
- **3 bananas, sliced**
- **1 tablespoon lemon juice**
- **1 pint strawberry ice cream, softened**
- **1½ cups frozen whipped topping, thawed**
- **Chocolate sauce**

Sprinkle bananas with lemon juice, stirring to coat. Arrange on bottom of pie crust. Spoon ice cream over bananas. Spread whipped topping over top. Freeze. Cover with plastic wrap if making several hours or days ahead. Remove from freezer 20 minutes before serving. Serve with chocolate sauce.

Per slice: Cal 353, Carb 42g, Fib 2g, Pro 4g, Fat 19g, Sod 172mg, Sug 24g

cookies & candies

Almond Butter Cookies   30 cookies

When my children were small we did a lot of camping and, of course, a lot of eating. We often joined other friends who also had four children. When you have a large family, I think you sometimes tend to gravitate toward others with large families. Anyway, needless to say, we went through a lot of healthy, good for you food, but also a lot of desserts and cookies. We sometimes went through two batches of brownies a day - we just couldn't keep the adults away from them.

- 1   (18.25-oz) box yellow cake mix
- ½   cup butter, melted
- ½   cup chopped almonds
- 3   large eggs, divided
- 1   (16-oz) box powdered sugar, sifted
- 1   (8-oz) package cream cheese, softened

Preheat oven to 350°F. In mixer bowl, blend cake mix, melted butter, almonds, and one egg. Pat mixture into a sprayed 13x9-inch baking dish.

Beat powdered sugar, cream cheese and remaining 2 eggs until well mixed; about 1 minute. Pour into baking dish, spreading evenly. Bake 40 to 45 minutes or until lightly browned. Cool. Cut into squares. Store in refrigerator.

Per bar: Cal 200, Carb 28g, Fib 0g, Pro 3g, Fat 9g, Sod 183mg, Sug 2g

cookie tips

Have eggs and butter at room temperature.

Measure accurately using glass measuring cups for liquid and dry measuring cups for dry ingredients.

Avoid using dark cookie sheets. They will absorb more heat and can cause over browning.

Grease cookie sheets and baking dishes only if instructed to do so.

Bake cookies on medium rack.

Cool cookies on a rack.

Always cool baking sheet before cooking a new batch.

Coconut Macaroons   36 macaroons

- ½   cup egg whites (about 4 large eggs)
- ¼   teaspoon salt
- ¾   cup sugar
- 1   teaspoon vanilla extract
- 4   cups shredded coconut

Preheat oven to 300°F. In medium saucepan, over low heat, combine egg whites, salt and sugar. Heat until warm, but not hot— you don't want to cook the egg whites. Remove from heat and stir in vanilla and coconut.

Drop into mounds, about the size of a walnut, onto greased baking sheet. Bake 20 to 25 minutes or until macaroons start to lightly brown on the bottom and around the edges. Cool on rack.

variation: Add ¾ cup finely chopped dates and/or ½ cup chopped walnuts.

Per cookie: Cal 74, Carb 8g, Fib 1g, Pro 1g, Fat 4g, Sod 61mg,Sug 7g

Finnish Jelly Fingers   7 to 8 dozen

I made hundreds of these for my daughter's wedding. They make a colorful addition to a cookie tray. The color of jam can be your choice; red, green, yellow, etc. If desired, drizzle the cookies with a powdered sugar glaze. Frozen cookies should not be frosted until ready to serve.

- 1 **cup butter, softened**
- ¾ **cup sugar**
- 1 **large egg**
- 2½ **cups flour**
- 1 **teaspoon baking powder**
-    **Jam**

Preheat oven to 375°F. In mixer bowl, cream butter and sugar. Add egg; beat thoroughly. Combine flour and baking powder. Add to butter mixture, stirring by hand. Cover and chill several hours or overnight.

Divide dough into 5 or 6 parts. Knead dough slightly to make it more workable. Roll into long ½-inch thick rolls. Carefully place on cookie sheet, allowing about 4 inches between rolls. With the side of your finger, make a well lengthwise down the roll, pressing almost to the bottom. Fill well with jam. Bake 10 to 12 minutes or until done but not brown around the edges.

Carefully place each roll on a breadboard. With a sharp knife, cut diagonally into 1¼-inch strips. Cool on rack.

Per cookie: Cal 38, Carb 5g, Fib 0g, Pro 0g, Fat 2g, Sod 21mg, Sug 2g

How to store cookies?

Soft and crisp cookies should be stored separately. Use tightly covered containers to prevent the drying out of soft cookies and the softening of crisp cookies. Cookies and cookie dough can also be frozen.

Chocolate Chow Mein Cookies   about 5 dozen cookies

Another kids' favorite. They also make a nice addition to a holiday cookie tray.

- 1 **cup butterscotch chips**
- 1 **cup semi-sweet chocolate chips**
- 1 **cup chopped walnuts**
- 1 **(5-oz) can Chow Mein noodles**

Melt chips in top of double boiler; stir until blended and smooth. Remove from heat. Add walnuts and Chow Mein noodles; gently stir until evenly coated. Drop by teaspoon onto wax paper-lined cookie sheet. Chill until firm. Store in refrigerator.

Per cookie: Cal 59, Carb 6g, Fib 0g, Pro 1g, Fat 4g, Sod 21mg, Sug 2g

Best Sugar Cookies   about 6 dozen cookies

- **2 cups butter, softened (do not substitute)**
- **2 cups sugar**
- **4 large eggs**
- **2 teaspoons vanilla extract**
- **1 teaspoon salt**
- **6 cups flour**

Preheat oven to 375°F. In mixer bowl, cream butter until smooth. Gradually add sugar, mixing well after each addition. Beat until light and fluffy. Add eggs and vanilla and mix well. Combine salt and flour. Add to creamed mixture, a little at a time and mix well. Cover and chill at least 6 hours.

On lightly floured surface, using a small amount of dough at a time, roll out to ⅛-inch thickness. Cut desired shapes with cookie cutters. Place on ungreased cookie sheets and bake 8 to 10 minutes or until just beginning to brown around edges.

Per cookie: Cal 99, Carb 12g, Fib 0g, Pro 1g, Fat 5g, Sod 73mg, Sug 4g

Cut out Cookies

Cut-out cookies (sugar cookies) are always fun to make. Young or old, it doesn't matter, we enjoy using the wonderful variety of cookie cutters available to us today.

The dough for cut-out cookies should be chilled before rolling out. Roll out only a small portion at a time and keep the rest chilled.

Roll dough on a lightly floured surface, rolling ⅛-inch thick or as specified in recipe. Cookie cutters should be dipped in flour or powdered sugar before cutting. Cookies can be served plain or decorated.

Shortbread   24 cookies

- **1 cup butter, softened**
- **½ cup sifted powdered sugar**
- **¼ teaspoon salt**
- **¼ teaspoon baking powder**
- **2 cups flour**

Preheat oven to 350°F. In mixer bowl, cream butter and powdered sugar. Beat until light. Combine remaining ingredients; add to butter mixture. Beat until thoroughly blended.

Divide mixture and pat evenly into two 9-inch pie pans. Prick all over with a fork. Bake 15 to 20 minutes or until a very light golden color. Cut into pie shaped wedges. Serve warm or cold.

Per cookie: Cal 115, Carb 11g, Fib 0g, Pro 1g, Fat 7g, Sod 86mg, Sug 3g

Mailing Cookies

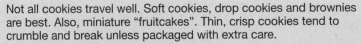

Not all cookies travel well. Soft cookies, drop cookies and brownies are best. Also, miniature "fruitcakes". Thin, crisp cookies tend to crumble and break unless packaged with extra care.

Have available plenty of filler material such as bubble wrap, styrofoam popcorn or paper towels.

Wrapping cookies back to back in plastic wrap and packing securely will minimize breakage. Be sure to mark the package Fragile.

Chocolate-Pecan Snowballs 48 cookies

A delightful chocolate surprise in the center of each snowball.

- 1 **cup milk chocolate chips**
- ¾ **cup powdered sugar, divided**
- ⅓ **cup chopped pecans**
- 1¼ **cups butter, softened**
- 1 **teaspoon vanilla extract**
- 3 **cups flour**

Preheat oven to 400°F. In a small heavy saucepan, melt chocolate chips over very low heat. Stir in ¼ cup of the powdered sugar and then the nuts. Chill just until firm enough to roll into balls. Using about a level teaspoonful, roll mixture into 48 small balls. Chill until ready to use.

Meanwhile, in a large mixer bowl, beat butter until smooth. Add vanilla and flour and beat until smooth. If mixture is too soft, chill a few minutes. Otherwise, divide into 48 balls.

Flatten each ball and wrap it around a chocolate ball, enclosing completely. Place about 1 inch apart on an ungreased baking sheet. Bake 10 to 12 minutes or until lightly browned.

Remove from baking sheet and cool about 5 minutes on rack. Roll in remaining powdered sugar and place on rack. Let cool completely, and then roll again in the powdered sugar.

Per cookie: Cal 103, Carb 10g, Fib 0g, Pro 1g, Fat 6g, Sod 38mg, Sug 4g

Butterscotch Drop Cookies 3½ dozen cookies

With these pantry items, you can always make these cookies at a moment's notice.

- 2 **cups butterscotch chips**
- ½ **cup creamy or chunky peanut butter**
- 2 **cups corn flakes**

Melt butterscotch chips and peanut butter in top of double boiler. Remove from heat and gently stir in corn flakes to coat. Drop by teaspoon on wax paper-lined cookie sheet. Chill until set.

Per cookie: Cal 83, Carb 9g, Fib 0g, Pro 1g, Fat 4g, Sod 31mg, Sug 0g

Christmas Holly Cookies 3 dozen cookies

These make a colorful addition to a tray of assorted holiday cookies.

- **35** **large marshmallows**
- **½** **cup butter**
- **1** **teaspoon vanilla extract**
- **1½** **teaspoons green food coloring (approx.)**
- **4** **cups corn flakes**
- **Red hot candies (for decoration)**

Melt marshmallows and butter in top of double boiler; stir to blend. Stir in vanilla extract and enough food coloring to make a dark green. Remove from heat and gently stir in cereal.

Working quickly, drop by teaspoon onto wax paper-lined cookie sheet. Decorate each cookie with 3 red hots for holly berries. Chill.

Per cookie: Cal 59, Carb 9g, Fib 0g, Pro 0g, Fat 2g, Sod 47mg, Sug 5g

Holiday Baking

Holiday baking can be an enormous task and it's the last thing you want to think about when you have a million other things to do.

Being organized is the best ingredient for stress-free cooking. Decide on the recipes you want to make that can be frozen. Depending on how much you want to do, starting in September and after the kids are in school, make a recipe or two a week and freeze. This will make for less stress in your life and your family will enjoy the goodies.

French Madeleines   6 dozen

These are absolutely delicious. They taste like crisp little butter cakes. Just before serving, sift powdered sugar lightly over top. The amount of vanilla extract called for is correct. Can freeze.

- **4** **large eggs**
- **2** **cups sugar**
- **2** **cups flour**
- **1½** **cups butter, melted**
- **1** **tablespoon vanilla extract**
- **Sifted powdered sugar**

Preheat oven to 425°F. Combine eggs and sugar in top of double boiler. Heat until lukewarm. Remove from heat and place mixture in mixer bowl. Beat until cooled.

Add flour gradually, mixing well after each addition. Add melted butter and vanilla, mixing until smooth.

Use special shell shaped Madeleine molds which have been sprayed, or small 1½-inch sprayed muffin tins. Fill molds two-thirds full. Bake 8 to 10 minutes until just lightly browned around the edges. Remove from oven; let stand about a minute. Tap pan to release cakes; cool on rack.

Per cookie: Cal 63, Carb 7g, Fib 0g, Pro 1g, Fat 4g, Sod 32mg, Sug 4g

Raisin Crunchies   about 3½ dozen cookies

- **2**   **cups semi-sweet chocolate chips**
- **½**   **teaspoon vanilla extract**
- **1½**   **cups raisins**
- **½**   **cup peanuts**
- **1**   **cup corn flakes**

Melt chocolate chips in top of double boiler, stirring until smooth. Remove from heat; stir in vanilla, raisins, peanuts and cereal. Drop by teaspoon onto wax paper lined cookie sheet. Chill until firm.

tip: If desired, spread mixture into a lightly buttered 8x8-inch dish. Chill before cutting into squares.

Per cookie: Cal 69, Carb 10g, Fib 1g, Pro 1g, Fat 3g, Sod 7mg, Sug 9g

Peanut Butter Drop Cookies   about 18 cookies

The basic cookie is very simple and delicious on its own, but if the mood strikes you, you can always add a few extra ingredients.

- **1**   **cup peanut butter**
- **1**   **cup sugar**
- **1**   **large egg**
- **1**   **teaspoon baking soda**
- **1**   **teaspoon vanilla extract**

Preheat oven to 350°F. In mixing bowl, combine all ingredients and mix until well blended. Form into walnut size balls and place on ungreased cookie sheet. Bake 12 to 15 minutes or until golden. They should be slightly soft in the center.

variation: Add chocolate chips and/or chopped nuts. Or, after removing from oven, top centers with chocolate chips, an M&M® candy or a chocolate kiss. YUM!

note: This recipe does not contain flour!

Per cookie: Cal 116, Carb 11g, Fib 1g, Pro 4g, Fat 7g, Sod 101mg, Sug 9g

Quick Chocolate Cookies

about 4 dozen cookies

My grandson Ben loves to make these cookies. They are quick and easy for him to make and he takes pride in making a delicious cookie that everyone enjoys.

1	(18.25-oz) box German Chocolate cake mix
½	cup vegetable oil
2	large eggs
½	cup flaked coconut
1	cup chopped walnuts or pecans

Preheat oven to 350°F. In a mixer bowl, beat the cake mix, oil, and eggs until blended. Add coconut and nuts and beat on low just until mixed. Drop dough by rounded teaspoons (less than walnut size), onto an ungreased baking sheet. Bake 12 to 14 minutes. Cookies should be slightly soft in the center.

variation: In place of coconut and nuts, Add ½ cup raisins and/or 1 cup chocolate chips to the dough.

Per Cookie: Cal 89, Carb 8g, Fib 0g, Pro 1g, Fat 6g, Sod 81mg, Sug 5g

Peanut Butter Cookies

about 36 cookies

Is there anyone who doesn't like peanut butter cookies? Let the kids make these for their school lunches or after school snacks.

½	cup butter, softened
1	cup packed light brown sugar
1½	cups chunky peanut butter
1	large egg
1¾	cup flour
1	teaspoon baking powder

Preheat oven to 350°F. Combine butter, brown sugar and peanut butter in a mixer bowl, beating until light in color. Add the egg and mix well. Combine flour and baking powder and mix just until flour is blended. Make walnut-size balls and place on ungreased baking sheets. Flatten with a fork in a crisscross pattern. Bake 10 to 12 minutes. Cookies should be slightly soft in the center.

variation: Place a single Hershey kiss® in the center of each cookie immediately after removing from oven.

Per Cookie: Cal 128. Carb 12g, Fib 1g, Pro 3g, Fat 8g, Sod 88mg, Sug 6g

Butter Pecan Cookies   3 dozen cookies

These are simple ingredients that turn into a very crisp butter flavored cookie. Delicious served with a glass of milk or your favorite ice cream.

- 1 **cup butter, softened**
- ¾ **cup sugar**
- ½ **teaspoon baking soda**
- ½ **teaspoon white vinegar**
- 1½ **cups flour**
- ¾ **cup chopped pecans, toasted**

Preheat oven to 325°F. In mixer bowl, beat butter about 1 minute. Add sugar, baking soda and vinegar and beat 7 to 8 minutes or until fluffy and turns almost white in color. By hand, stir in the flour and then the pecans. Drop onto an ungreased baking sheet making mounds slightly smaller than a walnut. Bake 18 to 20 minutes or until lightly browned around the edges.

Per Cookie: Cal 90, Carb 7g, Fib 0g, Pro 1g, Fat 7g, Sod 38mg, Sug 3g

Lemon Nut Cookies   48 cookies

Add this delicious cookie to your list of family favorite cookie recipes.

- 1 **(18.25-oz) box lemon cake mix**
- 2 **large eggs**
- ½ **cup vegetable oil**
- 1½ **teaspoons fresh lemon peel**
- ⅓ **cup finely chopped walnuts**

Preheat oven to 350°F. In large mixer bowl, combine first four ingredients. Beat on low until thoroughly mixed. Drop rounded teaspoons about 2 inches apart onto ungreased cookie sheets. They should be slightly smaller than a walnut.

With finger, make an indentation in middle of each cookie, pressing almost to the bottom. Fill with chopped nuts. Bake 9 to 12 minutes. Cookies should not brown, but will flatten slightly just before the cookies test done.

Per cookie: Cal 74, Carb 8g, Fib 0g, Pro 1g, Fat 4g, Sod 81mg, Sug 5g

Cranberry-Nut Shortbread Cookies about 48 cookies

A wonderful, not too sweet, shortbread cookie.

1¼　cups butter, softened
1　cup sifted powdered sugar
2¼　cups flour
½　cup dried cranberries
½　cup chopped pecans or hazelnuts

Preheat oven to 325°F. In mixer bowl, cream the butter and sugar. Gradually add the flour and beat just until mixed. Stir in the cranberries and nuts.

Form into 1-inch balls and place on an ungreased baking sheet. Spray the bottom of a small glass, dip in sugar and flatten each ball to a little more than ¼-inch thick. Bake 12 to 14 minutes or until just the bottoms are golden.

Per cookie: Cal 86, Carb 9g, Fib 0g, Pro 1g, Fat 6g, Sod 35mg, Sug 4g

Pecan Shortbread Cookies 48 cookies

Everyone loves these little cookies. Put on the coffee pot and have friends over for coffee, cookies and great conversation.

1¼　cups butter, softened
1¾　cups powdered sugar, divided
3　cups flour
1　cup chopped pecans, divided
1　lemon (2 tablespoons juice, 1 teaspoon peel)

Preheat oven to 350°F. In a large mixer bowl, combine butter and ¾ cup of the powdered sugar and beat until light and fluffy. Add flour and beat just until blended. Stir in ½ cup of the pecans. Press dough into an ungreased 15x10-inch baking pan. Sprinkle with remaining ½ cup pecans and bake 20 to 25 minutes or until light golden – watch carefully. Place pan on wire rack and while hot, cut into squares and then cut each square diagonally in half. Let cool in pan.

Combine remaining 1 cup powdered sugar with lemon peel and just enough lemon juice to make a glaze. Drizzle cookies with the glaze; let set slightly, and then remove from pan.

note: Cut cookies evenly by making 3 lengthwise cuts and five crosswise cuts. You should then have 24 squares. Then cut diagonally, cutting each square in half, to yield 48 cookies.

Per cookie: Cal 107, Carb 12g, Fib 0g, Pro 1g, Fat 6g, Sod 35mg, Sug 5g

Layered Chocolate Bars   45 bars

My mother regularly supplies me with wonderful fresh pecans that are put to good use in these chocolate pecan bars.

- **1   (18-oz) package sugar cookie dough, softened**
- **2   cups semi-sweet chocolate chips**
- **2   cups flaked coconut**
- **1   cup pecans**
- **1   (4-oz) can sweetened condensed milk**

Preheat oven to 350°F. Pat cookie dough evenly into a lightly sprayed 15x10-inch baking pan. Sprinkle with the chocolate chips, coconut and then the pecans. Pour condensed milk over the top. Bake 20 to 22 minutes or until lightly browned and center is set.

Per Bar: Cal 133, Carb 15g, Fib 1g, Pro 1g, Fat 8g, Sod 65mg. Sug 10g

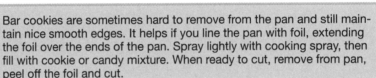

Bar Cookies

Bar cookies are sometimes hard to remove from the pan and still maintain nice smooth edges. It helps if you line the pan with foil, extending the foil over the ends of the pan. Spray lightly with cooking spray, then fill with cookie or candy mixture. When ready to cut, remove from pan, peel off the foil and cut.

Peanut Butter Krispie Bars   about 24 bars

This is a twist on an all time favorite recipe. You can melt the butter and marshmallows in the microwave if you prefer, but remember to stir frequently.

- **¼   cup butter**
- **40   large marshmallows**
- **5   cups crispy rice cereal**
- **¼   cup creamy peanut butter**

In a large saucepan, melt butter over low heat. Add marshmallows and cook, stirring constantly, until melted and smooth. Remove from heat and quickly stir in the peanut butter.

Add cereal and stir until well mixed. Spoon into a sprayed 13x9-inch baking dish and press evenly, using spatula or buttered hands - because mixture is hot. Cool and cut into squares.

Per Bar: Cal 94, Carb 15g, Fib 0g, Pro 1g, Fat 3g, Sod 78mg, Sug 8g

Coconut Nut Bars   30 bars

You can play around with this recipe by using a variety of chips and nuts.

- ¼ **cup butter, melted**
- 1½ **cups quick-cooking oats**
- 1½ **cups flaked coconut**
- 1 **(14-oz) can sweetened condensed milk**
- 1 **cup semi-sweet chocolate chips**
- ½ **cup chopped pecans or walnuts**

Preheat oven to 350°F. Pour butter into a 13x9-inch baking dish. Sprinkle oats evenly over butter (most of the oats will not be coated). Sprinkle coconut over the top. Pour condensed milk over coconut. Sprinkle with chocolate chips and pecans. Press down slightly.

Bake 20 to 25 minutes or until just lightly browned. Cool before cutting into bars.

Per Bar: Cal 145, Carb 17g, Fib 1g, Pro 2g, Fat 8g, Sod 46mg, Sug 13g

Quick Chocolate Bars   40 bars

Remember the Chocolate Revel Bars that are so popular and get gobbled up almost as soon as they come out of the oven? Well, these are just about as good and a whole lot easier to make.

- 1 **(18.25-oz) box white cake mix**
- ⅓ **cup vegetable oil**
- 2 **large eggs**
- ¼ **cup butter**
- 1 **(14-oz) can sweetened condensed milk**
- 1 **cup semi-sweet chocolate chips**

Preheat oven to 350°F. In a medium bowl, combine first three ingredients. Mix thoroughly with a stiff spatula or wooden spoon. Press two-thirds of the mixture into a sprayed 13x9-inch baking pan.

In small saucepan, melt butter over low heat. Add condensed milk and chocolate chips. Cook until mixture is melted, stirring until smooth. Pour evenly over crust. By hand, drop small pieces of dough over top. Bake 25 to 30 minutes or until lightly browned and chocolate filling feels somewhat firm. Cool and cut into bars.

Per Bar: Cal 130, Carb 18g, Fib 0g, Pro 2g, Fat 6g, Sod 108mg, Sug 14g

Peanut Butter Oatmeal Bars

about 30 bars

A great lunch box cookie. Just wrap in a little plastic wrap and pack.

- ⅔ **cup butter, melted**
- ¼ **cup, plus ⅓ cup creamy peanut butter**
- ¼ **cup light corn syrup**
- 1 **cup firmly packed light brown sugar**
- 4 **cups quick-cooking oatmeal**
- 1½ **cups semi-sweet chocolate chips**

Preheat oven to 350°F. In mixing bowl, combine butter, ¼ cup peanut butter, corn syrup, brown sugar and oatmeal. Press evenly into a sprayed 13x9-inch baking pan. Bake 10 to 12 minutes or until just starting to brown around the edges. Don't over bake or you won't be able to cut into nice neat bars. Place on rack and let cool while preparing frosting.

In a small saucepan, melt chocolate chips and the ⅓ cup peanut butter; stir to blend. Spread over cookie mixture and let cool. Cover and store in refrigerator until frosting is set.

Per Bar: Cal 176 Carb 22g, Fib 2g, Pro 3g, Fat 9g, Sod 57mg, Sug 14g

Chocolate Coconut Bars

about 30 bars

Bar cookies can save a lot of time in the kitchen. These attractive bars are not only good to eat but make a nice addition to any cookie tray.

- 1½ **cups graham cracker crumbs**
- ½ **cup butter, melted**
- 2⅓ **cups flaked coconut**
- 1 **(14-oz) can sweetened condensed milk**
- 2 **cups semi-sweet chocolate chips**
- ½ **cup creamy peanut butter**

Preheat oven to 350°F. Combine graham cracker crumbs and melted butter. Press into ungreased 13x9-inch baking dish. Sprinkle coconut over top. Pour condensed milk over coconut. Bake 25 to 30 minutes or until lightly browned.

Meanwhile, over low heat, melt chocolate chips with peanut butter. Pour over hot coconut layer. Let cool. Cut into bars.

Per Bar: Cal 181, Carb 19.3g, Fib 1.42g, Pro 3g, Fat 11.16g, Sod 96.45mg, Sug 15.92g

Chocolate Nut Bars

30 bars

I try to always have a cake mix on hand to make these quick and easy chocolate cookies.

- **1 (18.25-oz) box Devil's Food cake mix**
- **2 large eggs**
- **½ cup butter, melted**
- **1 cup semi-sweet chocolate chips**
- **1 cup chopped walnuts or pecans, divided**

Preheat oven to 350ºF. Combine first 3 ingredients in mixing bowl, stirring until all dry ingredients are moistened. Add chocolate chips and ¾ cup of the nuts. Press into a sprayed 13x9-inch baking pan. Sprinkle with remaining ¼ cup nuts.

Bake 20 to 25 minutes or until tester inserted in center comes out clean. Cool and cut into bars.

Per bar: Cal 160, Carb 16g, Fib 1g, Pro 3g, Fat 10g, Sod 156mg, Sug 11g

Raspberry Meringue Bars

4 dozen bars

- ¾ **cup shortening**
- ⅓ **cup sugar, plus ½ cup sugar**
- 2 **large eggs, separated**
- 1½ **cups flour**
- 1 **cup raspberry preserves**
- ⅓ **cup finely chopped walnuts**

Preheat oven to 350°F. In mixer bowl, cream shortening and ⅓ cup sugar. Add egg yolks and mix thoroughly. Stir in flour.

Pat mixture evenly into bottom of a 13x9-inch pan. Bake 15 minutes or until golden. Cool. Spread preserves evenly over crust. Beat egg whites until soft peaks form; gradually add the ½ cup sugar and beat until stiff but not dry; spread over preserves. Sprinkle with nuts. Bake 30 minutes.

Per bar: Cal 75, Carb 10g, Fib 0g, Pro 1g, Fat 4g, Sod 3mg, Sug 7g

Chocolate Peanut Squares

25 squares

Delicious! Those yummy Peanut Butter Cups have some competition here. These freeze well.

- ½ **cup butter, melted**
- 5½ **double graham crackers, crushed fine**
- 2 **cups sifted powdered sugar**
- ½ **cup chunky peanut butter**
- 1 **cup semi-sweet chocolate chips**

Pour melted butter over graham cracker crumbs, stirring to blend. Add powdered sugar and peanut butter; mix well. Pat into sprayed 8x8-inch pan, spreading evenly.

Melt chocolate chips in top of double boiler. Spread over top of mixture. Chill until firm, but not hard, about 30 minutes. Cut into squares. Cover and chill until ready to serve.

Per square: Cal 152, Carb 20g, Fib 1g, Pro 2g, Fat 8g, Sod 71mg, Sug 16g

Mike's Babe Ruth Bars   4 dozen

When Mike had friends stay over, they always made these cookies and devoured every one of them.

- **1 cup sugar**
- **1 cup light corn syrup**
- **1 cup chunky peanut butter**
- **6 cups Special K® cereal**
- **1 cup semi-sweet chocolate chips**
- **1 cup butterscotch chips**

Combine sugar and corn syrup in a 2-quart saucepan. Place over medium heat and bring to a boil, stirring occasionally. Remove from heat. Add peanut butter. Stir in cereal until evenly coated. Press mixture into a sprayed 13x9-inch pan. Cool.

Melt chips in top of double boiler. Spread over cookie mixture. Cool; then cut into bars.

Per bar: Cal 119, Carb 18g, Fib 1g, Pro 3g, Fat 5g, Sod 66mg, Sug 11g

Chocolate Walnut Brownies   about 24 brownies

When I made these brownies, while camping or boating, I was amazed at how many "new" friends showed up. Kids and adults!

- **1 cup butter**
- **1⅔ cups semi-sweet chocolate chips, divided**
- **2 cups sugar**
- **3 large eggs**
- **1 cup flour**
- **1 cup coarsely chopped walnuts**

Preheat oven to 350°F. Melt butter and ⅔ cup of the chocolate chips over very low heat. Remove from heat. Stir in sugar. Add eggs; stir until well mixed. Add flour and nuts.

Pour into a sprayed 13x9-inch baking pan. Sprinkle with remaining 1 cup chocolate chips. Bake 30 to 35 minutes or until tester inserted in center comes out almost clean (do not over bake). Cool.

Per brownie: Cal 178, Carb 19g, Fib 1g, Pro 2g, Fat 12g, Sod 53mg, Sug 15g

Brian's Peanut Butter Candy   3 dozen

1   **cup peanut butter, smooth or crunchy**
1   **cup light corn syrup**
1   **cup powdered milk**
1   **(or more) cup sifted powdered sugar**

Combine all ingredients and mix until thoroughly blended. Shape into balls and roll in additional powdered sugar. Place on baking sheet and chill until set.

Per candy: Cal 12, Carb 15g, Fib 0g, Pro 2g, Fat 4g, Sod 54mg, Sug 13g

Ben's Favorite Fudge   about 36 pieces

This or similar recipes have been printed over the years as See's® Fudge. I don't know how true that is, but I do know this has become one of my favorite fudge recipes. I had to experiment a bit to find the right temperature setting on my stove, which I found to be number five. This could vary from stove to stove. I also found that using a reliable cooking thermometer and cooking the sugar mixture to 234°F would ensure a perfect creamy fudge.

¼   **cup butter, sliced**
1   **cup semi-sweet chocolate chips**
1¼ **cups coarsely chopped pecans or walnuts**
2   **cups sugar**
1   **(5¾-oz) can evaporated milk**
10 **large marshmallows**

Place butter, chocolate chips and nuts in a large mixing bowl and set aside.

Place the sugar, milk and marshmallows in a heavy 3-quart saucepan. Bring to a boil over medium heat, stirring frequently. Cook about 6 minutes or until the temperature reaches 234°F, stirring constantly. Pour over ingredients in bowl and beat with a heavy wooden spoon or spatula until thoroughly mixed and butter and chocolate chips have melted. Pour into a buttered 8x8-inch baking dish. Chill until firm. Cut into square pieces.

hint: It is much easier to remove the fudge and cut into neat squares if you first line the bottom and sides of the dish with foil; lightly butter foil. Then, when firm, turn the dish upside down to remove.

Per square: Cal 101, Carb 14g, Fib 1g, Pro 1g, Fat 6g, Sod 16mg, Sug 12g

White Chocolate Clusters   about 48 candies

Real white chocolate (as opposed to almond bark) has a very low melting point. If allowed to get too hot, it will be grainy and sometimes almost crunchy. If this happens, don't try to revive it, you'll have no choice but to throw it away. This is expensive, so remember...Low Heat.

- **12 ounces white chocolate**
- **3 cups coarsely chopped pecans or walnuts**
- **⅓ cup semi-sweet chocolate chips**

Melt white chocolate in top of double boiler or in a heavy saucepan over very low heat. Remove from heat and add pecans. Gently stir in the chocolate chips.

Drop by tablespoon onto wax paper; cool.

variation: Omit chocolate chips and add dried cranberries, blueberries or other dried fruit.

Per candy: Cal 97, Carb 6g, Fib 1g, Pro 1g, Fat 8g, Sod 8mg, Sug 5g

Cran-Pecan Chocolate Bark   24 candies

Just a tiny bit of dried cranberries adds color as well as flavor.

- **12 ounces milk chocolate**
- **1 tablespoon shortening**
- **¼ cup dried cranberries**
- **¾ cup finely chopped pecans**

In small heavy saucepan, melt chocolate and shortening over very low heat. Remove from heat and stir in cranberries and ¼ cup pecans.

Pour into a buttered, then wax paper lined 11x7-inch baking dish; spread evenly. Sprinkle with remaining pecans; press lightly. Chill about 45 minutes to set. Remove and break into small pieces.

Per Piece: Cal 110, Carb 10g, Fib 1g, Pro 1g, Fat 7g, Sod 11mg, Sug 8g

Easy Toffee about 50 pieces

This doesn't last very long around our house, but will keep several weeks in a covered container.

2	**cups finely chopped walnuts, divided**
1	**cup firmly packed light brown sugar**
¾	**cup butter**
1¼	**cups semi-sweet or milk chocolate chips**

Sprinkle 1 cup of the walnuts evenly in well-buttered 8x8-inch dish.

Combine brown sugar and butter in small heavy saucepan. Bring to a boil over medium heat. Cook, stirring occasionally, to hard-ball stage, about 266°F on a candy thermometer. Pour hot mixture evenly over walnuts.

Sprinkle chocolate chips over top. Sprinkle remaining 1 cup walnuts over the chocolate chips. Press mixture down firmly using a knife or metal spatula. Let stand until firm (or chill). Break into small pieces.

Per piece: Cal 92, Carb 7g, Fib 0g, Pro 1g, Fat 7g, Sod 23mg, Sug 6g

Candied Walnuts 3½ cups

Do try these, they are delicious. Bet you can't eat just one! For best results, don't try making these on a rainy day. If walnut halves are large, break in half. In fact, I usually break most of them in half.

½	**cup sugar**
1	**cup firmly packed light brown sugar**
½	**cup sour cream**
1	**teaspoon vanilla extract**
3½	**cups walnut halves**

Combine sugar, brown sugar and sour cream in a heavy medium saucepan; stir to blend. Cook over medium heat, stirring constantly, until sugar is dissolved. Continue cooking, without stirring, to 238°F on candy thermometer.

Remove from heat; quickly stir in vanilla. Add walnuts and stir to coat. Turn out on waxed paper-lined baking sheet. Working with 2 forks, quickly separate walnuts. Let stand until coating is dry.

Per 2 tbsp: Cal 122, Carb 11g, Fib 1g, Pro 2g, Fat 8g, Sod 2g, Sug 10g

Microwave Peanut Brittle about 50 pieces

- 1 **cup sugar**
- ½ **cup light corn syrup**
- 1¾ **cup Spanish peanuts**
- 1 **teaspoon butter**
- 1 **teaspoon vanilla extract**
- 1 **teaspoon baking soda**

In a 4-cup glass measuring cup (or microwave safe bowl), combine sugar and corn syrup. Cook on high 4 minutes. Add peanuts and cook 4 minutes. Add butter and vanilla; cook 1 minute. Quickly fold in baking soda. Quickly spread on greased cookie sheet to cool. Break into pieces.

microwave variation: Use cashews or dry roasted peanuts. Mixed nuts are also very good. Cooking time may vary according to wattage of individual microwave ovens.

Per piece: Cal 49, Carb 6g, Fib 0g, Pro 1g, Fat 3g, Sod 6mg, Sug 6g

Orange Almond Bark about 50 pieces

Use a good quality chocolate-You'll be happy you did.

- 1 **orange (with nice rind)**
- 16 **ounces semi-sweet chocolate, chopped**
- 1½ **cups slivered almonds**
- ¼ **teaspoon coarse salt**
- 1 **cup dried tart cherries, chopped (optional)**

Line a large baking sheet with foil and chill. Using a large zester, cut zest from orange into 1-inch long strips. Place chocolate in double boiler and heat slowly until melted and smooth. Mix in half the nuts, half the zest and half the cherries (if using). Pour onto baking sheet and spread with a rubber spatula to about ¼-inch thick.

Sprinkle with remaining nuts, zest and fruit, then with coarse salt. Chill until firm; break into pieces. Store in refrigerator.

note: If you don't have a zester, you can use a vegetable peeler. Peel lightly to only get the zest (orange part). Then cut zest into very thin strips.

Per Piece: Cal 75, Carb 9g, Fib 1g, Pro 2g, Fat 4g, Sod 12mg, Sug 7g

Snowballs   2½ to 3 dozen

Snowballs are a must for the holidays. We have been enjoying this recipe for over thirty years. Buy coconut when it is on sale and double or triple the recipe. They can be made several months ahead and frozen.

- **1 cup semi-sweet chocolate chips**
- **⅓ cup canned evaporated milk**
- **1 cup sifted powdered sugar**
- **½ cup finely chopped walnuts**
- **1¼ cups flaked coconut**

Combine chocolate chips and milk in top of double boiler. Heat until melted, stirring to blend. Remove from heat. Stir in powdered sugar and walnuts. Chill slightly (until mixture just begins to hold its shape).

Drop by teaspoon onto mound of coconut. Roll in coconut; form into balls. Chill until set.

Per ball: Cal 71, Carb 9.g, Fib 1g, Pro 1g, Fat 4g, Sod 15mg, Sug 8g

Chocolate Bon Bons   about 7 dozen

This is an easy recipe but time consuming. You can make the Bon Bons ahead and freeze. Then at your convenience, you can dip them in the chocolate.

- **¼ cup butter, softened**
- **1 cup peanut butter**
- **2 cups sifted powdered sugar**
- **1 cup finely chopped peanuts**
- **2 cups semi-sweet chocolate chips**
- **1 tablespoon melted paraffin**

In mixer bowl, cream butter, peanut butter and powdered sugar. Stir in peanuts. If mixture is too soft, add a little more powdered sugar.

Roll into small balls and place on cookie sheet. Stick a wooden toothpick in center of each ball and freeze for at least one hour. (This will make the dipping process much easier.)

In top of double boiler, melt chocolate chips and paraffin and blend thoroughly. Remove 5 to 6 Bon Bons at a time from freezer. Dip one at a time in hot chocolate; remove excess by tapping edge of pan with side of toothpick. Place on waxed paper. Remove toothpick and fill in hole with additional chocolate, swirling to make a design. Place in refrigerator to set. Store in covered container in refrigerator or freeze.

Per bon bon: Cal 64, Carb 7g, Fib 1g, Pro 1g, Fat 4g, Sod 18mg, Sug 6g

brunch & lunch

eggs

soups

tarts

sandwiches

wraps

pizza

Basic Omelet   1 omelet

Any filling such as grated cheese and/or chopped ham, onion, green pepper, mushrooms, apple etc. can be added to top of omelet just before the eggs start to set.

- 3 **large eggs**
- ½ **teaspoon salt**
- ⅛ **teaspoon pepper**
- 1 **teaspoon water**
- 1 **tablespoon butter**

Slowly heat a 8 or 9-inch curved-sided nonstick skillet over medium heat. The pan must be hot enough for the butter to sizzle but not brown.

Combine first 4 ingredients in small bowl, mixing with fork until whites and yolks are just blended. Add butter to skillet; increase heat slightly. When melted, add eggs all at once. As eggs begin to set, pull edges slightly up and toward the center, letting uncooked egg flow underneath. When eggs are lightly set, fold in half and serve.

Per omelet: Cal 333, Carb 2g, Fib 0g, Pro 19g, Fat 27g, Sod 504mg, Sug 2g

Baked Bacon Omelet   4 to 6 servings

Have cooked bacon on hand in the freezer for these tasty omelets.

- 6 **large eggs, lightly beaten**
- ⅓ **cup Half & Half**
- 3 **slices bacon, cooked, crumbled**
- ¼ **teaspoon pepper**
- 1½ **cups (6-oz) Cheddar cheese, shredded**
- ¼ **cup chopped green onion**

Preheat oven to 400ºF. Combine eggs, Half & Half, and ⅓ cup water. Add bacon, pepper, cheese, and onion. Pour into a sprayed 8x8-inch baking dish. Bake 18 to 20 minutes or until center is set.

tip: Omelets are easier to make if cooked in a curve-sided nonstick skillet.

Per Serving: Cal 225, Carb 2g, Fib 0g, Pro 15g, Fat 18g, Sod 306mg, Sug 1g

Company Swiss Eggs   8 to 10 servings

It doesn't take long to have this dish prepared and baking in the oven. Add sweet rolls or a coffee cake, sausage links and sliced strawberries or melon. What a treat. Surprise your family and make this a special meal for them.

- 2 cups (8-oz) Gruyere or Swiss cheese, shredded
- ¼ cup butter
- 1 cup whipping cream
- ½ teaspoon salt
- ⅛ teaspoon pepper
- 12 large eggs, lightly beaten

Sprinkle cheese in a sprayed 13x9-inch baking dish. Dot with butter.

Combine cream, salt and pepper. Pour half of cream over cheese. Pour eggs over top; add remaining cream. Bake 30 to 35 minutes or until eggs are set.

Per serving: Cal 308, Carb 2g., Fib 0g, Pro 14g, Fat 26g, Sod 272mg, Sug 1g

Swiss Strata   8 servings

Being able to prepare a dish the night before and bake the next day is right up there with slow-cooking for me. It makes a company breakfast or brunch so much easier. Just add fresh fruit, coffee and juice.

- 1 (8-oz) loaf French bread
- 1 cup ham, cubed or cut into slices
- 1 cup (4-oz) Swiss cheese, shredded
- 6 large eggs, lightly beaten
- 1 cup whipping cream or half and half
- 1 cup milk

Preheat oven to 350°F. Tear bread into chunks and place in a sprayed 13x9-inch baking dish. Sprinkle with ham and cheese.

In medium mixing bowl, combine the eggs, whipping cream and milk. Pour over bread mixture. Cover and refrigerate overnight. Bake, uncovered, 40 to 45 minutes, or until golden.

hint: If you are unable to find an 8-ounce loaf of bread, purchase a 16-ounce loaf and use the other half for dinner or French toast.

Per serving: Cal 351, Carb 17g, Fib 1g, Pro 17g, Fat 23g, Sod 283mg, Sug 3g

Frittata
4 servings

- 6 **large eggs**
- 1 **cup milk**
- 1 **tablespoon butter, melted**
- ¼ **teaspoon salt**
- ⅛ **teaspoon pepper**
- 1 **cup (4-oz) Cheddar cheese, shredded**

Preheat oven to 400°F. With wire whisk, beat first 5 ingredients until blended. Pour into a sprayed deep-dish 10-inch pie dish. Sprinkle cheese over top. Bake 20 minutes or until lightly browned and cooked through.

tip: For variety, sprinkle top with parsley, ham, bacon, or sausage and cheese. Sliced vegetables and mushrooms can also be added.

Per serving: Cal 286, Carb 4g, Fib 0g, Pro 19g, Fat 21g, Sod 461mg, Sug 4g

Sausage Brunch Soufflé
6 servings

- 1½ **pounds seasoned bulk pork sausage**
- 6 **slices white bread with crust, cubed**
- 6 **large eggs**
- 2 **cups milk**
- 1 **tablespoon dry mustard**
- 1 **cup (4-oz) Cheddar cheese, shredded**

Preheat oven to 350°F. Brown sausage and drain off fat. Place bread cubes in sprayed 11x7-inch baking dish.

In mixing bowl, combine eggs, milk and mustard. Add sausage and pour mixture over bread cubes. Cover and chill several hours or overnight.

When ready to serve, bake 40 to 45 minutes or until lightly browned and mixture is set.

Per serving: Cal 330, Carb 15g, Fib 0g, Pro 19g, Fat 21g, Sod 725mg, Sug 5g

Ham & Cheese Bake   4 servings

Tired of the same old thing for breakfast? This recipe never fails to please. Serve as a breakfast, brunch or light dinner dish. Add fresh fruit or a fruit salad. A nice crisp roll or biscuit would also make a nice addition.

- 3   **cups frozen hash browns, thawed**
- 1   **cup (4-oz) Swiss cheese, shredded**
- 1   **cup finely diced ham**
- 1   **cup (4-oz) Monterey Jack cheese with peppers, shredded**
- 4   **large eggs, lightly beaten**
- 1   **cup half and half**

Preheat oven to 400°F. Place hash browns in a sprayed 1½-quart deep casserole. Bake 20 minutes. Remove from oven and reduce temperature to 350°. Sprinkle Swiss cheese over potatoes, then the ham and then the Monterey Jack cheese. In a small mixing bowl combine the eggs and half and half. Pour over the cheese. Bake, uncovered, about 45 minutes or until center is set.

note: It is sometimes hard to tell exactly when the center is set in this recipe. A knife inserted in the center should look fairly dry. The casserole will continue to cook somewhat in the center if allowed to stand about 10 minutes. Also good reheated.

Per serving: Cal 397, Carb 22g, Fib 1g, Pro 23g, Fat 24g, Sod 248mg, Sug 0g

Gourmet Italian Eggs   1 serving

Eggs are a great nutrient to start your day. High in protein and low in carbs. However, eating them fried, scrambled or poached gets boring. Try this recipe for a great treat.

- 3   **Large eggs**
- 1½   **teaspoons pesto**
- 1   **tablespoon chopped tomato**
- 1   **to 3 teaspoons Parmesan cheese, shredded**

In a small mixing bowl, whisk eggs with a fork until a smooth consistency. Heat a small skillet (non-stick, sprayed or buttered) over medium heat and add eggs. Reduce heat to medium low and continue cooking eggs, gently stirring. When eggs are within one minute of desired doneness add pesto and tomato; finish cooking. (You may add pepper at this stage, but salt is not necessary). Place eggs on plate and top with desired amount of Parmesan cheese.

note: multiply recipe as desired.

Per Serving: Cal 282, Carb 3g, Fib 0g, Pro 21g, Fat 20g, Sod 274mg, Sug 2g

Sausage Egg Scramble

4 servings

If Pepper Jack cheese isn't your favorite, substitute Cheddar or Colby.

- **4 ounces sausage**
- **¼ cup chopped onion**
- **2 tablespoons chopped green pepper**
- **6 large eggs**
- **½ cup (2-oz) Pepper Jack cheese, shredded**

Cook sausage, onion, and green pepper in a medium skillet; drain.

Combine eggs with ¼ cup water. Add to sausage and cook over medium heat, stirring occasionally. Sprinkle with cheese and serve.

Per Serving: Cal 226, Carb 3g, Fib 0g, Pro 16g, Fat 16g, Sod 360mg, Sug 2g

Heat and Hold Scrambled Eggs

6 servings

Scrambled eggs, if allowed to stand any time at all, will become watery. This recipe allows you more time, thus avoiding any last minute calamities.

- **¼ cup butter (do not substitute)**
- **12 large eggs**
- **1⅓ cups milk**
- **1 teaspoon salt**
- **⅛ teaspoon pepper**
- **2 tablespoons flour**

Melt butter in large skillet over low heat. Combine remaining ingredients in mixing bowl; mix until smooth. Pour mixture into skillet. As eggs cook, lift outside edges to allow uncooked eggs to flow underneath. Continue stirring until eggs are cooked, but still have a creamy texture. Serve, or cover and keep warm until serving time.

Per serving: Cal 194, Carb 4g, Fib 0g, Pro 11g, Fat 14g, Sod 443mg, Sug 3g

Orange French Toast

6 servings

A twist on French toast that makes it rich, but fresh.

- 4 **large eggs**
- ¾ **cup whipping cream**
- 1 **to 2 oranges (¼ cup juice, 1½ tsp zest)**
- ½ **teaspoon vanilla extract**
- ⅛ **teaspoon nutmeg**
- 1 **(16–oz) loaf French bread cut into 1-inch slices**

Preheat oven to 425°F. In a small bowl combine first 5 ingredients. Place bread slices in shallow pan, pour egg mixture over slices and turn to coat.

Place slices on generously sprayed or buttered baking sheet and bake 5 minutes on each side or until golden brown. Serve with powdered sugar or fruit.

variation: Use 2 tablespoons orange liqueur in place of nutmeg, and/or substitute cinnamon raisin bread for French bread.

Per serving: Cal 360, Carb 40g, Fib 2g, Pro 11g, Fat 17g, Sod 530mg, Sug 3g

Chocolate-Almond Stuffed French Toast

6 servings

A grown up French toast!

- 6 **(1¼-inch) slices French bread**
- 1 **(1.6-oz) milk chocolate bar, broken into 6 pieces**
- 4 **tablespoons slivered almonds**
- 4 **large eggs, beaten**
- ¾ **cup milk**
- ½ **cup Bailey's Irish Cream® or Kahlúa® liqueur**

Cut a pocket in each bread slice horizontally to, but not through, top crust. Fill each slice with 1 piece of chocolate and 2 teaspoons slivered almonds.

In a shallow dish combine eggs, milk and liqueur. Dip bread into egg mixture, coating each side thoroughly.

Place slices on a well buttered or sprayed griddle on low/medium heat for 4 to 5 minutes on each side or until golden brown.

Serve warm with syrup or sprinkled with powdered sugar.

note: Do not cook on high heat or slices will brown too fast, not cook through and will be soggy inside.

Per serving: Cal 462, Carb 65g, Fib 4g, Pro 15g, Fat 12g, Sod 646mg, Sug 10g

Oven French Toast   6 servings

This is a must have recipe when you have a hungry family to feed and not a lot of time. If desired, sprinkle with powdered sugar and top with your favorite syrup or sliced peaches.

- ⅔   **cup firmly packed brown sugar**
- ½   **cup butter, melted**
- 1½ **teaspoons cinnamon**
- 6   **large eggs, lightly beaten**
- 1¾ **cups milk**
- 1   **(1-lb) loaf French bread, cut into 1-inch slices**

Preheat oven to 350°F. Combine the brown sugar, butter and cinnamon and spread evenly in a 15x10-inch baking pan.

Combine eggs and milk in a 13x9-inch dish. Add bread slices and soak for 2 to 3 minutes. Place bread in baking pan. Bake 25 to 30 minutes or until golden.

Per Serving: Cal 526, Carb 63g, Fib 2g, Pro 15g, Fat 23g, Sod 682mg, Sug 27g

Oven Pancake   1 to 2 servings

If you haven't had these pancakes before, you are in for a treat. They make a great breakfast or light dinner. Serve with fruit and bacon or sausage links or fill with peach slices, drizzle with syrup and sprinkle with powdered sugar.

- ½   **cup flour**
- ½   **cup milk**
- 2   **large eggs**
- 3   **tablespoons butter**

Preheat oven to 425°F. Combine flour and milk in a small mixing bowl, mixing with fork just until blended (batter will still be lumpy). Stir in eggs. Place butter in a 9-inch pie pan and place in oven to melt. Remove from oven; pour in batter. Bake 15 minutes or until puffed and golden. Serve immediately. Pancake will puff up, but will fall shortly after removing from oven.

Per serving: Cal 368, Carb 26g, Fib 1g, Pro 11g, Fat 24g, Sod 215mg, Sug 4g

Egg Surprise Muffins   8 muffins

This recipe is surprisingly delicious as a family or a company dish. For brunch, serve with sausage links and fresh fruit. You can reheat in microwave (crust will be soft) or in the oven (crust will be crisper). Can be served with salsa. These muffins are wonderful hearty snacks for children. They can be cut in half and served warm and can be eaten out of hand.

- 1   (16.3-oz) can Grands® buttermilk biscuits
- 7   large eggs
    Salt and pepper
- ¾ cup (3-oz) Monterey Jack cheese with pepper, shredded
    Fresh or dried parsley for garnish

Preheat oven to 375°F. Press each biscuit into a 5-inch circle. Place in a sprayed muffin cup pressing on bottom and sides of each cup. Biscuits should extend slightly above the top of the cups.

Add ⅓ cup water to the eggs and lightly beat. Pour into a sprayed medium nonstick skillet. Sprinkle with salt and pepper. Cook, over medium low heat, stirring frequently, until cooked through. Remove from burner while eggs are still moist – they will continue to cook. Spoon into biscuit cups. Sprinkle with cheese, keeping the cheese inside the cups. Sprinkle with parsley and bake 11 to 13 minutes or until golden. Remove from cups and serve.

Per serving: Cal 293, Carb 25g, Fib 0g, Pro 12g, Fat 16g, Sod 732mg, Sug 1g

Breakfast Bacon Pizza   4 to 6 servings

A deliciously quick and easy pizza for breakfast, lunch or dinner.

- 1   (8-oz) can refrigerated pizza dough
- 6   large eggs, scrambled, but still moist
- 2   tablespoons finely chopped onion
- 3   tablespoons finely chopped green pepper
- 8   slices bacon, cooked and crumbled
- 1   cup (4-oz) Cheddar cheese, shredded

Preheat oven to 450°F. Unroll pizza dough and pat evenly onto a sprayed 12-inch pizza pan, forming a rim around the edges. Spoon the scrambled eggs over the crust. Sprinkle with onion, green pepper and then the bacon. Sprinkle cheese evenly over top. Bake 8 to 10 minutes or until crust is lightly browned.

hint: This doesn't reheat well, so enjoy the first time around.

Per serving: Cal 300, Carb 19g, Fib 0g, Pro 18g, Fat 16g, Sod 627mg, Sug 3g

Hot Breakfast
Ham Sandwich 2 to 4 servings

Serve with fresh fruit, coffee and orange juice

2   **English muffins, toasted**
    Dijon mustard
4   **slices sliced Deli ham**
4   **eggs, poached**
4   **slices Cheddar cheese**

Spread muffins with mustard. Top with ham, folded to fit. Top with egg, then cheese. Place under broiler to melt cheese.

Per sandwich: Cal 215, Carb 9g, Fib 1g, Pro 17g, Fat 12g, Sod 618mg, Sug 1g

Sausage Biscuits 5 servings

Sausage patties and maple syrup sounds a little weird, but that's how some kids like them.

1   **(10.2-oz) can of 5 jumbo size biscuits**
5   **sausage patties**
5   **slices Cheddar or American cheese**
    Maple syrup (optional)

Bake biscuits according to package directions.

Meanwhile cook sausage; drain.

Cut biscuits in half horizontally. Place a sausage patty on each biscuit half; then a slice of cheese and top with the other biscuit half. Serve with Maple syrup, if desired.

variation: Serve sausage patties topped with maple syrup. Add scrambled eggs and biscuits.

Per Serving: Cal 418, Carb 26g, Fib 0g, Pro 14g, Fat 28g, Sod 1005mg, Sug 0g

Company Maple Sausages
4 to 5 servings

These are best made fresh, but can be made ahead and reheated. Serve with scrambled eggs and sweet rolls.

16   pork sausage links
½   cup brown sugar
1   cup maple syrup

In a large skillet, brown sausages; drain off fat.

Combine brown sugar and maple syrup; pour over sausages. Bring to a boil, reduce heat and simmer until sausages are glazed and mixture has thickened.

Per serving: Cal 191, Carb 11g, Fib 0g, Pro 6g, Fat 14g, Sod 438mg, Sug 9g

The Perfect Scrambled Egg

Beat the eggs in a small bowl until frothy and evenly colored – about half a minute. You can use a fork or a whisk. Do not add salt yet.

Heat a small or medium size skillet over medium-low heat, and melt about 1 teaspoon of butter per egg. When the butter is melted, reduce heat to low and add beaten eggs.

Cook eggs at a low temperature. Cooking eggs at a high temperature will cause them to be rubbery and dry. Eggs cooked at a low temperature have a completely different texture than those cooked at high heat.

Wait until the first hint of eggs setting to begin stirring. Continue stirring until eggs are the doneness you desire – moist to dry.

Now is the time to add seasonings and other ingredients such as herbs, cheese, etc. Remove eggs from stove about a minute before you think they would be completely cooked as they will continue cooking once removed from heat.

Enjoy!

Quiche Lorraine   6 servings

My favorite Quiche. Serve with fresh fruit or a spinach salad and toasted French bread.

1	deep dish 9-inch pie crust
1½	cups (6-oz) Swiss cheese, shredded
12	slices bacon, cooked, crumbled
4	large eggs, lightly beaten
1¼	cups whipping cream
½	cup milk

Preheat oven to 325°F. Sprinkle cheese evenly over pie crust. Sprinkle bacon over top.

Combine eggs, cream and milk, stirring until well mixed. Pour over bacon. Bake 40 minutes or until filling appears almost firm in center when pan is gently shaken.

hint: To prevent a soggy crust, you may prefer to pre-bake the piecrust. Prick crust with fork and bake at 400°F for 10 minutes. Cool before adding filling

Per serving: Cal 458, Carb 21g, Fib 0g, Pro 17g, Fat 33g, Sod 534mg, Sug 1g

Easiest Quiche Ever   9 servings

This quiche is so simple it makes its own crust.

2	cups fresh vegetables
1	cup (4-oz) Cheddar cheese, shredded
2	cups milk
1	cup baking mix
4	large eggs

Preheat oven to 400°F. Cut vegetables into bite size pieces. Sprinkle vegetables and cheese in a sprayed 10-inch quiche dish or pie plate.

In a small bowl, mix remaining ingredients until smooth and pour over filling. Bake for 35 minutes or until knife inserted in the center comes out clean. Let stand 5 minutes before serving.

note: Good veggie choices would include broccoli, mushrooms, spinach, onion and zucchini.

Per serving: Cal 171, Carb 12g, Fib 1g, Pro 9g, Fat 10g, Sod 332mg, Sug 3g

Hot Pepper Quiche

6 servings

A nice Southwestern touch. Serve with sausage links and fresh fruit.

- **1 (9-inch) pie crust**
- **2½ cups (10-oz) Monterey Jack cheese with peppers, shredded**
- **3 large eggs, lightly beaten**
- **1 cup half and half**

Preheat oven to 350°F. Sprinkle cheese in pie crust. Combine eggs and half and half; mix thoroughly and pour over cheese. Bake 40 to 45 minutes or until golden and mixture is set. Remove and let stand 10 minutes before cutting.

variation: Add 1 cup chopped broccoli or 8 ounces cooked sausage.

Per serving: Cal 290, Carb 5g, Fib 0g, Pro 16g, Fat 23g, Sod 377mg, Sug 0g

Bacon Quiche Pizza

6 servings

- **1 (9-inch) pie crust**
- **2 cups (8-oz) Mozzarella cheese, shredded**
- **8 slices bacon, cooked and crumbled**
- **1½ cups sour cream**
- **4 large eggs**
- **2 teaspoons dried parsley or 2 tablespoons fresh**

Preheat oven to 425°F. Roll out or press pie crust to fit a 12-inch pizza pan, forming a ridge around the edge. Prick with a fork and bake 4 to 5 minutes. Remove from oven and sprinkle crust with cheese, then the bacon.

Combine sour cream and eggs. Add the parsley and pour over cheese. Bake 18 to 20 minutes or until lightly browned and cooked through.

Per serving: Cal 300, Carb 5g, Fib 0g, Pro 20g, Fat 20g, Sod 577mg, Sug 2g

Mexican Quiche   6 servings

- 8   large eggs, lightly beaten
- ¼   cup flour
- 1   teaspoon baking powder
- 2   cups (8-oz) Monterey Jack cheese, shredded
- ¼   cup butter, melted
- ¼   to ⅓ cup canned diced green chilies

Preheat oven to 350°F. Place eggs in a large mixing bowl, beat to mix. Stir in flour and baking powder. Fold in cheese. Add butter and green chilies. Pour into a sprayed 10-inch quiche pan. Bake 30 to 35 minutes or until custard is set. Let stand 5 minutes before cutting.

variations: Add finely chopped red and green pepper instead of green chilies.

Omit green chilies and use Monterey Jack cheese with jalapeños.

Serve quiche slices topped with salsa.

Per serving: Cal 339, Carb 6g, Fib 1g, Pro 17g, Fat 27g, Sod 533mg, Sug 1g

Sausage Mushroom Quiche   6 servings

- ¾   pound Italian sausage
- 8   ounces fresh mushrooms
- 1   (10-inch) pie crust
- 3   large eggs
- 1½   cups half and half
- ½   cup grated Parmesan cheese

Preheat oven to 375°F. Remove casings from sausage and slice the mushrooms. Add to medium skillet and cook until meat is cooked through. Drain off liquid.

Meanwhile, press crust into a deep 9-inch pie pan or a Quiche dish. Add meat mixture and spread evenly.

Slightly beat eggs to blend. Add half and half and Parmesan, stirring to mix. Pour over meat mixture. Bake 35 to 40 minutes or until knife inserted in center comes out clean.

Per serving: Cal 172, Carb 7g, Fib 1g, Pro 8g, Fat 13g, Sod 155mg, Sug 1g

Pineapple Oatmeal   4 servings

1 **(8-oz) can pineapple tidbits with juice**
1 **cup old-fashioned oats**
4 **teaspoons firmly packed light brown sugar**
¼ **teaspoon cinnamon**
⅓ **cup raisins**
¾ **cup milk**

In a medium saucepan, combine pineapple with juice and 1½ cups water. Bring to a boil and add oats, brown sugar, cinnamon, and raisins. Cook 5 minutes. Remove from heat, cover and let stand 5 minutes.

Spoon into serving bowls and top each serving with about 3 tablespoons of the milk.

Per serving: Cal 182, Carb 37g, Fib 3g, Pro 5g, Fat 3g, Sod 26mg, Sug 22g

Swedish Pancakes   about 12 large pancakes

Since I'm not a morning person, I like the convenience of making the batter the night before, but if you are rushed for time, go ahead and eliminate this step.

2 **cups flour**
4 **large eggs**
¼ **cup sugar**
½ **teaspoon salt**
2 **cups milk**
¼ **cup melted butter, plus additional butter for cooking**

In large mixer bowl, combine flour, eggs, sugar, salt and 1½ cups of the milk. Mix at medium speed until blended. Add remaining ½ cup milk and the ¼ cup butter. Cover and chill several hours or overnight. Batter should be fairly thin.

When ready to serve, if necessary, add a little more milk to the batter. Preheat medium skillet; add small dab of butter and spread to cover bottom. Pour about ¼ cup batter into skillet; spread thin by tipping pan, working quickly. When pancake appears a little dry on top, turn and cook other side. Roll up and keep warm while preparing remaining pancakes. Serve with syrup and fresh fruit.

Per pancake: Cal 171, Carb 21g, Fib 1g, Pro 5g, Fat 8g, Sod 170mg, Sug 6g

Roasted Corn Soup 7½ cups

This is a delicious savory soup. My favorite herb combination for this recipe is thyme and marjoram. If a heartier soup is desired add cooked cubed chicken, cooked crumbled bacon and/or cooked cubed potatoes.

- 2 **(10-oz) bags frozen corn**
- ¾ **cup chopped onion**
- 2 **to 3 teaspoons finely chopped fresh herbs**
- 8 **cups whole milk**
- 2 **tablespoons flour**

Preheat the oven to 450°F. Place corn on well greased baking sheet, and roast 10-20 minutes, or until corn just begins to brown.

In a large pot (using butter, water or spray) brown onion. Add milk and herbs; bring to a simmer.

In a small jar, place ⅓ cup cold water, add flour and shake until smooth. Slowly add to soup while stirring constantly until soup thickens. Add salt and pepper to taste.

note: Browning onion in butter will make a richer soup.

Per ½ cup: Cal 123, Carb 16g, Fib 1g, Pro 5g, Fat 5g, Sod 89mg, Sug 8g

Sausage-Corn Chowder 5½ cups

Lunch or dinner can be ready in less than 30 minutes. Just add bread and raw vegetables for a very satisfying meal.

- 12 **ounces sausage**
- ¾ **cup chopped onion**
- 1 **(10¾-oz) can condensed Cream of chicken soup with herbs**
- 1¾ **cup milk**
- 1 **(15-oz) can cream corn**

In a large saucepan, cook sausage and onion, breaking sausage up into small pieces; drain off fat.

Combine soup and milk until smooth. Add to sausage, along with the corn. Cook until heated through.

variation: If substituting ground beef or turkey, you may want to add additional seasoning or perhaps a can of Mexi-corn with its wonderful flavor of red and green peppers.

Per cup: Cal 273, Carb 25g, Fib 1g, Pro 15g, Fat 12g, Sod 1192mg, Sug 12g

Tomato Bread Soup

6 servings

- 4 **cups cubed seasoned Focaccia bread**
- 1 **medium onion, finely diced**
- 1 **pound zucchini, chopped**
- 1 **medium green pepper, chopped**
- 2 **(14-oz each) cans chicken broth**
- 1 **(14.5-oz) can diced tomatoes with basil, oregano & garlic**

Preheat oven to 375°F. On an ungreased baking sheet, spread bread cubes in a single layer. Bake 10 to 15 minutes or until toasted and crunchy.

Meanwhile, in a stock pot (using butter or cooking spray) sauté onions, zucchini and bell pepper until tender. Add chicken broth and canned tomatoes. Bring to a boil; reduce heat, simmer for 10 minutes.

To serve, put a few toasted bread cubes in individual soup bowls and ladle soup on top. Serve immediately. If desired, top with Parmesan cheese.

Per serving: Cal 254, Carb 50g, Fib 3g, Pro 10g, Fat 3g, Sod 1155mg, Sug 6g

Cheesy Wild Rice Soup

10 cups

Nothing warms the body like a hot bowl of soup on a cold winter night. For a complete meal, add a sandwich or salad and toasted bread or hot rolls.

- 1 **(6-oz) box long-grain and wild rice mix**
- ½ **cup chopped onion**
- 1½ **cups chicken broth**
- 2½ **cups Half & Half**
- 1 **(10¾-oz) can Cream of Potato soup**
- 2 **cups (8-oz) Cheddar cheese, shredded**

In medium saucepan, cook rice according to package directions; set aside.

Meanwhile, in a 3-quart saucepan, cook onion in a small amount of water until soft. Add chicken broth, Half & Half and soup. Heat, but do not boil (the cheese will curdle). Gradually add the cheese, stirring with each addition. Continue stirring until cheese is melted. Add the cooked rice.

note: If you want to eliminate a good portion of the sodium, omit the seasoning packet that comes with the rice, you will still have plenty of flavor.

Per cup: Cal 258, Carb 20g, Fib 1g, Pro 10g, Fat 15g, Sod 820mg, Sug 2g

Chicken Noodle Soup

10 servings

Our mom's were right...chicken soup is good for you.

- **4** **ounces linguine**
- **7** **cups chicken broth**
- **1** **small carrot, shredded**
- **½** **cup sliced celery**
- **1** **cup cubed, cooked chicken**
- **¼** **cup frozen peas**

Break pasta into 2-inch lengths and cook according to package directions. Drain and rinse.

In a large pot, combine broth, carrots, and celery. Bring to a boil, reduce heat, and simmer until vegetables are tender, about 5 to 6 minutes. Add peas, chicken, and pasta. Cook until heated through.

Per cup: Cal 125, Carb 12g, Fib 2g, Pro 9g, Fat 5g, Sod 751mg, Sug 2g

Chicken Tortellini Soup

15 cups

This recipe can easily be halved; in which case, you may still want to use all of the tortellini.
Some brands of process cheese can be shredded, but others are too soft and must be cubed. The shredded cheese will melt quickly and save a bit of time, but is usually more expensive.

- **1** **cup chopped onion**
- **1** **cup diced celery**
- **1** **(9-oz) package cheese tortellini**
- **6** **cups half and half**
- **24** **ounces process cheese spread, cubed**
- **4** **cups cubed cooked chicken**

In a small sprayed nonstick skillet, cook onion and celery until soft. Place in a large stockpot and add 6 cups of water.

Bring water to a boil; add tortellini and cook according to package directions. When pasta is cooked through, add half and half, cheese and chicken. Cook, stirring frequently, until heated through and cheese has melted. Stir from the bottom when serving (everything seems to settle there).

Per cup: Cal 420, Carb 20g, Fib 1g, Pro 23g, Fat 28g, Sod 1154mg, Sug 5g

Clam Chowder

6 to 8 servings

Tired of washing dishes? Almost any kind of soup is delicious served in bread bowls. Use 6 to 8-inch rounds of sourdough or French bread. Cut 1-1½ inches off the top, remove the soft bread, and fill with soup. No dishes!

1½	quarts chicken broth
2	cups finely chopped clams
2	cups small diced potatoes
½	cup small diced carrots
4	cups Half & Half
	Salt and pepper

Combine first 4 ingredients in large saucepan. Cook until vegetables are tender and mixture has thickened. Stir in Half & Half. Add salt and pepper to taste.

Per cup: Cal 240, Carb 17g, Fib 1g, Pro 10g, Fat 15g, Sod 1057mg, Sug 2g

Vegetable Chowder

8 cups

A vegetable soup can become a heartier main dish by adding cooked ground beef, chicken, or leftover pot roast. If you like even more flavor, use seasoned canned tomatoes.

¾	cup chopped onion
2	cups peeled, cubed potatoes
1	(28-oz) can diced tomatoes
2	cups mixed vegetables
	Salt and pepper to taste

In a sprayed 3-quart saucepan or stock pot, cook onion until soft, but not brown. Add potatoes, tomatoes, and 3 cups water. Bring to a boil, reduce heat, and simmer 15 minutes.

Add vegetables and cook 10 to 15 minutes or until potatoes are tender. Add salt and pepper to taste.

note: Canned diced tomatoes are sometimes a larger dice than you may want for soup. They can be cut in the can by using kitchen shears or lightly pulsed in a blender or food processor.

Per cup: Cal 96, Carb 22g, Fib3g, Pro 3g, Fat 0g, Sod 337mg, Sug 5g

Company Egg Drop Soup   4 cups

If desired, you can still make a delicious soup using just the first 3 ingredients.

- 3   **cups chicken broth**
- 2   **large eggs, beaten**
- ⅓   **cup chopped green onions**
- ¾   **cup sliced mushrooms**
- ¼   **cup chopped water chestnuts**
- 1   **tablespoon soy sauce**

In large saucepan, bring broth to a boil. Gradually add the eggs, stirring briskly after each addition. Add remaining ingredients and cook until mushrooms are tender.

Per cup: Cal 74, Carb 4g, Fib 1g, Pro 5g, Fat 4g, Sod 1012mg, Sug 2g

French Onion Soup   4 servings

- 5   **medium onions**
- 3   **tablespoons butter**
- 4   **cups beef broth**
-    **Salt and pepper**
-    **Toasted French bread slices or croutons**
- 1   **cup (4-oz) Swiss or Mozzarella cheese, shredded**

Thinly slice onions; separate into rings.

Heat butter in a 3-quart saucepan or pot and cook onions until tender and light golden. Add broth. Season with salt and pepper. Bring to a boil, reduce heat and simmer 10 minutes.

Top bread slices with cheese. Place under broiler and cook until cheese is melted and lightly browned. Pour soup into serving bowls and top with bread.

Per cup: Cal 239, Carb 20g, Fib 2g, Pro 14g, Fat 11g, Sod 1243mg, Sug 6g

Quick Soup Ideas

- Add ⅓ cup salsa to a can of cream of tomato soup.
- Add salsa to black bean soup and top with shredded Cheddar cheese.
- Cream soups- add 1 tablespoon dry white wine or sherry per serving.

Chicken-Broccoli Soup   6 cups

A nice creamy cheese soup.

- ½   **cup chopped onion**
- 1   **cup cubed cooked chicken**
- 1   **cup broccoli florets**
- 1½   **cups heavy cream**
- ¼   **teaspoon pepper**
- 1½   **cups (6-oz) Cheddar cheese, shredded**

Place onion and ½ cup water in a large saucepan. Cook until tender.

Add chicken, broccoli, cream, pepper, and 1¼ cups water. Bring to a boil, reduce heat, and cook until broccoli is tender. Gradually add cheese, stirring after each addition, until melted.

Per cup: Cal 357, Carb 4g, Fib 1g, Pro 14g, Fat 32g, Sod 215mg, Sug 1g

Baked Potato Soup   4 to 6 servings

As they do in restaurants, top with sour cream, cheese, chives and bacon just before serving.

- 4   **large baking potatoes, baked, then peeled and cubed**
- 2   **tablespoons butter**
- ¾   **cup finely chopped onion**
- 2   **tablespoons flour**
- 2   **cups Half & Half**
     Salt and pepper to taste

Melt butter in large saucepan and cook onion and celery until tender.

Combine flour with ¼ cup of the Half & Half, mixing until smooth. Add to mixture in saucepan. Add ½ cup water, salt and pepper. Bring mixture to a simmer, not a boil, and cook until heated through. Add the potatoes and then stir in the remaining Half & half. Continue cooking over low heat until hot, but do not boil.

Per cup: Cal 330, Carb 43g, Fib 3g, Pro 7g, Fat 15g, Sod 140mg, Sug 4g

Ground Beef Soup   6 servings

To expand the recipe, you can add thinly sliced celery and any leftover vegetables such as peas and corn. My daughter saves time, by using tiny new potatoes, unpeeled and quartered. Serve with French bread.

- 1½ **pounds lean ground beef**
- 1 **medium onion, chopped**
- 2 **cups cubed red potatoes**
- 1½ **cups sliced baby carrots**
- 1 **(28-oz) can tomatoes with basil, cut up**
  Salt and pepper

Brown ground beef and onion; drain off fat.

Put meat mixture, potatoes, carrots, and tomatoes in a large stock pot. Add about 3 cups of water. Cook 1 hour or until vegetables are tender. Add salt and pepper to taste.

tip: **Regardless of what they say about freezing potatoes, this recipe can be frozen.**

Per serving: Cal 328, Carb 20g, Fib 3g, Pro 27g, Fat 15g, Sod 524mg, Sug 6g

Chicken Velvet Soup   8 servings

- ⅓ **cup butter**
- ¾ **cup flour**
- 6 **cups chicken broth, divided**
- 2 **cups milk**
- 2 **cups diced cooked chicken**
  Salt and pepper

Melt butter in heavy Dutch oven or large saucepan. Add flour; stir quickly to blend. Cook over low heat until smooth. Add 2 cups of the chicken stock; stir to keep mixture smooth. Add milk. Cook, stirring frequently, until thickened.

Add remaining 4 cups chicken stock and the cubed chicken. Continue cooking until heated through. Add salt and pepper to taste.

Per serving: Cal 254, Carb 14g, 13.98g, Fib 0g, Pro 14g, Fat 15g, Sod 1214mg, Sug 4g

Bean Soup & Sausage   6 cups

Keep these ingredients on hand for a thick and hearty meal. Serve with toasted sourdough rolls and a fresh vegetable tray.

- 1   (12-oz) package sausage
- ¾   cup chopped onion
- 1   (15-oz) can black beans, drained
- 1   (15-oz) can Great Northern beans, drained
- 1   (14.5-oz) can Diced Tomatoes with Basil, drained
- 1   (14.5-oz) can beef broth

In a large saucepan, brown sausage and onion; drain off fat. Rinse beans and add to pan along with tomatoes and broth. Bring to a boil, reduce heat, and simmer 15 minutes to blend flavor.

Per cup: Cal 179, Carb 32g, Fib 8g, Pro 14g, Fat 2g, Sod 1463mg, Sug 5g

Chili Without the Beans   4 to 6 servings

If desired, this recipe can be cooked in a slow cooker. Serve with cornbread and a fresh vegetable tray.

- 2   pounds lean ground beef
- 1   medium onion, finely chopped
- 4   teaspoons chili powder
- 1   garlic clove, minced
- ½   teaspoon oregano, crushed fine
- 2   (16-oz) cans diced tomatoes, with liquid

Brown ground beef and onions; drain. Stir in chili powder, garlic, oregano, and tomatoes. Simmer 2 to 3 hours.

Per cup: Cal 370, Carb 10g, Fib 1g, Pro 36g, Fat 21g, Sod 526mg, Sug 5g

Beefy Salsa Chili   4 large servings

By adding a pound of ground beef to these pantry items, you have a family meal in less than 30 minutes.

- **1   pound lean ground beef**
- **1   cup chopped onion**
- **1   (15-oz) can Chili Makins®**
- **1   (14½-oz) can tomatoes, undrained**
- **1   cup thick and chunky salsa**
- **1   (15-oz) can black beans, drained**

In a large skillet, brown ground beef and onion; drain. Add remaining ingredients. Bring to a boil. Reduce heat and simmer 10 to 15 minutes to blend flavors and heat through.

Per cup: Cal 448, Carb 45g, Fib 11g, Pro 36g, Fat 20g, Sod 1735mg, Sug 11g

Chili Bowl   1 serving

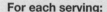

A young mother, who didn't think she could cook, told me she made these for a special friend. She was thrilled that it was so easy and so attractive that she told another friend that she absolutely had to buy my books. More important, this encouraged her to venture out and try other recipes that she was reluctant to try before.

For each serving:
- **Small round loaf of bread, unsliced**
- **Melted butter**
- **Prepared or canned chili, heated**
- **Chopped onion**
- **Shredded Cheddar cheese**
- **Sour cream**

Cut a 1 to 1½-inch slice off the top of the bread. Remove three-fourths of bread from center forming a bowl. Brush inside with melted butter. Bake 6 minutes to lightly toast the bread. Remove from oven. Fill with hot chili. Sprinkle with onion and cheese. Top with sour cream.

Sausage & Mushroom Tart

8 servings

½ **medium onion, thinly sliced**

1 **(1-lb) package Italian chicken sausage, removed from casing**

1 **(8-oz) package sliced mushrooms**

1 **sheet refrigerated pie crust**

1½ **cups (6-oz) Mozzarella cheese, shredded**

6 **tablespoons Blue cheese (optional)**

Preheat oven to 400°F. In a medium sprayed skillet, sauté onions. When they begin to soften, add sausage, stirring and breaking into small pieces. Just before sausage is cooked through, add mushrooms. Cook the mixture until mushrooms soften; drain.

Roll pie crust to a 12-inch circle on parchment paper. Spread the mixture within 1-inch of edge. Top with cheese. Fold and pinch edge of dough over mixture, leaving most of the mixture uncovered.

Bake 20 to 25 minutes or until sides are golden brown.

note: I prefer Isernio's® brand of chicken sausage for this recipe.

Per serving: Cal 279, Carb 20g, Fib 1g, Pro 9g, Fat 18g, Sod 704mg, Sug 2g

Tomato & Onion Tart

10 servings

A wonderful addition to a brunch buffet.

1 **sheet refrigerated pie crust**

2 **tablespoons butter**

1½ **lbs thinly sliced onions**

2 **cups (8-oz) Pepper Jack cheese, shredded**

1 **lb thinly sliced Plum tomatoes**

¼ **cup sliced olives (optional)**

Preheat oven to 375°F. Line a 10-inch tart pan with pie crust. Poke holes all over crust with a fork. Bake for 10 minutes. Remove from oven.

Meanwhile in a large skillet, melt butter and sauté onions, stirring occasionally until softened and light brown, about 20 minutes.

Spread onion mixture over pie crust and top with cheese. Fan tomato slices and sprinkle with olives. Season with salt and pepper to taste. Bake for 20 to 25 minutes or until crust is golden brown.

variation: Add one half red pepper to onion and brown, and/or substitute green chilies for black olives.

Per serving: Cal 260, Carb 21g, Fib 2g, Pro 7g, Fat 18g, Sod 315mg, Sug 4g

Stuffed Burgers   4 servings

If desired, serve on a lettuce leaf with dill pickles. Serve with potato salad, cole slaw or fresh fruit.

- 1½ **pounds lean ground beef**
- 1 **cup (4-oz) Cheddar cheese, shredded**
- 4 **tablespoons barbecue sauce**
- 4 **hamburger buns**

Divide meat into 8 equal portions and shape into thin patties.

Sprinkle cheese in center of half the patties. Press remaining patties over cheese and press to seal. Place on grill and cook to 160°F, turning once. Brush with barbecue sauce toward end of cooking time.

Per serving: Cal 594, Carb 23g, Fib 1g, Pro 48g, Fat 33g, Sod 720mg, Sug 3g

Reuben Burgers   4 servings

To reduce calories; eliminate the bun. They are equally as good.

- 1½ **pounds lean ground beef**
- 1 **cup sauerkraut, drained**
- 4 **slices Swiss cheese**
- 4 **hamburger buns**

Shape ground beef into 4 patties and grill or cook as desired, to 160°F.

Top each patty with sauerkraut, then cheese. Cover grill to melt the cheese.

Per serving: Cal 694, Carb 59g, Fib 4g, Pro 45g, Fat 29g, Sod 1099mg, Sug 4g

Tuna Burgers

6 burgers

- **1**   **can (6-oz) tuna, drained**
- **¼**   **cup finely chopped celery**
- **½**   **cup (2-oz) Cheddar cheese, shredded**
- **½**   **small onion, finely chopped**
- **⅓**   **cup mayonnaise (or to moisten)**
- **6**   **hamburger buns**

Preheat oven to 350°F. Combine first 5 ingredients, tossing with just enough mayonnaise to moisten. Fill buns with mixture. Wrap each separately in foil or place in baking pan and cover with foil. Bake 20 minutes or until heated through.

Per burger: Cal 287, Carb 22g, Fib 1g, Pro 13g, Fat 16g, Sod 455mg, Sug 3g

Safety First

Hamburgers, because they are made with ground meat must be cooked to an internal temperature of 160°F. This should kill any harmful bacteria. (Always use an accurate thermometer.) Cook any ground meat (beef, pork, poultry, etc.) to well done.

Swiss-Dill Burgers

4 servings

Serve hamburgers with your choice of condiments and fresh vegetables.

- **1**   **pound lean ground beef**
- **2**   **tablespoons sour cream**
- **¼**   **teaspoon dried dill weed**
- **4**   **slices Swiss cheese**
- **4**   **hamburger buns**

Combine first 3 ingredients, mixing lightly. Shape into 4 patties and grill until cooked to 160°F. Top with cheese and cook until melted.

Per burger: Cal 456, Carb 22g, Fib 1g, Pro 35g, Fat 24g, Sod 324mg, Sug 3g

Taco Burgers   4 servings

1   **pound lean ground beef**
½   **cup salsa**
4   **slices Cheddar cheese**
4   **hamburger buns**
1   **cup shredded lettuce**
2   **Plum tomatoes, chopped**

Combine ground beef and salsa. Form ground beef into 4 patties, about ¾-inch thick. Broil or grill until cooked to 160°F. Top with cheese and place on buns.

Top each with lettuce and tomato.

Per burger: Cal 472, Carb 26g, Fib 2g, Pro 35g, Fat 24g, Sod 534mg, Sug 5g

Delicious Sandwich Combinations

Top focaccia bread with sliced chicken, bacon, Mozzarella, mushrooms and Italian dressing

Top French bread with sliced chicken, bacon, Swiss cheese, tomato, red onion and honey mustard dressing

Sliced turkey on sour dough with bacon, avocado slices, lettuce, tomato and Italian dressing

Top focaccia bread with grilled chicken, Provolone, toasted red peppers, fresh basil, lettuce and tomato

Roast beef in pocket bread with caramelized onions, watercress and ranch dressing

Tuna salad on marbled rye bread with Monterey Jack cheese and tomato.

Grilled steak slices on hoagie rolls topped with sautéed onions and peppers, white Cheddar cheese and BBQ or Sloppy Joe sauce

Grilled Reuben Sandwiches

4 sandwiches

12 to 16 slices deli corned beef
8   slices dark rye bread
1   (8-oz) can sauerkraut, well drained
½   cup Thousand Island dressing
4   slices Swiss cheese
    Melted butter

Arrange 3 to 4 slices corned beef on 4 slices of the bread. Top each with ¼ of the sauerkraut. Drizzle with ¼ of the dressing and top with cheese. Top with remaining bread slices.

Brush both sides of bread with melted butter. Place in a heated nonstick skillet and lightly brown both sides. Check the cheese, but at this point it should be melted.

note: If the dressing is too thick to drizzle, you can either thin with a little milk or just spread it on the bread.

Per sandwich: Cal 723, Carb 57g, Fib 6g, Pro 40g, Fat 37g, Sod 2388mg, Sug 7g

French Toasted Sandwiches

4 sandwiches

4   thin slices ham (to fit bread)
4   thin slices cheese (to fit bread)
8   slices bread
2   large eggs, lightly beaten
½   cup milk or cream
    Butter

Place a slice of ham and cheese between each 2 slices of bread, making 4 sandwiches.

Combine eggs and milk. Dip sandwiches in egg mixture. Brown on both sides in heavy skillet or on grill, using butter as needed.

Per sandwich: Cal 362, Carb 28g, Fib 0g, Pro 18g, Fat 18g, Sod 710mg, Sug 6g

Grilled Roast Beef Sandwich 4 sandwiches

3   **tablespoons mayonnaise**
1   **tablespoon Dijon mustard**
8   **slices sourdough bread**
4   **slices Monterey Jack or Swiss cheese**
    Deli roast beef, 10 to 12 slices
    Butter, softened

Combine mayonnaise and mustard and spread on 4 of the bread slices. Top with cheese and roast beef. Cover with remaining bread. Butter both sides of sandwiches.

Cook sandwiches on a hot grill or in a large skillet until golden.

Per sandwich: Cal 455, Carb 33g, Fib 2g, Pro 24g, Fat 25g, Sod 1059mg, Sug 0g

Bread Bowl Sandwich 2 sandwiches

Are you tired of doing the same old thing for picnics? Give this a try...it's a little different and great for those hungry appetites.

1   **(5 to 6-inch) round loaf sour dough bread, unsliced**
1   **tablespoon mayonnaise**
4   **ounces deli sliced turkey**
1   **small Plum tomato, sliced**
    Lettuce

Cut a 1 to 1½-inch slice from top of bread. Remove bread from center, leaving a ¼-inch shell. Spread inside of shell with mayonnaise. Arrange folded slices of turkey on bottom. Top with tomato slices, then lettuce. Replace top. Cut in half to serve.

note: You can vary the type and size of the bread loaf, as well as the filling.

Per sandwich: Cal 178, Carb 17g, Fib 1g, Pro 12g, Fat 7g, Sod 638mg, Sug 2g

Favorite Barbecue Pork Sandwich

I have tried other prepared and purchased barbecue sauces with this sandwich, but Kraft® seems to work the best. And for that little zing, you do need the hot sauce too.

Kraft® Original barbecue sauce

Hot pepper sauce

Thinly sliced grilled pork loin roast

Shredded green cabbage

Hamburger buns

Several hours ahead or day ahead, combine barbeque sauce and several drops of hot sauce to taste. Cover and store in refrigerator.

When ready to serve the sandwiches, heat the sliced meat and warm the buns. Spread sauce on buns, top with sliced pork and then top meat with shredded cabbage. If at this point the sandwiches have cooled off, place briefly in the microwave to reheat.

Nutrition analysis will vary.

Open-Faced Smoked Salmon Sandwich   8 sandwiches

1   **loaf French bread (long narrow loaf)**

¼   **cup butter, softened or olive oil**

4   **to 6 oz thinly sliced smoked salmon**

8   **slices Mozzarella or Provolone cheese**

Chopped fresh parsley for garnish

Slice the bread, at an angle, into 6-inch long slices, making 8 slices. Spread one side of each slice with butter or oil. Place on baking sheet and broil until lightly toasted.

Remove from oven and top with salmon slices. Arrange cheese slices over salmon, cutting to fit. Return to broiler to melt the cheese. Sprinkle with parsley.

Per sandwich: Cal 284, Carb 29g, Fib 2g, Pro 14g, Fat 12g, Sod 697mg, Sug 2g

Make Ahead Toasted Cheese Sandwiches

This is the easiest way I know, to make a lot of sandwiches quickly.

Sliced cheese
Sliced bread
Melted butter

Do ahead: Place cheese between bread slices. Place on a baking pan and cover tightly. Chill until ready to serve.

When ready to serve, brush both sides lightly with butter. Place under broiler and broil each side until just golden.

tip: I have tried baking the sandwiches, but I think broiling is better for a crispy golden brown sandwich.

Chicken Club Sandwich   4 servings

If really in a hurry, use the frozen cooked chicken patties. Use hoagie rolls for fresh chicken breasts and round buns for the patties.

4	chicken breast halves, skinned, boned
3	tablespoons olive oil, divided
4	slices Swiss cheese
4	sandwich rolls, split
8	thin tomato slices
8	slices cooked bacon

Flatten chicken breasts to an even thickness. Cook in 2 tablespoons of the oil until cooked through, turning once. Place cheese on top and remove chicken from skillet.

Drizzle cut side of rolls with remaining oil. Top bottom halves with 2 slices of tomato, chicken and then bacon.

Per Sandwich: Cal 621, Carb 33g, Fib 2g, Pro 51g, Fat 30g, Sod 716mg, Sug 3g

Chicken-Pineapple Sandwiches
4 to 6 sandwiches

Chicken can be served on lettuce leaves as a salad or in melon halves garnished with strawberries or raspberries.

- 2 cups finely diced cooked chicken
- 1 can (8-oz) crushed pineapple, drained
- ¼ cup chopped slivered almonds
- Mayonnaise
- Lettuced leaves
- Choice of bread

In a small bowl, combine first 3 ingredients. Add just enough mayonnaise to moisten. Spread on half the bread slices; top with lettuce. Place remaining bread slices on top. Cut sandwiches in half diagonally.

Per sandwich: Cal 415, Carb 43g, Fib 3g, Pro 19g, Fat 18g, Sod 913mg, Sug 6g

Special Turkey Sandwich
1 sandwich

- 2 slices sourdough bread
- 1 tablespoon cream cheese, softened
- 2 tablespoons cranberry sauce
- 2 ounces deli sliced turkey
- Lettuce leaves

Spread one side of each bread slice with cream cheese. Spread with cranberry sauce. Add turkey and lettuce.

variation: Substitute bagels for the sour-dough bread.

Per sandwich: Cal 310, Carb 43g, Fib 2g, Pro 18g, Fat 8g, Sod 1031mg, Sug 7g

Hot Brie Turkey Sandwich

4 sandwiches

Different, but oh so good! Great for Thanksgiving leftovers. Serve with cranberry sauce, stuffing and pumpkin pie.

- **1**   **cup whipping cream**
- **1½** **cups (6-oz) Brie cheese**
-      **Salt and pepper**
-      **Turkey slices, heated, enough for 4 sandwiches**
- **4**   **(1-inch) slices French bread, lightly toasted, if desired**
- **1**   **cup fresh spinach leaves**

Heat whipping cream in medium saucepan; bring to a boil. Remove from heat.

While cream is heating, remove rind from Brie and cut cheese into small cubes. Gradually add to the cream, stirring to melt. Season with salt and pepper. Place bread slices on serving plates. Top with spinach, then the turkey slices. Spoon sauce over top.

Per Sandwich: Cal 635, Carb 53g, Fib 3g, Pro 23g, Fat 37g, Sod 1188mg, Sug 1g

Veggie Pita Sandwich

1 sandwich

- **1**   **Pita bread**
-      **Cream cheese, softened**
-      **Thinly sliced cucumber**
-      **Shredded lettuce**
-      **Sliced Swiss cheese**
-      **Thinly sliced tomatoes**

Spread inside of each Pita with a thin layer of cream cheese. Add remaining ingredients and enjoy.

Per sandwich: Cal 227, Carb 20g, Fib 3g, Pro 11g, Fat 12g, Sod 249g, Sug 4g

Polish Sausage Hoagies

2 sandwiches

Serve with coleslaw, fresh vegetable sticks and your favorite pickles.

- 1 **tablespoon olive oil**
- ¾ **cup chopped onion**
- ¼ **cup chopped green pepper**
- ⅓ **cup drained sauerkraut**
- 2 **cooked Polish sausages, heated**
- 2 **hot dog buns or hard rolls**

Heat oil in small skillet. Cook onion and green pepper until just tender. Add sauerkraut and heat through. Place sausages on buns and top with vegetable mixture.

Per sandwich: Cal 473, Carb 34g, Fib 3g, Pro 20g, Fat 29g, Sod 1724mg, Sug 6g

Turkey & Swiss Sandwich

4 sandwiches

Make this sandwich special by using fresh grown tomatoes when in season.

- 2 **tablespoons mayonnaise**
- 8 **slices pumpernickel or 7-grain bread**
- 8 **slices deli sliced turkey**
- 8 **slices bacon, cooked**
- 4 **slices Swiss cheese**
- 4 **to 8 thin slices tomato**

Spread mayonnaise on bread slices. Layer with turkey, bacon, cheese, and tomato. Top with bread slice.

Per sandwich: Cal 373., Carb 28g, Fib 4g, Pro 24g, Fat 19g, Sod 1065mg, Sug 7g

Soft Tacos 4 servings

Serve immediately to prevent tortillas from getting too soft.

- **1 pound lean ground beef**
- **4 (7-inch) tortillas**
- **¾ cup (3-oz) Cheddar cheese, shredded**
- **¼ cup sour cream**
- **¼ cup salsa**

Brown ground beef; drain. Spread beef in center of tortillas. Top with cheese, sour cream and salsa. Roll to enclose filling.

Per Taco: Cal 515, Carb 27g, Fib 2g, Pro 35g, Fat 28g, Sod 578mg, Sug 2g

Sloppy Joes 6 to 8 sandwiches

Prepare these for picnics, kid's birthday parties, and after game treats.

- **2 pounds lean ground beef**
- **1 cup finely chopped onion**
- **¾ cup chili sauce**
- **3 tablespoons prepared mustard**
- **1 to 2 teaspoons chili powder, or to taste**
- **Hamburger buns**

In a large skillet, cook ground beef and onion until browned; drain off fat. Add chili sauce, mustard, and chili powder, along with ½ cup water. Bring to a boil, reduce heat, and simmer 15 to 20 minutes or until liquid is absorbed, stirring occasionally. Serve on buns.

Per serving: Cal 408, Carb 31g, Fib 1g, Pro 30g, Fat 17g, Sod 1089mg, Sug 10g

Deli Sub Wrap 1 wrap

Meals in itself, but if really hungry, add dill pickles, raw vegetable sticks, and ½ cup fresh raspberries.

- 1 (7-inch) tortilla
- 2 slices deli roast beef, or other deli meat
- 1 thin slice Jarlsberg cheese or other cheese
- ½ cup alfalfa sprouts
- 1 teaspoon olive oil or mayonnaise
- 2 tablespoons chopped tomatoes

Top each tortilla with the next 3 ingredients. Drizzle with oil (you may use less). Roll tightly.

Per Wrap: Cal 437, Carb 26g, Fib 2g, Pro 27g, Fat 23g, Sod 782mg, Sug 2g

Tuna-Egg Wraps 4 wraps

- 1 (12-oz) can white tuna, drained
- ¼ cup finely chopped onion
- 2 hardboiled eggs, chopped
- ⅓ cup mayonnaise (or to taste)
- 4 (7-inch) tortillas

Combine first 4 ingredients. Spread equal amounts on tortillas and roll tightly.

Per Wrap: Cal 437, Carb 26g, Fib 2g, Pro 27g, Fat 23g, Sod 782mg, Sug 2g

Hot Dogs

For variety, top hot dogs with the following ingredients:

Chili, Cheddar cheese, diced onions

Sautéed onions

Sauerkraut and caraway seeds

Mustard, relish, chopped onion, peppers, and pickle spears (Chicago style)

Sauerkraut and Swiss cheese

Turkey Club Wrap   1 wrap

A restaurant favorite.

- 1   **(7-inch) tortilla**
- 1   **tablespoon mayonnaise**
- 2   **slices deli turkey**
- 2   **slices bacon, cooked, crumbled**
- 1   **Plum tomato, chopped**
- ½   **cup shredded lettuce**

Spread tortilla with mayonnaise. Layer ingredients in order listed. Roll tightly.

Per Wrap: Cal 379, Carb 32g, Fib 3g, Pro 18g, Fat 20g, Sod 1128mg, Sug 4g

Sausage Wraps   4 wraps

- 1   **(12-oz) package sausage**
- ⅓   **cup chopped onions**
- 1   **(4-oz) can sliced mushrooms, drained, chopped**
- 4   **(7-inch) tortillas**
- 1   **cup (4-oz) Monterey Jack cheese, shredded**

Brown sausage and onion; drain. Add mushrooms and heat through. Place ¼ of mixture on each tortilla; sprinkle with cheese. Roll tightly.

Per Wrap: Cal 425, Carb 30g, Fib 2g, Pro 19g, Fat 25g, Sod 1146mg, Sug 2g

Beef & Cheese Roll-ups

4 servings

Try using some of your favorite ingredients and you will might come up with some fantastic sandwich ideas.

- 4 **(7-inch) tortillas**
- ½ **cup soft herb cream cheese spread**
- 8 **slices deli roast beef**
- 1 **cup (4-oz) Monterey Jack cheese, shredded**
- 2 **cups shredded lettuce**

Spread each tortilla with 2 tablespoons cheese spread. Top with ingredients in order listed. Roll tightly.

Per serving: Cal 541, Carb 34g, Fib 6g, Pro 27g, Fat 31g, Sod 1134mg, Sug 2g

Taco Burger Wraps

4 wraps

The degree of heat in the salsa is up to you.

- 1 **pound lean ground beef**
- ½ **cup thick and chunky salsa**
- 4 **(7-inch) tortillas**
- ¾ **cup (3-oz) Cheddar cheese, shredded**
- 3 **Plum tomatoes, chopped**
- 1 **cup shredded lettuce**

Brown ground beef; drain. Add salsa and simmer until liquid is absorbed.
Fill with meat mixture and layer with cheese, tomatoes, and lettuce. Roll tightly.

Per Wrap: Cal 499., Carb 31g, Fib 3g, Pro 35g, Fat 26g, Sod 748mg, Sug 4g

Banana-Muffin Treat   2 to 4 servings

These delightful muffins are surprisingly delicious. They do take a little more time to prepare, but are worth it.

- **4**   **English muffins**
-     **Butter**
- **2**   **bananas, sliced**
- **8**   **slices Swiss cheese**
- **8**   **slices bacon, cooked, broken in half**

Toast, then lightly butter the muffins and place on a baking sheet. Arrange banana slices on muffins. Top with a slice of cheese. Criss-cross 2 slices bacon on top of cheese. Place under broiler just long enough to melt the cheese.

Per serving: Cal 369, Carb 30g, Fib 4g, Pro 20g, Fat 20g, Sod 423mg, Sug 8g

English Muffin Treats   4 sandwiches

- **2**   **English muffins, split and toasted**
-     **Mayonnaise**
- **4**   **(¼-inch) tomato slices**
- **4**   **thin onion slices**
- **4**   **slices of Cheddar cheese**
- **4**   **slices of bacon, cooked and broken in half**

Spread muffins with mayonnaise. Layer with slices of tomato, onion, and cheese. Place under broiler to melt cheese. Top each with 2 strips of bacon and serve.

tip: When cutting sandwiches, use a sharp or serrated knife to avoid squashing the bread.

Per serving: Cal 202, Carb 10g, Fib 1g, Pro 9g, Fat 14g, Sod 332mg, Sug 2g

Sausage Turnovers   8 turnovers

I don't know who likes these more, the kids or their parents. These are so convenient to have on hand in the freezer for lunch, dinner or a snack. For work or school, pack a few of these right from the freezer and microwave at lunch time.

- 1 **(12-oz) package sausage**
- ½ **cup chopped onion**
- 1 **(4-oz) can mushroom pieces, drained**
- 1 **cup (4-oz) Monterey Jack or Cheddar cheese**
- 1 **(16.3-oz) can refrigerated Grands® Biscuits**

Brown sausage and onion in a large skillet; drain. Add mushrooms and heat through.

Roll each biscuit into a 5-inch circle. Place ⅓ of the meat mixture just off center on biscuit. Sprinkle with some of the cheese. Fold one side over filling, stretching to fit; press edges firmly to seal, pricking 3 or 4 times with a fork. Place on baking sheet and bake 10 to 15 minutes or until lightly browned.

tip: These are quite a treat for the busy mother who is tired of feeding her children the same things day after day. Use your imagination and fill with a variety of fillings. Make a cheeseburger or taco (no lettuce). Fill with scrambled eggs and ham, bacon or sausage. Add chicken or tuna salad. Use leftovers, etc.

Per serving: Cal 324, Carb 26g, Fib 1g, Pro 11g, Fat 19g, Sod 961mg, Sug 6g

Beef-Sauerkraut Turnovers   8 turnovers

You will probably have some of the meat left over. It can be reheated and served over baked potatoes, or used as a filling for flour tortillas. Or, also buy a can of 5 biscuits and make additional turnovers.

- 1 **pound lean ground beef**
- 1 **cup chopped onion**
- 1 **(8-oz) can sauerkraut, drained**
- 1 **teaspoon salt**
- 1 **teaspoon caraway seeds**
- 1 **(16.3-oz) can buttermilk Grands® Biscuits**

Brown ground beef and onion; drain. Add sauerkraut, salt and caraway seeds; mix well. Cool.

Roll or pat each biscuit into a 5-inch circle. Top each with 1/3 cup meat mixture. Fold over to form a turnover. Press edges firmly to seal. Prick top 3 or 4 times and place on baking sheet. Bake 12 to 15 minutes or until golden.

Per serving: Cal 319, Carb 27g, Fib 1g, Pro 17g, Fat 16g, Sod 1086mg, Sug 1g

Cheeseburger Turnovers   5 turnovers

A half pound of ground beef will give you 5 sandwiches. Larger appetites will want two, but one should be enough for smaller appetites and children. These can also be reheated in the oven at 350°F.

- ½   **pound lean ground beef**
- ¼   **cup chopped onion**
- ½   **teaspoon salt**
- ⅛   **teaspoon pepper**
- 1   **(10.8-oz) can Grands® refrigerated biscuits**
- 5   **Cheddar cheese slices**

Preheat oven 350°F. In small skillet, brown ground beef and onion; drain. Season with salt and pepper.

Meanwhile, roll out biscuits on a floured surface, to a 5-inch circle. Place ground beef mixture on one side, top with cheese and fold biscuits over pressing firmly to seal. Prick top in 3 or 4 places and place on a baking sheet. Bake 10 to 12 minutes or until lightly browned.

Per serving: Cal 361, Carb 26g, Fib 1g, Pro 15g, Fat 21g, Sod 1012mg, Sug 5g

Cheesy Red Pepper Pizza Pocket   6 servings

- 1   **(10-oz) tube refrigerated pizza dough**
- ¾   **cup (6-oz) veggie herb spread**
- ½   **cup (2-oz) finely grated Parmesan cheese**
- 1   **cup (4-oz) Mozzarella cheese, shredded**
- 1   **medium bell pepper, thinly sliced**
-      **Olive oil**

Preheat oven to 400°F. Line baking sheet with parchment paper; spray with non-stick spray.

Unroll dough onto parchment. Spread half the veggie spread over half the dough, lengthwise, leaving ½-inch border. Sprinkle with half of parmesan cheese and half of mozzarella cheese, fold plain dough over filled half.

Spread remaining herb spread over the top, sprinkle with remaining cheese. Arrange slices of red pepper on the top. Brush with olive oil. Bake for 25 minutes or until golden brown. Slice to serve.

variation: Try different vegetable toppings, such as zucchini, red onion, canned artichoke hearts and/or mushrooms. Also, try different flavors of herb spread.

Per serving: Cal 381, Carb 28g, Fib 1g, Pro 11g, Fat 24g, Sod 1025mg, Sug 3g

Artichoke & Cheese Pizza

4 to 6 servings

- 2 teaspoons olive oil
- 1 large onion, thinly sliced, separated into rings
- 2 cups (8-oz) Mozzarella cheese, shredded
- 1 10 to 12 inch pizza crust or bread shell
- 1 (9-oz) can artichoke hearts, drained
- ⅓ cup freshly grated Parmesan cheese

Preheat oven to 425°F. Heat oil in medium skillet and cook onion until soft, stirring frequently. Drain off any liquid.

Sprinkle 1 cup of the Mozzarella cheese over pizza crust. Top with artichoke hearts, onion and the remaining Mozzarella. Sprinkle with Parmesan cheese. Bake 10 to 12 minutes or until pizza is heated through and cheese is melted.

Per slice: Cal 256, Carb 30g, Fib 1g, Pro 18g, Fat 7g, Sod 711mg, Sug 2g

Pizza Dough

Make your own pizza dough or use refrigerated canned pizza dough, large biscuits, English muffins, tortillas, frozen bread dough, or easiest of all, purchased baked pizza crusts. Pizza crusts can be prebaked or unbaked. If unbaked, the cooking time will be a few minutes longer. Check closely the last few minutes.

Pizza Toppings
- Barbecue sauce, cooked chicken, chopped red onion and Mozzarella cheese.
- Pesto sauce, cooked chicken, chopped tomatoes, and Mozzarella cheese.
- Pizza sauce, cooked chicken, Canadian bacon, pineapple tidbits and Mozzarella cheese.
- Pizza sauce, cooked sausage, onion, green pepper and Mozzarella cheese.
- Pizza sauce, chopped plum tomatoes, fresh basil, Parmesan or Mozzarella cheese.

Chicken Pesto Pizza 4 to 6 servings

1 **(13.8-oz) refrigerated pizza crust**
⅓ **cup pesto**
1½ **cups (6-oz) Mozzarella cheese, shredded**
1½ **cups cubed cooked chicken**
1 **(6-oz) jar marinated artichokes, drained.**
3 **Plum tomatoes, chopped**

Preheat oven to 425ºF. Place pizza crust on baking sheet and spread with pesto. Sprinkle with remaining ingredients in order given and bake 10 to 15 minutes or until crust is golden brown and cheese is melted.

variation: Substitute barbecue sauce for the pesto and chopped green pepper for the artichokes.

Per slice: Cal 371, Carb 31g, Fib 3g Pro 26g, Fat 16g, Sod 1098mg, Sug 4g

Garlic Bread Pizza Wedge 24 wedges

These are best served in small servings with soup or salad or as an appetizer.

1 **(14-oz) purchased, Italian pizza crust**
⅓ **cup finely chopped red onion**
2 **large garlic cloves, minced**
1 **teaspoon dried oregano, crushed**
1 **cup mayonnaise**
1 **cup freshly grated Parmesan cheese**

Preheat oven to 450ºF. Place bread shell on an ungreased 14-inch pizza pan.

Cook onion in a small amount of water until softened.

Combine onion with remaining ingredients and spread over the crust. Bake 8 to 10 minutes or until quite golden and the bottom of the shell has become crisp. Cut into 24 wedges. Serve hot.

Per wedge: Cal 120, Carb 8g, Fib 0g, Pro 2g, Fat 8g, Sod 199mg, Sug 1g

Deep Dish Pizza   6 to 8 servings

The easy baking mix crust is a nice change from your typical pizza crust.
Also, very inexpensive to make.

3	cups baking mix
¾	cup cold water
1½	pounds lean ground beef
½	cup finely chopped onion
1	(14-oz) jar pizza sauce or spaghetti sauce
1	(12-oz) package Mozzarella cheese, shredded

Preheat oven to 425°F. Mix baking mix and water until soft dough form; beat 20 strokes. Place on floured board and knead about 20 times. With floured hands, press dough evenly on bottom and up sides of a sprayed 15x10-inch jelly roll pan.

Lightly brown ground beef and onions; drain off fat. Spread pizza sauce over dough. Distribute meat over top. Sprinkle with cheese. Bake about 20 minutes or until lightly browned. Watch cheese carefully the last 5 minutes.

Per serving: Cal 498,Carb 52g, Fib 4g, Pro 39g, Fat 15g, Sod 1050mg, Sug 7g

Tortilla Pizzas

Flour tortillas

Pizza sauce

Mozzarella cheese, shredded

Choice of meat

Choice of vegetable

Grated Parmesan cheese

Preheat oven to 400°F. Place tortillas on baking sheet and bake 5 to 6 minutes or until lightly toasted. Remove from oven and turn over. Spread with pizza sauce, sprinkle with cheese. Top with meat and/or vegetables. Sprinkle with Parmesan.

Increase heat to 450° and bake 10 to 12 minutes or until cheese is melted and pizza is lightly browned.

Meat choices:

Cooked ground beef, cooked sausage, Canadian bacon, Pepperoni, Bacon, Ham, Chicken

Vegetable choices:

Sliced tomatoes, Onions, Mushrooms, Red, yellow or green pepper, ripe olives, Avocado, Artichokes

Nutrition analysis will vary.

beef, pork & seafood

You may substitute ground chicken or turkey for these ground beef recipes. The flavor may be different, but still good.

Cheesy Shepherd's Pie   8 servings

A favorite for dinner and midnight snacking. I often triple the recipe and with two teenage boys it gets devoured in a few days!

- 1   to 1½ lbs lean ground beef
- 3   (4-oz) packages Roasted Garlic & Parmesan instant mashed potatoes
- 2   teaspoons Worcestershire sauce
- 1   (10.75-oz) can Cream of Mushroom soup
- 1   (12-oz) package frozen peas and carrots
- 9   slices Cheddar cheese

Preheat oven to 350°F. In a 9 or 10-inch oven proof skillet, begin browning ground beef over medium heat. Meanwhile, prepare mashed potatoes according to directions on package. Set aside.

Finish browning ground beef and drain.

Add Worcestershire sauce, soup and vegetables to ground beef and stir. Top with cheese, then potatoes. Bake for 30 minutes or until heated through and potatoes are lightly browned.

variation: You may substitute homemade mashed potatoes for instant.

Per ½ cup: Cal 218, Carb 10g, Fib 1g, Pro 15g, Fat 13g, Sod 340mg, Sug 1g

Popover Pizza Casserole   6 servings

- 1   pound ground beef
- 2   cups pizza sauce
- 1   (12-oz) package Mozzarella cheese, shredded
- 1   cup flour
- 1   cup milk
- 2   large eggs

Preheat oven to 425°F. In medium skillet, lightly brown ground beef; drain off fat. Add pizza sauce and bring to a boil. Lower heat; cook 2 to 3 minutes. Pour into sprayed 13x9-inch baking pan. Sprinkle cheese over top.

Combine flour, milk and eggs; mix well. Pour over cheese. Bake 25 to 30 minutes or until heated through.

Per serving: Cal 431, Carb 27g, Fib 3g, Pro 40g, Fat 17g, Sod 840mg, Sug 7g

Salisbury Steak
4 servings

If desired, cook on outdoor grill and serve with a mushroom sauce. For mock Filet Mignon, wrap 1 slice of bacon around each patty before cooking. Serve with baked potatoes and tossed green salad.

- 1½ **pounds lean ground beef**
- ¾ **cup quick cooking oats**
- ¼ **cup finely chopped onions**
- 1 **large egg, beaten**
- ½ **cup tomato juice**
- **Salt and pepper to taste**

Combine ingredients in large mixing bowl. Shape into 4 thick oval patties. Place on broiler rack and cook to 160°F, turning once.

Per serving: Cal 451, Carb 15g, Fib 2g, Pro 41g, Fat 24g, Sod 180mg, Sug 2g

Cornbread Salsa Bake
6 servings

- 1 **(8½-oz) box corn muffin mix**
- 1 **large egg**
- ⅓ **cup milk**
- 1 **pound lean ground beef**
- 1 **cup thick and chunky salsa**
- 1 **cup (4-oz) Cheddar cheese, shredded**

Preheat oven to 400°F. In a bowl, combine muffin mix, egg and milk, stirring just until moistened. Spread in a sprayed 8x8-inch baking dish. Bake 10 to 12 minutes or until golden.

Meanwhile, lightly brown ground beef; drain off fat. Add salsa and simmer 7 to 8 minutes or until excess liquid has cooked off. Pour over baked cornbread. Sprinkle with cheese. Return to oven just long enough to melt the cheese.

note: If desired, serve additional salsa to spoon over the top.

Per serving: Cal 419, Carb 32g, Fib 1g, Pro 25g, Fat 20g, Sod 851mg, Sug 10g

Quick Meat Loaf 6 servings

Serve with mashed potatoes, broccoli and a molded fruit salad.

- 1½   pounds lean ground beef
- 1½ teaspoons salt
- ¼ teaspoon pepper
- ½ cup quick-cooking oats
- ¼ cup milk
- 1 large egg

Preheat oven to 350°F. Combine ingredients and shape into loaf in a sprayed 13x9-inch baking dish. Bake 45 to 60 minutes or until meat reaches 160°F.

Per serving: Cal 284, Carb 6g, Fib 01g, Pro 27g, Fat 16g, Sod 3745mg, Sug 1g

Southwestern Meat Loaf 6 servings

Wondering what in the world to do with that bit of left over salsa. Try it in meatloaf for a southwestern touch. Makes a great sandwich too.

- 1½ pounds lean ground beef
- ¾ cup thick and chunky salsa
- 1 large egg, lightly beaten
- 10 saltine crackers, crushed
- ¾ cup (3-oz) Cheddar cheese, shredded

Preheat oven to 350°F. Combine ingredients in a large bowl and mix just until blended. Place in a sprayed 9x5-inch loaf pan. Bake 60 to 70 minutes or until meat reaches at least 160°F. Carefully pour off fat; let stand about 5 minutes for easier slicing.

Per serving: Cal 337, Carb 6g, Fib 0g, Pro 30g, Fat 201g, Sod 459mg, Sug 1g

Hamburger Chili Dish   4 servings

- **1   pound lean ground beef**
- **2   cups coarsely chopped onion**
- **1   (14½-oz) can stewed tomatoes with liquid**
- **2   teaspoons chili powder**
- **1   teaspoon salt**
- **½   cup uncooked rice**

In large skillet, lightly brown ground beef and onion; drain. Add tomatoes (cut up, if too large) and remaining ingredients. Add 1 cup water. Bring to a boil; reduce heat and simmer, covered, for 30 minutes. Uncover; cook 10 minutes or until most of the liquid is absorbed.

note: Recipe can be baked in the oven, if desired, at 350°F for about the same amount of time.

Per serving: Cal 400, Carb 36g, Fib 3g, Pro 29g, Fat 15g, Sod 852mg, Sug 9g

Beef Rice Casserole   6 to 8 servings

- **1½   pounds lean ground beef**
- **½   cup chopped onion**
- **1½   cups uncooked long grain rice**
- **1   (10¾-oz) can condensed cream of mushroom soup**
- **1   (10¾-oz) can condensed cream of celery soup**
- **2   soup cans water**

Preheat oven to 350°F. Brown ground beef and onion; drain off fat. Spoon into a sprayed 2-quart casserole. Add the uncooked rice.

Combine soups in mixing bowl; gradually stir in water until blended and smooth. Pour over rice mixture. Bake 1 hour and 15 minutes or until liquid is absorbed and rice is tender.

Per serving: Cal 382, Carb 37g, Fib 1g, Pro 22g, Fat 15g, Sod 592mg, Sug 1g

Company Beef Casserole

12 servings

You can also assemble this recipe in two 8x8-inch square pans and freeze one. Half of the recipe will make 6 servings.

1½	pounds lean ground beef
1	(15½-oz) jar spaghetti sauce
12	ounces small egg noodles
1	(3-oz) package cream cheese, softened
1	cup sour cream
16	ounces Mozzarella cheese, shredded

Preheat oven to 350°F. Brown ground beef; drain. Add spaghetti sauce; simmer 20 minutes. Meanwhile, cook noodles; drain.

Beat cream cheese until smooth. Add sour cream; mix well. Spread half the noodles in sprayed 13x9-inch baking dish. Cover with half the cream cheese mixture; top with half the cheese. Spread all the meat sauce over cheese. Layer remaining noodles, cream cheese mixture and cheese. Bake 30 minutes or until heated through.

Per serving: Cal 371, Carb 23g, Fib 1g, Pro 28g, Fat 17g, Sod 549mg, Sug 3g

Make 2 - Freeze 1

For quick emergency meals, always have lasagna or other precooked meal in the freezer. For individual servings: bake lasagna, cool, slice into desired size squares and wrap tightly in plastic wrap. Remove amount needed, thaw and reheat.

Your Own Seasoned Taco Meat   10 servings

You won't have to purchase expensive seasoning mixes for this recipe (provided you have the other seasonings among your collection of spices).

- 1¼   pounds lean ground beef
- 1½   cups chopped onion
- 1½   teaspoons garlic salt
-   2   teaspoons chili powder
-   ¼   teaspoon cumin
-   ¼   teaspoon crushed red pepper flakes, or to taste

In medium skillet, brown ground beef and onion; drain. Add 1 cup water along with remaining ingredients. Bring to a boil, reduce heat and simmer 18 to 20 minutes or until liquid is absorbed.

Use for Tacos, Taco Burgers, Mexican Pizzas, Meat Turnovers and a topping for baked potatoes.

Per serving: Cal 125, Carb 3g, Fib 1g, Pro 12g, Fat 7g, Sod 182mg, Sug1g

Beefy Pasta Bake   6 to 8 servings

You can do all kinds of things with this casserole. Add any combination of chopped green pepper, pimiento, olives, corn, peas, etc. Use regular or spiral shaped noodles, top with buttered soft bread crumbs or grated cheese. Or, just follow the recipe.

- 1½   pounds lean ground beef
-   ¾   cup finely chopped onion
-   1   cup sour cream
-   1   (10¾-oz) can Cream of Mushroom soup
-   1   (10¾-oz) can Cream of Chicken soup
-   5   cups rotini noodles, cooked, drained

Preheat oven to 350ºF. Brown ground beef and onion in large skillet; drain off fat. Stir in remaining ingredients.

Pour into a sprayed 3-quart casserole or 13x9-inch baking dish. Bake 45 minutes or until heated through.

note: If really in a hurry, heat ingredients in skillet and omit step two.

Per Serving: Cal 503, Carb 54g, Fib 3g, Pro 25g, Fat 20g, Sod 630mg, Sug 3g

Ground Beef Salsa Dinner
6 to 8 large servings

This recipe will be a standby for many busy cooks. It makes a lot, which also makes for wonderful leftovers. To make ahead: Cook as directed and spoon into a sprayed 13x9-inch baking dish. When ready to serve, bake at 350° for 30 minutes. Add cheese and bake about 5 minutes.

- 8 ounces rotini noodles
- 1½ pounds lean ground beef
- 1 cup chopped onion
- 2 cups salsa
- 1 (11-oz) can Mexicorn, drained
- 1 cup (4-oz) Cheddar cheese, shredded

Cook pasta according to package directions; drain.

Meanwhile, in a 12-inch deep skillet, brown ground beef and onion; drain. Add salsa and corn; heat through. Add pasta then sprinkle with cheese. Cover and cook 5 minutes or until cheese is melted.

Per serving: Cal 395, Carb 34g, Fib 2g, Pro 27g, Fat 16g, Sod 586mg, Sug 6g

Southwestern Chili
4 to 6 servings

A delicious warming chili to be served on a cold blistery day.

- 1 pound lean ground beef
- 1 (15-oz) can dark kidney beans, drained
- 1 (14.5-oz) can diced tomatoes, undrained
- 1 cup thick and chunky salsa
- ¾ teaspoon chili powder (or to taste)
  Salt and pepper

In a large skillet, brown ground beef; drain. Add kidney beans, tomatoes and salsa. Add chili powder and stir until well mixed. Bring to a boil; reduce heat, cover and simmer about 15 minutes. Taste for flavor, and if desired, season with salt and pepper.

Per serving: Cal 270, Carb 21g, Fib 6g, Pro 22g, Fat 10g, Sod 543mg, Sug 4g

Linda's
Beef Curry Casserole

6 servings

This casserole has become a family favorite.

1	pound lean ground beef
1½	cup cooked long-grain rice
1½	teaspoons salt
1½	teaspoons curry powder (or to taste)
1	(8-oz) can crushed pineapple, undrained
½	cup raisins

Preheat oven to 350°F.In a large skillet, brown ground beef; drain off fat. Add salt and curry to meat. Stir in pineapple and raisins. Reduce heat and simmer 3 to 4 minutes. Add rice and place mixture in a sprayed 2-quart deep casserole dish. Bake covered for 30 minutes to heat through and blend flavors.

Per Serving: Cal 348, Carb 37g, Fib 2g, Pro 22g, Fat 12g, Sod 639mg, Sug 15g

Hamburger Hot Dish

6 to 8 servings

You can do all kinds of things with this casserole. Add any combination of chopped green pepper, pimiento, olives, corn, etc. Use regular or spiral shaped noodles, top with buttered soft breadcrumbs or grated cheese. Or, just follow the recipe. If really in a hurry, heat ingredients in skillet and omit step two.

1½	pounds lean ground beef
¾	cup finely chopped onion
1	cup sour cream
1	(10¾-oz) can condensed cream of mushroom soup
1	(10¾-oz) can condensed cream of chicken soup
4	cups noodles, cooked, drained

Preheat oven to 350°F. Brown ground beef and onion in large skillet; drain off fat. Stir in remaining ingredients.

Pour into sprayed 3-quart casserole or 13x9-inch baking dish. Bake 45 minutes or until heated through.

Per serving: Cal 395, Carb 29g, Fib 2g, Pro 24g, Fat 19g, Sod 339mg, Sug 3g

Layered Hamburger Bake

6 servings

- 2 **pounds lean ground beef**
  Prepared mustard
  Salt and pepper
  Thin onion slices
  Sliced tomatoes
  Sliced green pepper rings

Preheat oven to 350°F. Pat half of the ground beef into a deep 8 or 9-inch round cake pan. Spread with a little mustard; sprinkle with salt and pepper. Cover with onion slices, then tomato slices and green pepper rings.

Pat remaining ground beef evenly over top. Arrange additional tomato slices over ground beef. Bake 30 minutes or until ground beef reaches 160°F.

note: If a smaller or larger recipe is desired, decrease or increase ingredients and size of pan accordingly.

Per serving: Cal 347, Carb 4g, Fib 1g, Pro 35g, Fat 21g, Sod 171mg, Sug 2g

Tater Tot Casserole

6 servings

This is a very old recipe, but when my granddaughter, Paulina, had it for the first time at a friend's house, she loved it. I decided to bring it out of my file box for everyone to enjoy.

- 1½ **pounds lean ground beef**
- 1 **medium onion, thinly sliced**
  Salt and pepper
- 1 **can Cream of Celery or Mushroom soup**
- 1 **(16-oz) package Tater Tots**

Preheat oven to 350°F. In a skillet, brown the ground beef, and then drain. Spoon into a sprayed 11x7-inch baking dish. Separate onion slices into rings and arrange over meat. Sprinkle with salt and pepper. Give the soup a stir and spread over onion. Cover with Tater Tots. Bake 30 to 40 minutes or until heated through.

Per serving: Cal 368, Carb 25g, Fib 2g, Pro 22g, Fat 21g, Sod 767mg, Sug 2g

Italian Meatballs

4 servings

Meatballs are easy to cook when you bake them in the oven.

- 1 **pound lean ground beef**
- ½ **cup fine dry bread crumbs**
- 1 **teaspoon Italian seasonings**
- 1 **large egg, lightly beaten**
- 2¼ **cups purchased chunky spaghetti sauce, divided**
- 2 **ounces Mozzarella cheese, cut into 16 cubes**

Preheat oven to 400°F. In large mixing bowl, combine ground beef, bread crumbs, Italian seasoning, egg and ¼ cup of the spaghetti sauce. Mix lightly.

Shape a small amount of mixture around each cheese cube, making 16 meatballs (the cheese should be completely enclosed). Place on a shallow baking pan and bake 18 to 20 minutes. Meanwhile, heat remaining spaghetti sauce, add meatballs and serve over pasta.

note: If desired, make smaller meatballs, spear with a pick and serve as an appetizer.

Per serving: Cal 424, Carb 2g, Fib 2g, Pro 33g, Fat 21g, Sod 812mg, Sug 10g

Stuffed Green Peppers

4 servings

For a colorful festive dish, use red, yellow and red peppers.

- 1½ **pounds lean ground beef**
- 1 **cup chopped onion**
- ½ **cup cooked rice**
  Salt and pepper to taste
- 4 **large green peppers**
- 2 **(8-oz each) cans tomato sauce**

Preheat oven to 325°F. In a skillet, brown ground beef and onion; drain. Add cooked rice and season to taste.

Meanwhile, cut green peppers in half lengthwise. Remove seeds. Place cut side up, in sprayed 13x9-inch baking dish. Fill with meat mixture. Pour tomato sauce over top. Add ¼ cup water to baking dish. Bake 60 minutes or until peppers are tender.

note: Any leftover meat mixture can be spooned around the green peppers.

Per serving: Cal 466, Carb 26g, Fib 5g, Pro 41g, Fat 22g, Sod 775mg, Sug 10g

Chili-Corn Bread Casserole
4 to 6 servings

- **2 (15-oz) cans chili with beans**
- **1 (11-oz) can Mexican corn**
- **¼ cup fresh cilantro, chopped**
- **1 (8½-oz) box corn muffin mix**
- **1 large egg**
- **⅓ cup milk**

Preheat oven to 400°F. Heat chili and corn in medium saucepan, add cilantro. Pour into a sprayed 11x7-inch baking dish. Mix cornbread according to package directions and spread as evenly as possible over the chili. Bake 12 to 15 minutes or until golden.

Per serving: Cal 330, Carb 64g, Fib 8g, Pro 13g, Fat 5g, Sod 1305g, Sug 15g

Beefy Italian Pasta
6 servings

If using the cheese, you may want to omit the salt.

- **1½ pounds lean ground beef**
- **1 (14.5-oz) can diced Italian tomatoes, with juice**
- **1 teaspoon salt**
- **¼ teaspoon pepper**
- **2 cups uncooked rotini**
- **12 ounces process cheese spread, cubed (optional)**

In a large skillet (with a lid), brown ground beef; drain.

Add tomatoes, salt and pepper and bring to a boil. Add pasta and reduce heat to a medium simmer. Cover and cook 12 to 15 minutes or until pasta is tender and most of the liquid is absorbed.

If using, stir in the cheese and heat through until melted.

Per Serving: Cal 493, Carb 33g, Fib 1g, Pro 34g, Fat 25g, Sod 1480mg, Sug 7g

Southwestern Beef & Rice

6 servings

Can be made in about 15 minutes and is a lot better than Hamburger Helper.

- 1   pound lean ground beef
- 1   cup cooked rice
- 1   (15-oz) can kidney beans, drained
- 1   cup thick and chunky salsa
- ½   cup (2-oz) Cheddar cheese, shredded

In a large skillet, brown ground beef; drain off fat. Add rice, kidney beans and salsa; heat through. Add cheese and stir just until melted.

Per serving: Cal 330, Carb 25g, Fib 6g, Pro 25g, Fat 13g, Sod 412mg, Sug 3g

Spaghetti Cheese Casserole

8 large servings

My grandchildren like this casserole because it has fewer tomato chunks (ugh!) and more cheese (yum!).

- 1   (12-oz) package thin spaghetti
- 1   pound lean ground beef
- 1   cup chopped onion
- 2½ cups spaghetti sauce with mushrooms
- 2   cups (8-oz) Cheddar cheese, shredded
- 2   cups (8-oz) Mozzarella cheese, shredded

Preheat oven to 350°F. Cook pasta according to package directions. Meanwhile, in a large skillet, cook ground beef and onion until browned; drain. Add spaghetti sauce, bring to a boil, reduce heat and simmer 10 to 15 minutes.

Drain pasta; add meat mixture and toss to mix. This doesn't mix very well so you will need to rearrange some of the meat in the casserole. Place half of the mixture in a sprayed 13x9-inch baking dish. Top with half of each cheese. Add remaining meat mixture. Sprinkle with remaining cheese. Dish will be quite full. Bake 20 to 30 minutes or until heated through.

Per serving: Cal 489, Carb 44g, Fib 3g, Pro 35g, Fat 20g, Sod 831mg, Sug 7g

Chili Bake

6 servings

- ⅓ **cup butter**
- 5 **large eggs, lightly beaten**
- ½ **cup yellow cornmeal**
- ¾ **cup flour**
- 1¼ **cups milk**
- 2 **(15-oz) cans chili with beans**

Preheat oven to 425°F. Place butter in a 10-inch cast iron or ovenproof skillet. Place in oven to melt.

Meanwhile, combine eggs, cornmeal, flour, and milk until smooth. Remove skillet from oven. Carefully pour batter into pan. Spoon chili into center leaving about a 1½-inch margin around the edge. Bake 18 to 20 minutes, or until puffed and lightly browned. Serve immediately.

Per serving: Cal 394, Carb 49g, Fib 8g, Pro 17g, Fat 17g, Sod 785mg, Sug 8g

Have on Hand in Freezer

Breaded chicken strips and nuggets

Marinated chicken breast or flank steak

Homemade soups

Casseroles

Spaghetti sauce

Cooked chicken cubes or strips

(use in Caesar salad, fajitas, casseroles, etc.)

Skillet Ground Beef & Potatoes

4 large servings

This hearty dish of meat and potatoes can be prepared quickly and is sure to please hungry appetites.

- 1 **pound lean ground beef**
- ½ **cup chopped onion**
- 3 **cups frozen O'Brien potatoes, thawed**
- 1¼ **cups salsa**

In a large skillet, brown ground beef and onion; drain. Add potatoes and cook 8 to 10 minutes or until tender. Add salsa and heat through.

Per serving: Cal 385, Carb 33g, Fib 3g, Pro 28g, Fat 15g, Sod 406mg, Sug 3g

Ground meat safety

When meat is ground, more of the meat is exposed to the harmful bacteria. Bacteria multiply rapidly in the "Danger Zone" — temperatures between 40 and 140 °F. To keep bacterial levels low, store ground beef at 40 °F or less and use within 2 days, or freeze. To destroy harmful bacteria, cook ground beef to a safe minimum internal temperature of 160 °F. (www.fsis.usda.gov)

When working with any raw meat, be sure to thoroughly clean your hands, counters and utensils to prevent any cross contamination.

Southwestern Muffin Cups · 8 servings

- 1 **pound lean ground beef**
- ¾ **cup thick and chunky salsa**
- 1 **(16.3-oz) package Grands® buttermilk biscuits**
- ¾ **cup (3-oz) Cheddar cheese, shredded**

Preheat oven to 375°F. Brown ground beef in medium skillet; drain. Add salsa and bring to a boil. Reduce heat and simmer while preparing biscuits.

On cutting board or other smooth surface, pat each biscuit into a 5-inch circle. Spray cooking spray in 8 of the muffin cups. Press a biscuit into each one, pressing well onto bottom and up sides of each cup, extending over the top a little.

Spoon equal amounts of ground beef mixture into muffin cups. Sprinkle with cheese making sure the cheese stays inside the biscuits. Bake 10 to 12 minutes or until biscuits are golden.

note: Can be reheated in microwave oven, but the crust will be soft.

Per serving: Cal 355, Carb 25g, Fib 0g, Pro 19g, Fat 19g, Sod 846mg, Sug 1g

Hamburger Salsa Dish · 4 servings

A great family recipe when you have less than 30 minutes to cook dinner. Also good reheated.

- 1 **pound lean ground beef**
- 1 **(10¾ oz) can Southwest style Chicken Vegetable soup**
- ¾ **cup frozen corn**
- ½ **cup thick & chunky salsa**

Brown ground beef in a large skillet; drain. Add remaining ingredients along with ½ cup water. Cook 10 to 12 minutes, over low heat.

Per serving: Cal 343, Carb 20g, Fib 3g, Pro 29g, Fat 16g, Sod 819mg, Sug 4g

Ground Beef Stovetop Dinner
6 servings

Nothing fancy here, but you'll enjoy this quick and easy recipe on those days when you have to eat and run.

1   (7.2-oz) package rice pilaf or beef-flavored rice mix
1   pound lean ground beef
½   cup chopped celery
¾   cup chopped onion
½   cup (2-oz) Cheddar or Monterey Jack cheese, shredded

Cook rice according to directions on package. Meanwhile, brown ground beef, celery and onion in a deep 10-inch skillet; drain off fat. Add rice; if necessary; cook a little longer to heat through. Sprinkle cheese over top. Cover and let stand until cheese has melted.

Per serving: Cal 324, Carb 27g, Fib 1g, Pro 23g, Fat 14g, Sod 645mg, Sug 2g

Really Quick Meals

Taco Salad

Purchased
Roasted Chicken

Hamburgers,
salad, fresh veggies

Quick
Homemade Soup

Easy Skillet Dinner

Purchased Fried
Chicken - add coleslaw
and baked beans

Chicken, Beef
or Pork kabobs

Potato Taco Bake
6 servings

This is one of the easiest dishes ever- and very flexible (see additions below). Add a salad or a green veggie and you're done!

1   pound ground beef
1   (4.7-oz) package scalloped potatoes
1   (14.5-oz) can seasoned tomatoes diced, undrained
¾   cup milk
2   tablespoons taco seasoning
2   cup Cheddar cheese, shredded

Preheat oven to 350°F. In a large oven proof skillet, cook beef over medium heat until no longer pink; drain.

Stir in the potatoes and contents of sauce mix, tomatoes, milk, taco seasoning and ⅔ cup water.

Cover and bake for 60 minutes or until potatoes are tender. Sprinkle with cheese. Bake uncovered, 5 minutes longer or until cheese is melted. If desired, serve with sour cream and/or guacamole.

variation: (increase water to 1 cup) and add:

   1 cup frozen corn or 1 can corn, drained

   1 can beans, drained

   1 can green chilies

Per Serving: Cal 465, Carb 24g, Fib 2g, Pro 33g, Fat 26g, Sod 1133mg, Sug 5g

Dinner Nachos

2 servings

- ¾ **pound lean ground beef**
- ⅓ **cup taco sauce**
- 4 **cups tortilla chips**
- 1 **small tomato, coarsely chopped**
- ⅓ **cup sliced ripe olives**
- 2 **cups (8-oz) Cheddar cheese, shredded**

Preheat oven to 400°F. Lightly brown ground beef; drain. Add taco sauce.

Spread tortilla chips on a 12-inch pizza pan or large baking sheet. Spoon meat over top. Sprinkle with tomato, olives and then cheese. Bake 10 minutes or until cheese is melted.

Per serving: Cal 529, Carb 16g, Fib 2g, Pro 36g, Fat 35g, Sod 786mg, Sug 2g

Ground Beef & Onion

4 servings

- 1 **pound lean ground beef**
- ½ **cup fresh bread crumbs**
- 1 **teaspoon salt**
- ⅛ **teaspoon pepper**
- 2 **tablespoons butter**
- 2 **large onions, thinly sliced**

Combine ground beef, bread crumbs, salt and pepper. Shape into 4 patties.

Melt butter in a large skillet; add onion and cook until tender and lightly browned. If desired season with salt. Remove and keep warm. Add meat patties to skillet and cook to 160°F. Arrange on serving dish and top with onions.

Per serving: Cal 369, Carb 15g, Fib 1g, Pro 28g, Fat 21g, Sod 800mg, Sug 3g

Easy Goulash

6 servings

Easy, but good. Great for boating and camping.

- 1 **pound lean ground beef**
- 1 **(15-oz) can kidney beans, drained**
- 1 **(10.75-oz) can vegetable soup**

Brown ground beef in skillet; drain off fat. Add kidney beans and soup. Simmer 15 to 20 minutes.

Per serving: Cal 295, Carb 25g, Fib 8g, Pro 24g, Fat 11g, Sod 496mg, Sug 5g

cooking beef

The best guarantee, for the best results, when cooking any meat is an accurate thermometer. Time charts are good guidelines, but there can be several variables:

How cold is the meat? (Was it just removed from the refrigerator or has it been sitting out at room temperature)

Is your oven temperature accurate?

Is the cut long and narrow or short and thick?

A thermometer is the best way to ensure the same degree of doneness time after time. Experiment to find just the right temperature that your family prefers.

Remove At:

"I have found that removing the meat from the source of heat when it reaches 135°F, covering it with foil and allowing it to stand 10 to 15 minutes produces medium rare and removing it at 140°F produces medium."

For juiciest meat always allow the 10 to 15 minutes standing time.

The temperature will rise during standing time.

beef roasting chart

Cut of Meat	Weight (Pounds)	Oven Temp.	Approx. Cooking Time	
			Med. Rare (135°F)	Medium (140°F)
Eye Round Roast	2-3	325°F	1½-1¾ hrs	not advised
Rib Eye Roast (small end)	4-6 6-8	350°F	1¾-2 hrs 2-2½ hrs	2-2½ hrs 2½-3 hrs
Rib Eye Roast (large end)	4-6 6-8	350°F	2-2½ hrs 2¼-2½ hrs	2½-3 hrs 2¾-3¼ hrs
Rib Roast (Prime Rib)	6-8 8-10	350°F	2¼-2½ hrs 2½-3 hrs	2¾-3 hrs 3-3½ hrs
Round Tip Roast	4-6 6-8	325°F	2-2½ hrs 2½-3 hrs	2½-3 hrs 3-3½ hrs
Tenderloin	2-3 4-5	425°F	35-40 min. 50-60 min.	45-50 min. 60-70 min.
Tri-Tip Roast	1½-2	425°F	30-40 min.	40-45 min.

Prosciutto Wrapped
Rosemary Steak 4 servings

Impressive, delicious and easy!

2 **to 3 tablespoons Dijon mustard**
1 **to 2 tablespoons fresh rosemary, finely chopped**
4 **thin slices prosciutto**
4 **small steaks**

In a small bowl, combine Dijon mustard and rosemary. Using a knife or small spatula spread a thin layer of Dijon mixture on each side of the steaks. Place steaks in container and let marinate in refrigerator 12-24 hours

Preheat broiler or grill. Wrap one piece of prosciutto around each steak. Broil or grill until desired doneness, about 5-7 minutes per side. If desired, serve with gorgonzola butter.

Per serving:Cal 236, Carb 0g, Fib 0g, Pro 23g, Fat 16g, Sod 275mg, Sug 0g

Gorgonzola Butter

Wonderful served on beef, chicken, seafood, vegetables and even bread.

• 8 ounces crumbled Gorgonzola cheese

• ½ cup butter, softened

Combine ingredients in small mixing bowl and enjoy! Store in refrigerator.

Beef Kabobs   4 servings

Wooden skewers can be used for Kabobs, but they must first be soaked in water for at least 20 minutes.

1	(1½ lbs) top sirloin
1	cup dry white wine
⅔	cup vegetable oil
⅓	cup soy sauce
2	large garlic cloves, crushed
1	medium onion (8 wedges)

Cut meat into 16 cubes. In medium bowl, combine wine, oil, soy sauce and garlic. Add meat and toss to coat. Cover and marinate in refrigerator at least 2 hours. Drain the marinade into a small saucepan; bring to a boil and cook 5 minutes.

Meanwhile, thread meat alternately with onion on skewers, starting and ending with meat. Place kabobs on grill and cook about 3 minutes per side or until desired degree of doneness, basting frequently with the marinade.

tip: Place a scoop of rice on center of plate. Top with a Beef Kabob, then spoon peas on both sides.

Per serving: Cal 389, Carb 6g, Fib 1g, Pro 51g, Fat 17g, Sod 121mg, Sug 2g

Basic Pot Roast   6 to 8 servings

We all need a good basic pot roast recipe.

1	(3 to 4 lbs) rump, chunk or round beef roast
	Flour
¼	cup oil
1	large onion, cut into 8 wedges
	Salt and pepper to taste
1½	teaspoons of thyme or an herb blend

Preheat oven to 350ºF. Dip roast in flour and brown in oil in heavy pot or Dutch oven. Add remaining ingredients along with 1 cup water. Cover; bake 2 to 2½ hours or until meat is tender. Add more water if necessary. If desired, potatoes and carrots can be added last hour of cooking time.

Per serving: Cal 342, Carb 2g, Fib 0g, Pro 49g, Fat 14g, Sod 65mg, Sug 1g

Standing Rib Roast   4 servings

1   standing rib roast (4 ribs)
Seasoning, if desired

Preheat oven to 350°F. Place roast, rib side down, on rack in a shallow roasting pan. Sprinkle with seasoning, if desired. Bake to desired degree of doneness. See Meat Chart, page 168.

Cover lightly with foil and let roast stand 15 to 20 minutes before carving. Allow ¾ to 1 pound per person.

Per serving: Cal 862, Carb 0g, Fib 0g, Pro 46g, Fat 74g, Sod 136mg, Sug 0g

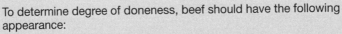

Beef

To determine degree of doneness, beef should have the following appearance:

Rare-130°F	Meat will be soft in center and still red. Very moist, but probably not much more than lukewarm in center.
Medium-Rare-135°F	Meat will be pink in center, but darker around the edges. Somewhat firmer than rare, but still very juicy. Also considered safer than meat cooked to rare stage.
Medium-140°F	Meat may still be somewhat pink in center, but with more darker meat around the edge. The texture is more firm than medium-rare.
Medium-Well-165°F	Meat will be darker throughout with very little, if any pink in center. Depending on cut of meat, can be quite dry.
Well Done-170°F	Don't! But if you insist, know that the meat will be overcooked and very dry unless that particular cut of meat has a lot of fat.

Beef Tenderloin with Mustard Caper Sauce

6 servings

This wonderful sauce can be made 1 to 2 hours ahead and kept warm in a well-insulated thermos. Leftover sauce can be gently reheated. In addition to beef tenderloin, the sauce can be served with pork chops, pork tenderloin, beef and pork kabobs, beef fondue, and prime rib.

- **1 beef tenderloin (3 lbs), purchase the butt section**
- **2 tablespoons butter, divided**
- **3 green onions, divided**
- **2 cups heavy cream**
- **3 tablespoons Dijon mustard**
- **1½ tablespoons capers, drained**

Preheat oven to 425°F. Remove tenderloin from refrigerator and trim, if necessary, and pat dry. Melt 1 tablespoon of the butter and brush over meat. Place on rack in a small roasting pan. Bake about 35 to 44 minutes or until meat thermometer registers 135° for medium rare (or 140° for medium.) Remove from oven and cover lightly with foil. Let stand 10 to 15 minutes before carving.

Meanwhile, melt the remaining 1 tablespoon butter in a medium saucepan and cook 1 tablespoon chopped white part of the onion, until soft. (Thinly slice some of the green part of the onion and set aside for garnish.) Add cream and bring to a boil. Reduce heat and simmer 10 to 15 minutes or until mixture thickens, stirring occasionally. Remove from heat and add Dijon mustard and capers.

Spoon some of the sauce on each dinner plate and top with a slice of beef tenderloin. Sprinkle with sliced green onion for garnish.

note: You must use pasteurized heavy cream or the sauce may not thicken.

Per beef serving: Cal 554, Carb 0g, Fib 0g, Pro 41g, Fat 42g, Sod 98mg, Sug 0g
Per 2 tbsp sauce Cal 93, Carb 1g, Fib 0g, Pro 1g, Fat 10g, Sod 71mg, Sug 0g

 menu

**Beef Tenderloin with
Mustard Caper Sauce
Scalloped Potatoes Deluxe
Lemon Broccoli
Caesar Salad
Hot Rolls
Ice Cream Amaretto Dessert**

Beef Fajita Meat

4 servings

This is a popular recipe in restaurants as well as home entertaining. Chicken breasts halves can be substituted for the beef. Favorite condiments served with Fajitas are: Guacamole, salsa, chopped onion and tomato or sour cream. Or try the Onions and Pepper Sauté on page

1	pound skirt steak, flank steak, or sirloin steak
½	cup fresh lime juice
¾	teaspoon garlic salt
½	teaspoon freshly ground black pepper
½	teaspoon paprika or to taste
	Chopped cilantro

Place beef in shallow dish. Combine next 4 ingredients and pour over meat. Cover and refrigerate several hours or overnight.

Remove meat from marinade; drain thoroughly. Cook to desired degree of doneness. Meat can be grilled, broiled or cooked in a skillet with a small amount of oil. Slice diagonally into strips. Garnish with chopped cilantro. Serve with warm flour tortillas.

Per Serving: Cal 357, Carb 16g, Fib 2g, Pro 35g, Fat 17g, Sod 136mg, Sug 0g

Beef Stroganoff

4 servings

1½	pounds beef tenderloin or sirloin
6	tablespoons butter, divided
1	cup chopped onion
¼	cup flour
1¾	cups beef broth
1	cup sour cream

Cut meat across the grain into ¼-inch strips about 1½-inches long.

Heat butter in large skillet. Add onion and cook until tender; remove and set aside. Add remaining butter to skillet. Add half the meat and lightly brown; remove and repeat with remaining meat. Return all the meat to skillet, but do not drain off fat.

Add onion and flour to skillet; stir to mix. Slowly add the broth, stirring until smooth. Cook until thickened, stirring occasionally. Reduce heat. Add sour cream and heat through, but do not boil or it may curdle. Serve over rice or noodles.

Per serving: Cal 494, Carb 8, Fib 1g, Pro 24g, Fat 39g, Sod 417mg, Sug 3g

Stuffed Flank Steak

6 servings

For a two ingredient recipe, this one has a lot of flavor. Any leftover steak makes delicious sandwiches.

1 to 1½ pound flank steak

¾ pound bulk Italian sausage

Preheat oven to 350°F. Place steak on waxed paper, rounded side down. Pound to flatten slightly.

Crumble sausage over steak to within 1 inch of edge. Starting with the short end, roll meat tightly. Tie with string (or dental floss) in 5 to 6 places, making sure ends are tied to enclose filling. String should be tight, making a compact loaf. Place seam side down on rack in roasting pan. Bake 75 to 85 minutes or until both meats are cooked through. Slice into ¼-inch slices to serve.

Per serving: Cal 327, Carb 1g, Fib 0g, Pro 35g, Fat 20g, Sod 296mg, Sug 0g

Teriyaki Tri-Tip Steaks

4 servings

1½ pounds tri-tip beef steak

½ cup soy sauce

2 tablespoons brown sugar

½ teaspoon ground ginger

Place meat in a large resealable bag. Combine remaining ingredients with ¼ cup water. Pour over meat. Seal. Marinate in refrigerator for 6 to 8 hours. Discard marinade.

Grill over hot coals until cooked to desired doneness, turning once.

Per Serving: Cal 319, Carb 9g, Fib 0g, Pro 37g, Fat 14g, Sod 2710mg, Sug 9g

Broiled Sirloin Steak

4 to 6 servings

The steak can be grilled over direct heat, basting with the butter sauce.
If desired, use individual sirloin steaks or steaks of choice.

- 1 **sirloin steak, 1½ inches thick**
- 1 **tablespoon Worcestershire sauce**
- ¼ **cup butter, melted**
- 1 **teaspoon salt**
- ⅛ **teaspoon pepper**
- ½ **teaspoon garlic powder**

Place steak on rack in a roasting pan.

Combine remaining ingredients. Brush steak generously with the sauce. Broil about 3½-inches from broiling unit 8 to 10 minutes. Turn steak, brush with sauce and broil 8 to 10 minutes, depending on desired degree of doneness. Transfer to a hot serving platter; pour remaining butter sauce over top.

Per serving: Cal 455, Carb 0g, Fib 0g, Pro 40g, Fat 32g, Sod 316mg, Sug 0g

Steak & Mushroom Sauce

2 servings

If you want to impress your guest, you can flame the brandy after adding it to the skillet. But, watch carefully -I've heard of singed eyebrows and curtains burning!

- 2 **New York steaks**
- ¼ **cup butter**
- ½ **cup chopped onion**
- 8 **mushrooms, sliced**
- 2 **teaspoons Worcestershire sauce**
- 2 **tablespoons brandy**

Melt butter in a large skillet. Brown steak quickly on one side. Reduce heat; add onion and mushrooms. Cook 2 minutes. Turn steaks and cook about 6 minutes or to desired degree of doneness. Add Worcestershire sauce and brandy. Cook about 2 minutes.

Per serving: Cal 897, Carb 7g, Fib 1g, Pro 60g, Fat 64g, Sod 350mg, Sug 3g

menu

Pepper Steak
Asparagus & Red Peppers
Garlic Mashed
Potatoes
Pear-Gorgonzola Cheese Salad
Easy Dinner Rolls
Almond Angel Food Cake

Pepper Steak   2 servings

- **2 New York cut steaks, about 1½-inch thick**
- **2 tablespoons black peppercorns, coarsely ground**
- **1 teaspoon salt**
- **3 tablespoons butter**
- **3 tablespoons oil**
- **⅓ cup cognac**

Sprinkle both sides of steak with peppercorns, pressing into the meat. Let stand 15 to 20 minutes.

Sprinkle one side of meat with salt. Heat butter and oil in skillet over medium-high heat. Place steaks, salted side down, in the hot oil and cook for 3 minutes. Salt steaks, turn, and cook 3 minutes. Reduce heat to medium; cook about 3 minutes on each side. Check for desired degree of doneness and cook longer, if necessary, bearing in mind that they will continue to cook when removed from the skillet. Remove and keep warm. Remove pan from heat, add cognac and carefully ignite; pour over steaks.

Per serving : Cal 872, Carb 4g, Fib 2g, Pro 60g, Fat 61g, Sod 764mg, Sug 0g

Beef Jerky

- **1 flank steak**
- **½ cup soy sauce**
- **½ teaspoon garlic powder**
- **1 teaspoon lemon pepper**

Preheat oven to 150°F. Cut flank steak lengthwise (with the grain) in long thin strips no more than ¼-inch thick. Combine remaining ingredients in mixing bowl. Add meat; marinate 1 hour. Baste occasionally if meat is not completely covered with sauce.

Arrange meat strips on rack; place on cookie sheet. Bake 12 hours. The time can vary a little depending on how your oven bakes. Meat should be cooked through and dry, but not brittle. Cool and store in a covered container.

Coffee Beef Stew   10 servings

The coffee taste is very mild in this recipe. Serve with a Waldorf salad and garlic bread for a complete meal.

- **4 pounds stew meat**
- **1 (1.25-oz) package meat marinade**
- **²/₃ cup brewed coffee**
- **2 (10.75-oz) cans Tomato Bisque soup**
- **1 large onion, chopped**
- **4 large potatoes, peeled, cubed**

Preheat oven to 300°F. Combine all ingredients in a Dutch oven; stir and cover. Bake for 3 to 4 hours or until meat and potatoes are tender. If desired, garnish with freshly chopped parsley.

note: You may cook this dish in a slow cooker, rather than the oven, for 7 to 8 hours.

Per cup: Cal 485, Carb 29g, Fib 2g, Pro 34g, Fat 25g, Sod 719mg, Sug 9g

Swiss Steak   4 to 6 servings

- **2 pounds round steak, 1 inch thick**
- **¼ cup flour**
- **Salt and pepper**
- **3 tablespoons oil**
- **½ cup chopped onion**
- **1 (16-oz) can tomatoes, with juice, cut up**

Preheat oven to 350°F. Combine flour, salt and pepper; pound into meat. Brown meat on both sides in hot oil in large Dutch oven or skillet. Top with onion and tomatoes. Bake, covered, for 1¾ hours or until tender. Add water if necessary.

tip: If desired, add 1/4 cup chopped green peppers the last 15 minutes.

Per serving: Cal 316, Carb 8g, Fib 0g, Pro 33g, Fat 16g, Sod 297mg, Sug 3g

Lamb with Mustard & Apple

Juice 6 servings

An unexpected combination of flavors that work very well with lamb.

6	lamb chops (approx. 2-lbs)
¼	cup soy sauce
½	cup apple juice concentrate
¼	cup Dijon mustard
1	tablespoon minced garlic
1	sprig fresh rosemary

Wash and pat lamb chops dry. Sprinkle with salt and pepper. In a hot skillet (using butter or spray) sear lamb chops on both sides.

Transfer chops to slow cooker. In a small bowl mix together soy sauce, apple juice concentrate, Dijon mustard and garlic. Pour over chops.

Add rosemary sprig to the slow cooker. Cover and cook for 5 hours or until chops are tender.

Per serving: Cal 309, Carb 2g, Fib 0g, Pro 40g, Fat 14g, Sod 265mg, Sug 0g

Company Lamb Chops

4 servings

4	lamb chops, 1½ inches thick
1	teaspoon salt
¼	teaspoon pepper
3	tablespoons prepared mustard
3	tablespoons honey

Trim fat from lamb chops. Season with salt and pepper. Broil 7 minutes on one side; turn and broil 6 minutes or to desired degree of doneness. Do not overcook; it's okay if lamb is pink in the center.

Combine mustard and honey; spread over lamb chops. Broil 2 minutes longer.

Per serving: Cal 137, Carb 9g, Fib 0g, Pro 14g, Fat 5g, Sod 443mg, Sug 8g

cooking pork

Remove At:

"I have found that removing the pork from the source of heat when it reaches 145°F, covering it loosely with foil and allowing it to stand 10 to 15 minutes produces the best results."

For juiciest meat always allow the 10 to 15 minutes standing time. The temperature will rise during standing time.

pork roasting chart

Cut	Oven Temp	Pounds	Approx. Cooking time	Remove at:
Crown Roast	350° F	6-10	20 minutes per pound	145° F
Center Loin Roast	350° F	3-5	20 minutes per pound	145° F
Boneless Top Loin Roast	350° F	2-4	20 minutes per pound	145° F
Whole leg (fresh ham)	350° F	12	20 minutes per pound	145° F
Boston Butt	350° F	3-6	45 minutes per pound	145° F
Tenderloin	425° F	½-1½	25-35 minutes total	145° F
Half Ham (precooked)	325° F	6-8	1 hour total	130° F -140° F
Ground Pork				160° F

Company Pork Tenderloin and Noodles   6 servings

Pork Tenderloin makes an elegant company dish and this one is especially easy to prepare.

- **2   pork tenderloins, about 1½-lbs total weight**
- **2   tablespoons melted butter, divided**
- **1   cup apricot preserves**
- **¼   cup light corn syrup**
- **¼   tablespoons Grand Marnier®**
- **8   ounces egg noodles**

Preheat oven to 450°F. Place tenderloins in a small shallow baking pan. Brush with 1 tablespoon butter. Bake for 20 minutes. Combine next 3 ingredients and pour over meat. Bake 10 to 15 minutes or until meat teat done (160°F).

Meanwhile, cook pasta according to package directions; drain and toss with remaining tablespoon of butter. Place on serving plate. Cut pork tenderloins diagonally into ½-inch slices. Overlap, arranging two rows of meat on top of noodles. Spoon apricot sauce over top.

tip: Cooking time may vary according to the size of the tenderloins. The ones used in this recipe were rather small, ¾-lbs each.

Per Serving: Cal 478, Carb 71g, Fib 1g, Pro 27g, Fat 9g, Sod 242mg, Sug 46g

Pork Roast Dijon   6 servings

An easy family or company recipe.

- **1   (2½-lb) boneless pork loin roast**
- **2   teaspoons Dijon mustard**
- **½   teaspoon dried rosemary**
- **Salt and pepper**

Preheat oven to 350°F. Place roast on a rack in a roasting pan; spread with mustard and sprinkle with rosemary, salt, and pepper.

Bake 40 to 50 minutes or until meat reaches 145°F. Cover loosely with foil and let stand 15 minutes before slicing.

Per Serving: Cal 279, Carb 0g, Fib 0g, Pro 30g, Fat 17g, Sod 165mg, Sug 0g

Cashew Ham Bake
4 to 6 servings

- **1**   **large ham slice, 1-inch thick**
- **½**   **cup orange marmalade**
- **¼**   **cup coarsely chopped cashews**

Preheat oven to 300°F. Place ham on rack in a roasting pan. Bake 30 minutes.

Spread marmalade over top and sprinkle with cashews. Bake 15 minutes.

note: Serve with buttered peas, Dinner Hash Browns, and a crisp green salad.

Per serving: Cal 187, Carb 10g, Fib 2g, Pro 9g, Fat 13g, Sod 471mg, Sug 5g

Italian Sausage Dinner
4 servings

This hearty and flavorful dish can be prepared quickly and is great anytime. Serve with hot bread to sop up the juices.

- **4**   **to 6 Italian sausages**
- **1**   **tablespoon oil**
- **2**   **medium onions, sliced, separated into rings**
- **1**   **green pepper, cut into strips**
- **5**   **plum tomatoes, sliced**
-     **Salt and pepper**

Brown sausages in hot oil in medium skillet. Add onion and green pepper and continue cooking until vegetables are just tender. Add tomatoes and season with salt and pepper. Cook until heated through.

Per serving: Cal 187, Carb 10g, Fib 2g, Pro 9g, Fat 13g, Sod 471mg, Sug 5g

Baked Hot Dogs and Sauerkraut

4 servings

The caraway seeds and Swiss cheese soften the tartness of the sauerkraut.

- **1 (32-oz) jar refrigerated sauerkraut, drained**
- **2 teaspoons caraway seeds**
- **8 hot dogs**
- **1½ cups (6-oz) Swiss cheese, shredded**

Preheat oven to 350°F. Place well-drained sauerkraut in sprayed 10x7-inch baking dish. Sprinkle with caraway seeds and toss with a fork to mix. Place hot dogs over sauerkraut and sprinkle with cheese. Bake 25 to 30 minutes or until heated through and cheese is melted.

Per serving:Cal 247, Carb 17g, Fib 4g, Pro 12g, Fat 15g, Sod 1203mg, Sug 4g

Maple Ham

10 servings

For the holidays, you may want to purchase a 12 pound ham, otherwise, a 7 or 8 pound ham is an ideal size.

- **1 (7-lb) fully cooked bone-in ham**
- **1 teaspoon dry mustard**
- **2 teaspoons cider vinegar**
- **½ cup maple syrup**

Preheat oven to 350°F. Trim ham of excess fat. Score top of ham. Place, fat-side up, on a rack in a shallow roasting pan.

Bake 15 to 20 minutes per pound or until temperature reaches 140°F, about 1½ hours.

Meanwhile, combine remaining ingredients and spoon over ham last 30 minutes of cooking time. I usually add this after ham has baked about an hour. Then I baste a couple of times. Let stand 10 minutes before slicing.

Per Serving: Cal 534, Carb 11g, Fib 0g, Pro 56g, Fat 28g, Sod 123mg, Sug 10g

Ham Noodle Casserole   6 servings

For a quick economical meal, this is an excellent way to use up any leftover ham.

8	ounces ¼-inch wide egg noodles
1	cup finely chopped onion
2	large eggs
1	cup sour cream
¾	cup (3-oz) Swiss or Monterey Jack cheese, shredded
1½	cups cubed cooked ham

Preheat oven to 350°F. Cook noodles according to directions on package; drain. Meanwhile, cook onion in a small nonstick skillet until tender.

In mixing bowl, combine eggs and sour cream. Add onion, cheese and ham. Add noodles and mix well. Pour into a sprayed 2-quart casserole. Cover and bake 35 minutes. Uncover and bake 10 minutes or until heated through and mixture is set.

Per serving: Cal 404, Carb 32g, Fib 1g, Pro 22g, Fat 19g, Sod 94mg, Sug 3g

menu

Stuffed Spareribs
Almond Rice Pilaf
Lemon Broccoli
Jiffy Cornbread Muffins
Dome Cake

Stuffed Ribs   6 servings

2	racks baby back ribs
	Salt and pepper
½	cup butter
1¼	cups chopped onion
¾	cup chopped celery
1	(8-oz) package seasoned bread cubes

Preheat oven to 400°F. Trim ribs of excess fat, rinse and pat dry. Sprinkle lightly with salt and pepper and set aside.

Melt butter in a large 12-inch skillet. Add onion and celery and cook until just tender. Add bread cubes and 1 cup water, toss until bread cubes are moistened.

Place one rack of ribs, meaty side down, on a shallow roasting pan. Spoon stuffing evenly over ribs. Top with remaining rack of ribs, meaty side up. Press down slightly to cover and check to make sure the stuffing is inside the ribs and not spilling out the sides. Bake 50 to 60 minutes (no need to turn) until nicely browned and cooked through. Cut into 2 rib servings, cutting through the bottom ribs.

Per serving: Cal 874, Carb 31g, Fib 2g, Pro 44g, Fat 62g, Sod 1020mg, Sug 6g

Chicken Fried Pork

4 servings

This recipe is similar to Chicken Fried Steak (Beef), only here I have used pork. It can be made for any number of servings, using any size boneless pork, pounded to ¼-inch thickness.

- **2   thick cut (1-1½-inches) boneless pork chops**
- **Salt and pepper**
- **½   cup flour**
- **Vegetable oil**

Cut pork lengthwise into 2 thin chops. Place between plastic wrap and pound to ¼-inch thickness. Sprinkle both sides with salt and pepper. Dredge in flour, coating both sides and shaking off excess. Heat ¼-inch oil in a heavy large skillet. Add pork and fry until nicely browned, about 3 to 4 minutes on each side.

note: If gravy is desired, pour off all but 2 tablespoons of the fat. Add 1 cup milk. Heat until boiling, scraping up all the browned bits. Cook until thickened. (No need to add flour, as the flour from the cooked pork chops is usually enough to thicken.)

Per serving: Cal 242, Carb 12g, Fib 1g, Pro 20g, Fat 13g, Sod 130mg, Sug 1g

Pork Chop Casserole

4 servings

- **1   (14-oz) jar sauerkraut, drained**
- **4   (¾-inch) pork chops**
- **1   granny smith apple, thinly sliced**
- **1   tablespoon butter**
- **1   large onion, thinly sliced**
- **½   cup apple juice or apple cider**

Place sauerkraut in the bottom of a lightly sprayed slow cooker. Arrange pork chops over top. Sprinkle with salt and pepper to taste. Add apple slices

In a medium skillet, heat butter and sauté onions until just lightly browned. Spoon over apples. Pour apple juice over the top. Cover and cook on low 7 to 8 hours or until pork chops are tender.

Per serving: Cal 233, Carb 15g, Fib 4g, Pro 17g, Fat 12g, Sod 732mg, Sug 10g

Mustard Glazed Ham

8 to 12 servings

1 **4 to 6 pound ham**
½ **cup firmly packed light brown sugar**
¼ **cup orange juice**
½ **teaspoon dry mustard**

Preheat oven to 325°F. Place ham on rack, fat side up. Bake 20 minutes per pound or until heated through, temperature should reach 140°F.

Meanwhile, combine remaining ingredients. Brush ham generously with glaze during last 30 minutes of baking time. Continue basting every 10 minutes. Let stand 20 minutes before slicing.

Per 4 oz : Cal 225, Carb 1g, Fib 0g, Pro 22g, Fat 14g, Sod 1524mg, Sug 1g

Quick Glaze

Pour 3 cups apple cider or Coca Cola® over ham; basting occassionally during the last hour to glaze.

Baked Herb Pork Chops

2 to 4 servings

4 **loin-cut pork chops, about ½-inch thick**
   Salt and pepper
1 **tablespoon red wine or red wine garlic vinegar**
1 **tablespoon Dijon mustard**
1 **teaspoon Italian seasoning**

Preheat oven to 450°F. Rinse pork chops and pat dry. Sprinkle both sides lightly with salt and pepper. Place in a sprayed 8x8-inch baking dish.

Combine remaining ingredients and brush over meat. Bake, covered, for 10 minutes. Remove from oven, turn pork chops, and continue baking, uncovered 5 to 8 minutes or until temperature reaches 145°F. (Do not overcook or meat will be dry and tough.)

Per serving: Cal 169, Carb 0g, Fib 0g, Pro 18g, Fat 10g, Sod 162mg, Sug 0g

Oven Spareribs   4 to 6 servings

     3   to 4 pounds pork spareribs
     ½   cup ketchup
     ½   cup firmly packed light brown sugar
     2   tablespoons Worcestershire sauce
     1   tablespoon white vinegar
         Dash hot pepper sauce

Preheat oven to 350°F. Cut spareribs into 2-rib servings. Place ribs in a large roasting pan, meaty side down. Bake 45 minutes.

Turn ribs, meaty side up. Combine remaining ingredients and brush over ribs. Bake 20 to 30 minutes or until cooked through and tender.

Per serving: Cal 600, Carb 11g, Fib 0g, Pro 41g, Fat 43g, Sod 272mg, Sug 11g

Stuffing-Topped Pork Chops   4 servings

A lot of flavor with just a few ingredients.

     4   loin cut pork chops, 1-inch thick
     3   cups herb seasoned bread cubes
     ¼   cup chopped onion
     ¾   cup vegetable or chicken broth
     ¼   cup butter, melted
     1   (10¾-oz) can condensed cream of mushroom soup

Preheat oven to 350°F. Trim pork chops of excess fat. Rinse and pat dry. Lightly brown on both sides in a large sprayed skillet. Place in a shallow roasting pan.

In mixing bowl, combine bread cubes with the onion, broth and butter. Let stand 3 or 4 minutes for the liquid to soften the bread somewhat. Divide into four equal amounts. Roll each into a rather compact, but not firm, ball. Place on pork chops and pat to cover most of the meat.

Combine soup with ½ can water, mixing until smooth. Spoon over and around pork chops. Cover tightly with foil and bake 25 minutes. Remove foil and bake, uncovered, 15 minutes or until tender. Watch carefully and do not overcook. The internal temperature when removing from oven should be no higher than 145°F. The temperature will then continue to rise.

note: The onion is somewhat crisp in this recipe. If desired, after browning the pork chops, add onion to skillet and cook until soft.

variation: For special dinners, I sometimes add ⅓ cup chopped pecans to the stuffing mixture.

Per serving: Cal 675, Carb 41g, Fib 4g, Pro 42g, Fat 37g, Sod 1454mg, Sug 4g

Natasha's Orange Fennel Salmon

6 servings

- 1 **(2-lb) salmon fillet, skinless**
- 1 **cup thinly sliced fennel, bulb and sprigs**
- 1 **cup thinly sliced carrots**
- ½ **cup thinly sliced onion**
- 1 **teaspoon coriander powder**
- 1 **medium orange thinly, sliced**

Preheat oven to 375°F. Divide salmon fillet into 6 equal parts. Cut 6 rectangular pieces of parchment paper large enough to wrap each fillet and vegetables.

In the center of each parchment paper, put a few slices of fennel, carrots and onion. Lay the fish fillet on top. Sprinkle with coriander powder, salt and pepper.

Top each fillet with a couple of slices of orange. Fold paper lengthwise to enclose fish then seal by crimping ends of paper several times. Repeat with all 6 fillets.

Place on baking sheet. Bake for 12-15 minutes or until fish flakes easily with fork. Serve immediately.

substitute: If you don't have coriander powder, you may substitute dried cilantro.

Per serving: Cal 319, Carb 5g, Fib 1g, Pro 34g, Fat 17g, Sod 89mg, Sug 3g

Pesto Salmon

2 servings

Desperately easy to make, wonderful to eat!

- 6 **tablespoons pesto**
- 2 **(6-oz) salmon fillets, skinned**

Preheat oven to 450°F. Spread 3 tablespoons pesto in a sprayed 8x8-inch baking dish. Add salmon and spread with remaining pesto. Bake 10 to 12 minutes or until cooked through.

Per Serving: Cal 411, Carb 1g, Fib 0g, Pro 40g, Fat 26g, Sod 205mg, Sug 0g

Teriyaki Salmon Steaks

4 servings

Serve with almond Rice Pilaf, Steamed Green Beans and Sally Lunn Muffins.

- **4 salmon steaks, 1-inch thick**
- **¼ cup oil**
- **2 tablespoons lemon juice**
- **2 tablespoons soy sauce**
- **½ teaspoon dry mustard**
- **½ teaspoon ground ginger**

Place salmon in a sprayed 11x7-inch baking dish. Combine remaining ingredients; pour over top. Marinate 1 hour in refrigerator, turning occasionally.

Drain off marinade. Place salmon on rack in broiling pan. Broil 5 minutes, turn and broil 5 minutes more or until cooked through. Brush lightly with additional oil if salmon appears dry.

Per serving: Cal 291, Carb 0g, Fib 0g, Pro 31g, Fat 17g, Sod 139mg, Sug 0g

Cooking Time for Fish

Measure fish at its thickest point. Estimate 10 minutes total cooking time per inch

Total cooking time applies to whatever cooking method is being used—baking, broiling, frying, etc. If baking a salmon or other fish and the fish measures 3 inches at its thickest point, bake 30 minutes at 450°. If broiling steak 1½-inches thick divide the total time and broil 7½ minutes on each side. Test with a wooden toothpick; if it comes out clean and dry, fish is done. Cooking times may vary somewhat according to the thickness and size of the fish, the temperature of the fish at cooking time and how hot your oven bakes. Watch carefully though, and remember that the fish will continue to cook somewhat after removing from heat. The internal temperature of fish should be 137°F.

Baked Salmon Steaks

4 servings

- **4 (6-oz) salmon steaks**
- **2 tablespoons butter, melted**
- **½ teaspoon Worcestershire sauce**
- **1 teaspoon fresh lemon juice**

Preheat oven to 450°F. Place salmon in a sprayed shallow baking pan.

Combine remaining ingredients and brush salmon with some of the sauce. Bake 10 minutes, basting occasionally with the sauce. Test for doneness after 8 minutes.

Per Serving: Cal 384, Carb 0g, Fib 0g, Pro 37g, Fat 25g, Sod 136mg, Sug 0g

Salmon Loaf   4 to 6 servings

- **1**   **(14-oz) can salmon**
- **1**   **(10¾-oz) can condensed cream of mushroom soup**
- **1½   cups soft breadcrumbs**
- **¼   cup finely chopped celery**
- **2   tablespoons finely chopped onion**
- **2   large eggs**

Preheat oven to 350°F. Combine ingredients and spoon into sprayed 7x5-inch loaf pan. Bake 45 to 50 minutes or until center is firm. Let stand 5 minutes. Turn out on serving plate.

Per serving: Cal 194, Carb 10g, Fib 1g, Pro 16g, Fat 10g, Sod 747mg, Sug 1g

Salmon Steaks   4 servings

- **4   salmon steaks, about 6 ounces each**
- **2   tablespoons oil**
- **2   tablespoons fresh lemon juice**
- **1   small garlic clove, minced**
- **2   tablespoons minced fresh basil**

Pat salmon steaks dry with a paper towel and place on a broiler pan, skin-side down.

Combine remaining ingredients and brush some of the mixture over the salmon. Broil, about 8 to 10 minutes, or until steaks test done, basting once or twice with the sauce. You do not have to turn the steaks.

variation: Substitute halibut for the salmon.

Per serving: Cal 312, Carb 1g, Fib 0g, Pro 31g, Fat 20g, Sod 73mg, Sug 0g

Lemony Fish with Capers

6 servings

This dish has a great blend of flavors. I use salted butter which eliminates the need to add salt.

- ½ cup butter
- 1 tablespoon capers, minced
- 2 tablespoons green onion, minced
- 1 tablespoon Dijon mustard
- 3 tablespoons fresh lemon juice, divided
- 6 fish fillets (6-oz each)

Preheat oven to 400°F. In a food processor combine butter, capers, green onion, mustard and 2 tablespoons lemon juice. Coat a 13x9-inch baking dish with half the mixture. Place fillets in baking dish. Dot each fillet with remaining mixture.

Bake 15 to 20 minutes or until fish is flaky. Transfer fillets to platter (keep warm).

In a small saucepan add drippings and remaining 1 tablespoon lemon juice; reduce over medium heat, stirring with whisk. Pour over fish and serve immediately.

Per serving: Cal 251, Carb 3g, Fib 0g, Pro 24g, Fat 15g, Sod 272mg, Sug 1g

Favorite Halibut

4 servings

This recipe is good with almost any white fish.

- 1 (1-lb) halibut, 1-inch thick
- ½ teaspoon garlic salt
- 3 tablespoons sour cream
- 1 green onion, chopped
- 2 tablespoons grated Parmesan cheese

Place halibut in a sprayed shallow baking dish. Sprinkle with garlic salt.

Combine sour cream and onion; spread over fish. Sprinkle with Parmesan. Bake 10 minutes or until cooked through.

Per Serving: Cal 258, Carb 1g, Fib 0g, Pro 18g, Fat 19g, Sod 245mg, Sug 1g

Halibut-Shrimp Bake

4 servings

4	small halibut steaks or fillets
½	cup fresh lemon juice
½	cup butter, melted
½	cup sour cream
½	cup (2-oz) Cheddar cheese, shredded
⅓	cup tiny shrimp, cooked

Preheat oven to 350°F. Place halibut in a shallow baking pan. Combine butter and lemon juice; pour over halibut. Bake 10 to 12 minutes or until fish tests done.

Top each steak or fillet with some of the sour cream. Sprinkle with cheese. Place under broiler and cook just until cheese melts. Garnish top with shrimp.

Per serving: Cal 546, Carb 4g, Fib 0g, Pro 44g, Fat 37g, Sod 403mg, Sug 2g

Easy Bake Parmesan Sole

4 servings

Serve with Hazelnut Asparagus, Oven Roasted New Potatoes and Caesar Salad.

4	fillet of sole
2	tablespoons butter
⅓	cup dry breadcrumbs
2	tablespoons grated Parmesan cheese
1	teaspoon paprika

Preheat oven to 450°F. Wash fillets; brush both sides with melted butter.

Combine remaining ingredients in a pie dish. Dip fillets in crumbs and place in a sprayed shallow baking pan. Bake 10 minutes or until fish flakes easily with a fork. If coating is dry, brush with a little melted butter.

Per serving: Cal 204, Carb 2g, Fib 0g, Pro 29g, Fat 8g, Sod 212mg, Sug 0g

Trout Amandine
4 servings

- **4**   **trout (about 8-oz each)**
- **½**   **cup butter, melted**
- **⅓**   **cup slivered almonds**
- **1**   **tablespoon lemon juice**

Wipe trout dry with paper towels. Brush both sides with melted butter. Place on sprayed broiler pan. Broil 4 inches from heat, about 8 to 10 minutes or until fish tests done, being careful not to overcook. (Do not try to turn fish.)

Meanwhile, brown almonds lightly in remaining butter; add lemon juice. Pour over fish.

Per serving: Cal 515, Carb 2g, Fib 1g, Pro 51g, Fat 33g, Sod 195mg, Sug 0g

Jamaican Jerk Mahi-Mahi
4 servings

Jerk seasoning isn't for everyone, but it takes beautifully to grilled fish, pork, and chicken. Team with a fruity salsa. In case you are wondering, jerk seasoning is not the same as Cajun seasoning.

- **4**   **(1-inch) mahi-mahi fillets or steaks**
- **1**   **tablespoon oil**
- **2**   **tablespoons Jamaican jerk seasoning**

Lightly spray the grill rack. Place over medium-hot heat.

Brush mahi-mahi with oil. Sprinkle with seasoning and rub in. Grill fish, turning once, until opaque in the center, about 3 to 4 minutes per side.

note: Any firm white fish may be substituted for the mahi-mahi.

Per Serving: Cal 203, Carb 0g, Fib 0g, Pro 38g, Fat 5g, Sod 599mg, Sug 0g

Cheesy-Salsa Fish Fillet   4 servings

Try one of the new tropical salsas on the market; such as Peach Mango - delicious!

- **4 fish fillets (perch, sole, etc.)**
- **⅓ cup seasoned bread crumbs**
- **1 tablespoon oil**
- **¾ cup chunky salsa**
- **4 slices Mozzarella cheese**

Coat fillets with bread crumbs shaking off excess. Brown in oil in a medium skillet, turning once.

Top with salsa and cook through, topping each with a cheese slice toward end of cooking time.

Per Serving: Cal 232, Carb 10g, Fib 2g, Pro 26g, Fat 9g, Sod 596mg, Sug 2g

Tuna Mornay   4 servings

Delicious served over hot buttered toast, rice or noodles.

- **2 (6½-oz) cans tuna, drained**
- **¼ cup butter**
- **¼ cup flour**
- **2 cups milk**
- **¼ cup (1-oz) Swiss cheese, shredded**
- **Salt and pepper**

Melt butter in medium saucepan. Stir in flour and cook for 1 minute. Remove from heat; add milk, stirring to blend. Return to heat, continue cooking, stirring frequently, until thickened. Add cheese; stir until melted. Add salt and pepper to taste. Stir in tuna and heat through.

Per serving: Cal 324, Carb 12g, Fib 0g, Pro 30g, Fat 16g, Sod 531mg, Sug 6g

Tuna Rice Casserole

4 servings

Serve with Crisp Green Salad and hot rolls.

- 1 (6½-oz) can tuna, drained
- 1 (10¾-oz) can condensed cream of mushroom soup
- 1 cup cooked rice
- 1 small onion, chopped
- 1 cup crushed potato chips

Preheat oven to 350°F. Gently combine ingredients until mixed. Spoon into a sprayed 1-quart casserole. If desired, top with additional crushed potato chips. Bake 30 to 45 minutes or until heated through.

Per serving: Cal 236, Carb 27g, Fib 1g, Pro 13g, Fat 8g, Sod 750mg, Sug 2g

Tuna Cashew Casserole

4 to 6 servings

- 1 (6½-oz) can tuna, drained
- 1 (10¾-oz) can condensed cream of mushroom soup
- 1 cup thinly sliced celery
- ¼ cup finely chopped onion
- 1 (3-oz) can Chow Mein Noodles
- 1 (3-oz) package cashews, split

Preheat oven to 350°F. Combine soup with ¼ cup water. Add remaining ingredients, reserving ⅓ of the Chow Mein Noodles. Pour mixture into a sprayed 2 quart casserole. Sprinkle reserved noodles over top. Bake 30 minutes or until heated through.

Per serving: Cal 236, Carb 18g, Fib 2g, Pro 13g, Fat 13g, Sod 601mg, Sug 2g

Red Snapper with Mushrooms and Peppers   4 servings

1	**pound fillet of red snapper**
1	**tablespoon light soy sauce**
¼	**teaspoon ground ginger**
2	**medium peppers, 1 red and 1 green, julienned**
6	**ounces fresh mushrooms, sliced**

Place fillet in shallow baking pan. Combine soy sauce and ginger; brush over fish. Place under broiler and cook 8 to 10 minutes, depending on thickness of fish, or until fish flakes easily with a fork.

Meanwhile, in large sprayed non-stick skillet, cook peppers and mushrooms until crisp tender. Serve vegetables over fish.

Per serving: Cal 134, Carb 5g, Fib 2g, Pro 24g, Fat 2g, Sod 165mg, Sug 3g

Mushroom Fillet Dish   4 to 6 servings

2	**pounds fillets (white fish)**
1	**medium onion, finely chopped**
8	**ounces fresh mushrooms, sliced**
1	**cup (4-oz) Swiss cheese, shredded**
	Salt and pepper
1	**cup whipping cream**

Preheat oven to 400°F. Sprinkle onion evenly in a sprayed 11x7-inch baking dish. Arrange three-fourths of the mushrooms over onions. Sprinkle with half the cheese. Place fillets over the top; sprinkle with salt and pepper. Add remaining mushrooms and cheese. Pour cream over top. Bake 20 minutes or until cooked through.

Per serving: Cal 387, Carb 5g, Fib 1g, Pro 42g, Fat 21g, Sod 185mg, Sug 2g

Tequila Shrimp

6 servings

Impressive and easy. Delicious served over rice.

- ¼ cup finely chopped green onion
- 2 tablespoons capers with juice
- ½ cup Tequila
- Juice of 3 limes and 1 teaspoon lime zest
- 2 tablespoons butter
- 1 pound raw shrimp, shelled, deveined

In a mixing bowl, combine green onion, capers with juice, Tequila, lime juice and zest. Add shrimp; marinate for 30 minutes.

In a medium skillet melt butter. With slotted spoon remove shrimp from marinade; cook shrimp until they turn opaque or to desired doneness. Remove from skillet, place into serving bowl and keep warm.

Pour marinade into same skillet and boil 5 minutes. Pour over shrimp. Serve immediately.

Per serving: Cal 152, Carb 2g, Fib 0g, Pro 12g, Fat 4g, Sod 263mg, Sug 0g

Shrimp Scampi

4 to 6 servings

- 2 pounds shrimp, peeled and cleaned
- ⅓ cup oil
- 2 small garlic cloves, minced
- 1 teaspoon salt
- ½ teaspoon pepper
- ¼ cup fresh lemon juice

Heat oil in large skillet. Stir in garlic, salt, pepper and lemon juice. Add shrimp. Cook until shrimp turns pink. Reduce heat and cook until liquid is almost absorbed (do not overcook shrimp). Serve hot.

tip: For added color, sprinkle with chopped parsley or garnish dish with parsley sprigs.

Per serving: Cal 223, Carb 1g, Fib 0g, Pro 24g, Fat 13g, Sod 645mg, Sug 0g

Bacon Prawns

1 serving

Jumbo prawns are so large you need allow only 3 to 4 per person. Try cooking the prawns on a grill and serve with corn on the cob and rice pilaf.

Bacon - 1 slice per prawn
Raw Prawns - allow 3 to 4 per person
Melted butter with parsley or desired herbs

Partially cook bacon, until limp, but not crisp. Drain on paper towels.

Shell prawns, except for the tails and de-vein. Wrap a bacon strip around each prawn; secure with a wooden toothpick. Place on broiler rack, baste with butter mixture and cook, turning once, until prawns are opaque and turn pink. Brush occasionally with butter mixture.

Per 4 prawns: Cal 82, Carb .0g, Fib 0g, Pro 8g, Fat 5g, Sod 297mg, Sug 0g

When buying fresh prawns or shrimps look for the following signs before making your choice:

The shells should be firm and glossy and not broken or slippery.

There should be no discoloration of the heads or the shells, as this is an indication that the meat is starting to go bad.

They should smell fresh and salty. Avoid if there is any hint of a smell of ammonia.

The eyes should be prominent and shiny and not shrunken inwards or missing.

Breaded Butterflied Shrimp

3 servings

Serve with tartar sauce, coleslaw and Au Gratin Potatoes.

1   **pound shrimp**
   Salt and pepper
1   **large egg, lightly beaten with 1 tablespoon water**
½   **cup fine dry breadcrumbs**
   Oil

Remove shells from shrimp, leaving tails intact; de-vein. Cut two-thirds of the way through the center of each shrimp and flatten. Season with salt and pepper. Dip in crumbs, egg and again in crumbs.

Deep fry in oil (350°F) for about 3 minutes or until golden. Drain and serve.

Per serving: Cal 167, Carb 6g, Fib 0g, Pro 14g, Fat 9g, Sod 257mg, Sug 0g

Baked Shrimp Scampi 4 servings

For a more affordable dish, substitute medium-size shrimp for the jumbo.

- **2 pounds uncooked jumbo shrimp, peeled, deveined, butterflied**
- **⅓ cup butter, melted**
- **2 tablespoons olive oil**
- **¼ cup fresh lemon juice**
- **3 medium garlic cloves, minced**

Preheat oven to 450ºF. Place shrimp in a 13x9-inch baking dish. Combine remaining ingredients and pour over shrimp. Gently toss to coat. Spread evenly over pan and bake 6 to 10 minutes or until shrimp is pink and cooked through.

note: Watch carefully. If the shrimp is overcooked, it will be tough.

Per serving: Cal 167, Carb 6g, Fib 0g, Pro 14g, Fat 9g, Sod 257mg, Sug 0g

Scallops & Ginger 4 servings

Choose scallops that are pink or cream colored. Avoid the bright white ones that have probably been bleached in various preservatives.

- **1¼ pounds bay scallops**
- **¼ cup butter**
- **3 to 4 slices fresh ginger**
- **Salt and pepper**

Rinse scallops and pat dry.

Heat butter in medium skillet. Add ginger and sauté briefly. Add scallops and continue to cook until scallops are heated through. Add salt and pepper to taste.

Per serving: Cal 127, Carb 0g, Fib 0g, Pro 24g, Fat 3g, Sod 264mg, Sug 0g

Scallop Piccata   2 servings

To make this a true piccata dish, you probably should add capers, but if you don't have a jar in your cupboard, you may not want to add them since they are quite expensive.

- **1   teaspoon minced shallots**
- **2   tablespoons butter, divided**
- **4   ounces (10 to 15) bay scallops**
- **2   tablespoons white wine**
- **1   teaspoon lemon juice**

In a medium skillet, sauté the shallots in 1 tablespoon butter. Add scallops and brown. Remove and keep warm.

Deglaze by adding the wine to the hot skillet and stirring quickly. Add lemon juice, then add the remaining butter and cook until slightly thickened. Return scallops and quickly heat through, if needed.

Per Serving: Cal 176, Carb 2g, Fib 0g, Pro 12g, Fat 11g, Sod 225mg, Sug 0g

menu

Baked Salmon Steaks
Applesauce
Garlic mashed Potatoes
Lemon Broccoli
Rice Chex Dessert

Crab Divan   4 servings

Fresh crab can be substituted for canned crab.

- **1   (6½-oz)can crab, drained**
- **2   cups broccoli florettes, cooked**
- **½   cup mayonnaise**
- **1   teaspoon prepared mustard**
- **1   tablespoon finely chopped onion**
- **½   cup (2-oz) Cheddar cheese, shredded**

Preheat oven to 350°F. Arrange broccoli in bottom of a sprayed 1-quart casserole. Distribute crab evenly over top.

Combine mayonnaise, mustard and onion; spread over crab. Sprinkle with cheese. Bake 20 to 30 minutes or until heated through.

Per serving: Cal 315, Carb 3g, Fib 1g, Pro 14g, Fat 27g, Sod 451mg, Sug 1g

poultry & pasta

Turkey Roasting

Guaranteed Success

Defrost Fresh or frozen - it's up to you. Fresh turkey is a little bit higher priced, but it will not take days of refrigerator space to thaw. The safest recommended method to thaw turkey is in the refrigerator. Allow 24 hours for each 5 pounds. For example, a 15-pound turkey will take 3 days to thaw. If you are running tight on space or time, an alternative method is to thaw the turkey in cold water. Allow approximately 30 minutes per pound, and change water every hour or two.

Prepare When turkey is thawed, you may prepare it for roasting. First, be sure to remove the paper sack inside of the turkey containing the giblets. Remove any other pieces, such as the neck, that may be inside the turkey. Next, rinse the turkey both inside and out. Dry with paper towels. (Be sure to thoroughly clean all surfaces that have come into contact with the raw turkey.)

Safety First It is now recommended that poultry not be stuffed with dressing, but rather the dressing be baked separately in a casserole dish or even a slow cooker. However, if you still insist on stuffing your bird, the dressing must reach an internal temperature of 165°F thus killing any harmful bacteria. (Do not pack the dressing, but spoon in lightly.) But, reaching this safe temperature may cause the breast meat to be overcooked and dry.

Be Sure To test for doneness, an instant read thermometer should read 170°F when inserted into the thickest part of the thigh. When done, remove from oven, cover with foil and let stand 30-60 minutes before carving. (If allowing to stand more than 30 minutes, remove from oven when temperature reaches 165°F. Meat will continue to cook and meat will be moist.. Slicing any meat right out of the oven, will cause the juice to run and the meat to be dry

roasting turkey

Traditional Method   (325°F)

Place turkey, breast side up, in shallow baking pan. Brush with oil or butter. Bake at 325° until cooked through. Remove from oven, cover with foil and let stand 30-60 minutes before carving.

Pounds	Hours	Remove from oven
8-12	2¼ - 2¾	170°F (thigh)
12-16	2¾ - 3¼	170°F (thigh)
16-20	3¼ - 3¾	170°F (thigh)
20-24	3¾ - 4½	170°F (thigh)

PLEASE NOTE: For safety reasons, dressing should not be stuffed in the turkey, but baked separately. However, if you do stuff your turkey, the dressing must reach an internal temperature of 165°F. 30-60 minutes before carving.

Foil Wrapped Method   (450°F)   (Faster than traditional)

Using wide, heavy-duty foil, cut 2 long strips. Place one piece lengthwise in large shallow roasting pan and one piece crosswise in pan. Place turkey, breast side up, on top of foil. Brush with oil or butter. Bring 2 opposite ends of foil up over turkey; fold ends together to seal. Bring remaining two ends of foil up and seal.
Bake at 450° until cooked through. Remove from oven, cover with foil and let stand 30-60 minutes before carving.

Pounds	Hours	Remove from oven
8-12	1¼-2	170°F (thigh)
12-16	2-2¼	170°F (thigh)
16-20	2¼-2½	170°F (thigh)
20-24	2½-2¾	170°F (thigh)

Orange Glazed Turkey Breast

12 servings

A wonderful marmalade glaze with a touch of black pepper.

- 1 **(6-lb) whole turkey breast**
- 2 **teaspoons oil**
- ⅓ **cup orange marmalade**
- 1 **tablespoon prepared mustard**
- 2 **teaspoons Worcestershire sauce**
- ½ **teaspoon cracked pepper**

Preheat oven to 350°F. Place turkey breast, breast-side up, on a rack in a roasting pan. Brush with oil. Cover with foil and bake 1½ to 2 hours.

Combine remaining ingredients and brush over turkey. Cook 30 to 40 minutes or until temperature reaches 160°F, basting frequently with the pan drippings. Cover with foil and let stand 15 minutes before slicing.

Per serving: Cal 368, Carb 6g, Fib 0g, Pro 52g, Fat 14g, Sod 147mg, Sug 5g

Oh So Easy Turkey Dinner – 6 servings

No matter how careful we are, we always have some leftovers after that big turkey dinner - at least I hope we do. This isn't anything fancy, but it is easy, quick and does use up some of those leftovers.

- 4 **cups leftover stuffing**
- 8 **slices turkey or enough to cover stuffing**
- 1½ **cups whole berry cranberry sauce**
- 2 **cups gravy, heated**

Preheat oven to 350°F. Layer ingredients in order given in a sprayed 7x11-inch baking dish.

Cover with foil and bake 25 to 30 minutes or until heated through.

note: Amounts can vary somewhat according to the size of turkey slices or how much you have. If the stuffing is dry you may want to use more gravy.

Apple Brandy Cornish Hens

6 servings

3	Cornish hens, halved
2	tablespoons flour
3	tablespoons butter
1½	cup heavy cream
2	cups apples, peeled, cored and diced
1	cup apple brandy

Preheat oven to 325°F. Season flour with salt and pepper. Dredge hens in flour, coating both sides and shaking off excess.

Heat butter in a large skillet. Add two to three hen halves at a time (being sure not to crowd) and fry until nicely browned, about 3 to 4 minutes on each side. Remove and place in a large baking dish.

Drain fat from skillet, leaving some of the brown bits. Add cream, chopped apples and apple brandy. Heat mixture to simmer: pour over hens.

Bake, covered for 1 hour or until hens are tender. Remove hens to a warm platter and cover loosely with foil.

Pour apple mixture into small saucepan. Stir over medium high heat until sauce is reduced and slightly thickened. Serve sauce over hens.

Per Serving: Cal 780, Carb 22g, Fib 1g, Pro 36g, Fat 56g, Sod 165mg, Sug 17g

Roast Chicken

This is one of the easiest meals to prepare. Once the chicken is baking you can turn you attention to the rest of the meal. Prepare on a Sunday and use any leftover chicken for sandwiches the next day.

1	(3 to 4-lb) chicken
1	tablespoon oil
	Paprika

Preheat oven to 350°F. Clean chicken and wipe dry. Place on rack in baking pan. Brush with oil and sprinkle with paprika.

Bake 1 to 1½ hours or until temperature reaches 170°F. Let stand 10 minutes before serving.

Hawaiian Chicken   6 to 8 servings

- 8   **chicken breast halves, skinned, boned**
- 1   **(6-oz) can frozen orange juice, thawed**
- 2   **tablespoons butter, melted**
- 2   **(8-oz) cans crushed pineapple, with juice**
- 1½   **teaspoons ground ginger**
- 1   **tablespoon soy sauce**

Preheat oven to 375°F. Place chicken pieces, skin-side up, in a roasting pan. The one that came with your oven is just about the right size.

Combine remaining ingredients. Pour over chicken and bake about 60 minutes or until chicken is cooked through, basting frequently.

Per serving: Cal 240, Carb 18g, Fib 1g, Pro 27g, Fat 6g, Sod 253mg, Sug 16g

Chicken Marmalade   4 servings

Serve with Lemon Broccoli and steamed new potatoes.

- 1   **chicken, cut up**
- ¼   **cup butter, melted**
- 1   **cup orange marmalade**
- ¼   **cup packed brown sugar**
- ½   **teaspoon dry ginger**

Preheat oven to 350°F. Place chicken, skin-side down, in a sprayed 13x9-inch baking dish. Brush with butter. Bake 15 minutes. Turn chicken, baste with butter, and bake 15 minutes.

Combine remaining ingredients and brush on chicken. Bake 20 minutes or until tender and richly glazed, basting frequently.

Per serving: Cal 621, Carb 43g, Fib 0g, Pro 42g, Fat 31g, Sod 216mg, Sug 40g

Chicken Enchiladas in Cream

6 servings

This delightful dish features a combination of popular ingredients. Serve with a tossed green salad, rolls and Strawberry Margarita Pie.

- 3 **cups cubed cooked chicken**
- 1 **cup green chili salsa (this is a red salsa)**
- 1 **(4-oz) can chopped green chilies**
- 10 **(8-inch) flour tortillas**
- 2½ **cups whipping cream**
- 2 **cups (8-oz) Monterey Jack cheese, shredded**

Preheat oven to 350°F. Combine chicken, salsa and green chilies. Fill each tortilla with a portion of the chicken mixture. Roll up and place, seam-side down, in sprayed 13x9-inch baking dish. Pour cream over top. Sprinkle evenly with cheese. Bake 45 minutes or until golden and most of the cream is absorbed.

Per serving: Cal 508, Carb 29g, Fib 2g, Pro 20g, Fat 34g, Sod 824mg, Sug 2g

Ben's Chicken Parmesan

4 servings

- 4 **chicken breast halves, skinned, boned**
- 3 **tablespoons grated Parmesan cheese**
- 1¼ **cups spaghetti sauce**
- 1 **cup (4-oz) Mozzarella cheese, shredded**
  Parsley

Preheat oven to 350°F. Place chicken in a sprayed 11x7-inch baking dish.

Combine Parmesan and spaghetti sauce; pour over chicken. Cover. Bake 30 minutes or until cooked through.

Top with cheese and a sprinkle of parsley. Bake 5 minutes to melt cheese.

Per serving: Cal 305, Carb 9g, Fib 1g, Pro 45g, Fat 9g, Sod 724mg, Sug 5g

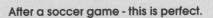

Quick Chicken Mozzarella

After a soccer game - this is perfect.

Use desired amounts of the following ingredients:
Frozen breaded chicken breast patties
Mozzarella cheese slices
Prepared spaghetti or pizza sauce

Cook chicken patties as directed on package using a medium skillet and cooking on top of stove.

Place a cheese slice on top of each patty. Pour desired amount of sauce around the patties and heat through.

Sweet Pepper Chicken   6 servings

This is colorful, delicious and low calorie. Serve over rice.

- 4   **chicken breast halves, skinned and boned**
- ¼   **cup white vinegar**
- ½   **cup firmly packed brown sugar**
- 1   **(20-oz) can pineapple chunks, save juice**
- 2   **tablespoons cornstarch**
- 2   **bell peppers, ½ red pepper and ½ green pepper, cut into narrow strips**

Cut chicken into bite-size pieces. Cook over medium-high heat in a sprayed nonstick skillet, until cooked through, stirring frequently. Set aside. In medium saucepan, combine vinegar and brown sugar with ½ cup water. Bring to a boil; reduce heat. Drain pineapple. Combine cornstarch with pineapple juice; mix until blended. Stir into saucepan. Add pineapple and peppers. Cook, over low heat, until sauce has thickened and peppers are crisp-tender.

Per serving: Cal 244, Carb 31g, Fib 1g, Pro 23g, Fat 3g, Sod 63mg, Sug 28g

Make Your Own Buttermilk

No need to purchase a quart when you need a cup. Make your own by mixing 1 tablespoon of vinegar or lemon juice with 1 cup of milk and letting it sit until it curdles, about 10 minutes.

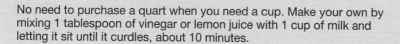

Italian Chicken Casserole   4 servings

If doubling recipe, use two 13x9-inch baking dishes, not one large. For a more tender moist chicken, use bone-in chicken breast with skin.

4	chicken breast halves, bone in
1	cup uncooked long-grain rice
1	(.65-oz) Italian salad dressing mix
2½	cups boiling water
1	(10¾-oz) can Cream of Chicken soup
	Salt and pepper

Preheat oven to 350°F. Spread rice in a sprayed 13x9-inch baking dish. Combine salad dressing mix, water and soup; mix well. Pour over rice. Place chicken, skin-side up, on top of rice. Sprinkle with salt and pepper. Cover dish with foil, and bake 60 minutes.

Remove foil and bake 20 to 30 minutes or until liquid is absorbed and chicken is tender.

Per serving: Cal 421, Carb 50g, Fib 1g, Pro 39g, Fat 6g, Sod 746mg, Sug 3g

Cooking Tips

Marinating adds flavor and makes for a more moist chicken.

Cooking with skin on adds more flavor, but not fat. The fat does not transfer to the meat during cooking.

Leaving the skin on helps to create a more tender and moist meat.

For accurate doneness, use a good thermometer. Chicken or turkey breasts should be cooked to 160°F. Don't overcook or it will be dry and tough. Watch closely the last few minutes of cooking time.

Use tongs when turning chicken pieces. A fork will pierce the meat and allow too much of the juice to escape.

Chicken & Coconut   4 servings

Serve with Almond Rice Pilaf, Broccoli Meringue and Sweet-Sour Spinach Salad.

4	chicken breasts, halved, skinned, boned
	Salt and pepper
	Oil
⅓	cup fine dry bread crumbs
⅓	cup flaked coconut
¼	cup butter, melted

Preheat oven to 350°F. Sprinkle chicken with salt and pepper. Brush with oil.

Combine bread crumbs and coconut. Roll chicken in mixture to coat. Place in a sprayed 13x9-inch dish; drizzle with melted butter. Bake 30 to 40 minutes or until tender.

Per serving: Cal 278, Carb 3g, Fib 0g, Pro 30g, Fat 16g, Sod 164mg, Sug 2g

Chicken Mounds   4 servings

Almost as good as turkey and dressing and a whole lot easier. Serve with mashed potatoes, Baked Acorn Squash or Minted Petite Peas, Strawberry Nut Salad and Key Lime Pie.

4	small whole chicken breasts, leave skin on
	Salt and pepper
3	cups seasoned stuffing mix
½	cup butter, melted
½	cup finely chopped pecans

Preheat oven to 350°F. Sprinkle chicken with salt and pepper; set aside.

Combine remaining ingredients with ½ cup water. Divide into 4 equal portions. Shape into mounds in a shallow baking pan. Place chicken, skin-side up, over stuffing. Cover with foil; bake 30 minutes. Remove foil; bake 20 minutes or until chicken is lightly browned and tender.

Per serving: Cal 668, Carb 35g, Fib 5g, Pro 36g, Fat 42g, Sod 913mg, Sug 3g

Linda's Phyllo Chicken

6 to 8 servings

This is one of my daughter's favorite company recipes. She likes to prepare it the day before and bake just before serving. Very elegant and even good cold.

- **6**   **chicken breast halves, cooked, cubed**
- **2½** **cups broccoli florettes**
- **2**   **cups sour cream**
- **10** **sheets Phyllo**
- **1**   **cup butter, melted**
- **1**   **cup freshly grated Parmesan cheese**

Preheat oven to 350°F. Steam the broccoli until it turns bright green and is not quite crisp tender. Rinse with cold water to stop the cooking process. Cut florettes into small pieces and set aside. Combine the chicken and sour cream and set aside.

Lay out one sheet of phyllo (keep remaining phyllo covered with wax paper and a slightly damp towel to prevent drying out). Brush with melted butter. Top with second sheet of phyllo and brush with butter. Repeat until you have 5 sheets. Spread phyllo with half the chicken mixture, leaving a 2-inch border all the way around. Sprinkle with half the broccoli and half the Parmesan cheese. Fold the 2-inch border over, covering outer edge of filling. Brush with butter. Starting with short end, roll up jelly-roll style. Place, seam-side down, on baking sheet. Brush with butter. Repeat with second half of ingredients.

Bake at 375°F 20 to 25 minutes or until golden (may take longer if rolls have been refrigerated). Slice each roll into 4 to 6 slices.

Per serving: Cal 499, Carb 18g, Fib 1g, Pro 34g, Fat 31g, Sod 460mg, Sug 4g

menu

Linda's Phyllo Chicken
Wild Rice
Baked Carrots
Sally Lunn Muffins
Cranberry-Nut Cake

Sesame Chicken 8 servings

This has always been a favorite recipe in our family. It is richly glazed, tender and delicious. If you want to make an impressive dish for company, you can sprinkle with sesame seeds before baking and then serve on an attractive dish garnished with parsley sprigs.

- 1 teaspoon fresh ginger or ⅛ teaspoon dried ginger
- ¼ cup light soy sauce
- 2 tablespoons sherry
- 1 tablespoons brown sugar
- 2 tablespoons sesame oil
- 16 chicken legs, skinned

Preheat oven to 350°F. In a small bowl, combine first four ingredients and set aside. Heat oil (it should be very hot) in large skillet and quickly brown chicken, turning once.

Place in a sprayed 13x9-inch baking dish. Bake 15 minutes. Baste with sauce. Continue baking 15 minutes or until cooked through, basting every 5 minutes.

Per serving: Cal 400, Carb 2g, Fib 0g, Pro 51g, Fat 20g, Sod 410mg, Sug 2g

Herb Chicken Bake 4 servings

- 1 chicken, cut up
- ⅓ cup butter
- 1 (10¾-oz) can cream of chicken Soup with herbs
- 1 (4-oz) can sliced mushrooms (optional)

Preheat oven to 350°F. Place chicken pieces, skin-side down, in a 13x9-inch baking dish. Slice butter and arrange on chicken. Bake 20 minutes. Turn chicken and bake 20 minutes.

Stir soup and mushrooms together; spoon over chicken. Bake 20 minutes or until chicken is cooked through.

Per serving: Cal 518, Carb 4g, Fib 1g, Pro 44g, Fat 35g, Sod 574mg, Sug 1g

Entertaining

Can be a lot of work, but you don't have to do everything. People love to contribute, so take them up on it. Have them bring an appetizer, salad, side dish or dessert. You won't be so rushed and you can also enjoy the party. Besides, it's always fun to try everyone else's favorite dishes.

Chicken Broccoli Casserole

8 servings

This delightful dish features a combination of favorite ingredients made even better by the addition of a special tossed green salad and toasted French bread. This is a large recipe and should be baked in a deep 13x9-inch baking pan or dish.

- 1 (20-oz) package frozen chopped broccoli
- 5 cups cooked long-grain rice
- 2½ cups cubed cooked chicken
- 2 (10¾-oz) cans Cream of Chicken Soup
- 1 cup mayonnaise
- 2 cups (8-oz) Mozzarella cheese, shredded, divided

Preheat oven to 350°F. Place frozen broccoli in a colander and run under hot water; drain thoroughly. Spread on bottom of a sprayed 13x9-inch baking dish. Spoon rice over top.

Combine chicken, soup, mayonnaise and 1 cup of the cheese. Pour over rice. Sprinkle with remaining cheese. (Dish will be quite full.) Bake 30 to 35 minutes or until heated through. Watch carefully last few minutes. Cover with foil if cheese is browning too fast.

Per serving: Cal 495, Carb 40g, Fib 3g, Pro 24g, Fat 27g, Sod 637mg, Sug 2g

Ritz® Baked Chicken

4 servings

Tell your children they can't eat the rest of the box of Ritz® crackers. You're going to use them for dinner tonight. This is an easy recipe, so it is actually something they could do.

- 4 chicken breast halves
- ½ cup sour cream
- 1 tablespoon Worcestershire sauce
- 1 tablespoon lemon juice
- 1 cup crushed Ritz® crackers

Preheat oven to 350°F. Combine sour cream, Worcestershire sauce and lemon juice. Dip chicken in mixture; roll in cracker crumbs. Place on baking sheet and bake 30 to 40 minutes or until cooked through.

Per serving: Cal 330, Carb 11g, Fib 0g, Pro 32g, Fat 16g, Sod 241mg, Sug 3g

Chicken Pineapple Supreme 1 serving

1   **chicken breast half, skinned and boned**
    Salt and pepper
1   **pineapple ring**
1   **broccoli spear, cooked crisp tender**
½   **slice Swiss cheese**
    Paprika

Place chicken between two pieces of plastic wrap. Gently pound to about ¼-inch thickness. Place, rounded side down, in heated sprayed nonstick skillet. Cook, over medium heat, until browned and cooked through, turning once. Total cooking time shouldn't take more than 8 to 10 minutes. Sprinkle lightly with salt and pepper.

Place a pineapple ring on each chicken breast. Top with a broccoli spear. Place a cheese slice diagonally over the broccoli. Sprinkle cheese lightly with paprika. Cover skillet and cook just long enough to melt the cheese.

Per serving: Cal 332, Carb 24g, Fib 8g, Pro 46g, Fat 7g, Sod 456mg, Sug 11g

menu

Chicken Pineapple Supreme
Almond Rice Pilaf
Sally Lunn
Muffins
Sweet-Sour Spinach Salad
Cherry Parfaits

Oven Barbecued Chicken   6 servings

1½   **chickens, cut up**
¾   **cup honey**
1   **cup ketchup**
¼   **cup light corn syrup**
2   **tablespoons Worcestershire sauce**
    juice of 1 lemon

Preheat oven to 350°F. Place chicken, skin-side down, in a sprayed 13x9-inch baking dish. Combine remaining ingredients and pour over top. Marinate at least one hour, basting occasionally.

Pour off marinade and reserve. Bake chicken 30 minutes. Turn chicken and baste with marinade. Continue baking 30 minutes longer or until chicken is tender and richly glazed, basting frequently.

Per serving: Cal 440, Carb 12g, Fib 0g, Pro 42g, Fat 24g, Sod 155mg, Sug 11g

chicken

Chicken Pecan   4 servings

- **4**   **chicken breast, boned, skinned**
- **6**   **tablespoon butter, plus ¼ cup**
- **½**   **cup Dijon mustard, divided**
- **1¼**   **cups very finely chopped pecans**
- **½**   **cup sour cream**
- **½**   **cup heavy whipping cream**

Preheat oven to 450°F. Place each chicken breast between plastic wrap and pound until the overall thickness is the same. Set aside.

Microwave 6 tablespoons of butter until it is soft, but not melted. Combine butter with ¼ cup Dijon mustard. Brush both sides of chicken generously with this mixture and coat with pecans until thoroughly covered.

Heat ¼ cup butter in a large skillet. Add chicken and cook over medium heat until browned on both sides. Transfer chicken to a shallow baking dish, reserving pan juices, but removing all but a small amount of the nuts remaining in the pan. Bake chicken 10 to 12 minutes or until cooked through.

Meanwhile, add sour cream, heavy cream and the remaining ¼ cup Dijon mustard to skillet. Cook until heated through, but do not boil. Spread a small amount of sauce on each plate and top with chicken.

Per serving: Cal 852, Carb 7g, Fib 4g, Pro 39g, Fat 74g, Sod 711mg, Sug3g

Tropical Chicken Kabobs   6 servings

This is easy, colorful and delicious. A great company dish. Serve with rice pilaf, fresh asparagus and salad.

- **6**   **chicken breast halves, boned, skinned**
- **1**   **(20-oz) can pineapple chunks**
- **1**   **teaspoon ground ginger**
- **1**   **orange bell pepper, cut into 1½-inch squares**
- **1**   **onion, cut into 1½-inch squares**
- **½**   **cup orange juice concentrate**

Cut chicken into 1½-inch pieces and place in a large bowl. Open pineapple and drain juice over chicken pieces. Save pineapple for later. Add ginger to chicken and stir. Marinate at least 30 minutes.

On skewers, alternately thread chicken, pineapple, peppers and onions. Grill over medium heat, basting with orange juice concentrate, about 20 to 30 minutes or until cooked through.

Per serving: Cal 220, Carb 20g, Fib 2g, Pro 28g, Fat 3g, Sod 66mg, Sug 17g

Chicken Madeira   4 servings

This makes a delicious mild flavored sauce that you will be tempted to eat with a spoon. Enjoy the chicken and sauce served over rice or pasta.

- **4   chicken breast halves, skinned and boned**
-     **Lemon pepper**
- **3   tablespoons butter**
- **1¾ cups heavy cream, divided**
- **¼   cup Madeira wine**
- **2   cups sliced fresh mushrooms**

Sprinkle both sides of chicken with lemon pepper. Melt butter in a 10-inch heavy skillet. Add chicken and brown lightly on both sides (do not overcook). Remove chicken from skillet. Add 1 cup of the cream and the Madeira; stir to blend.

Bring mixture to a simmer, return chicken to pan and cook 20 minutes over medium low heat. Add remaining ¾ cup cream and the mushrooms. Cook about 10 minutes or until chicken is cooked through.

If sauce is a little on the thin side, remove chicken and keep hot. Cook sauce over medium high heat until thickened, about 3 to 4 minutes. Serve sauce over chicken.

Per serving: Cal 648, Carb 6g, Fib 1g, Pro 38g, Fat 1g, Sod 268mg, Sug 2g

Clarified Butter

Clarified butter is great for browning since it tends to burn less than regular butter. I try to keep some in the refrigerator at all times. Or you can use half oil and half butter.

Baked Chicken Curry   4 servings

- **1   chicken, cut up**
- **½   cup butter, melted**
- **1   teaspoon lemon juice**
- **2   cloves garlic, minced**
- **1   teaspoon salt**
- **2   teaspoons curry powder (or to taste)**

Preheat oven to 350°F. Place chicken, skin-side down, in a sprayed 13x9-inch baking dish.

Combine remaining ingredients. Brush chicken with some of the sauce. Bake 30 minutes, basting once. Turn chicken, bake 20 minutes, or until chicken is tender, basting every 10 minutes.

Per serving: Cal 530, Carb 1g, Fib 0g, Pro 42g, Fat 38g, Sod 630mg, Sug 0g

Chicken with Sour Cream Gravy   4 servings

Serve the gravy over the chicken and mashed potatoes or rice. Add hot
buttered peas and rolls and you have a delicious meal without any fuss.

- 1   **chicken, cut up**
- 3   **tablespoons butter**
-      **Seasoning salt**
- 3   **tablespoons flour**
- ¼   **cup sour cream**

Heat butter in a large skillet. Brown chicken on both sides. Sprinkle with
seasoning salt. Add ½ cup water; bring to a boil. Reduce heat and cook,
covered, 20 minutes. Turn chicken; continue cooking 15 to 20 minutes or until
cooked through. Remove chicken and keep warm.

In small jar, combine flour and ½ cup water; shake to mix well. Gradually add
to liquid in skillet. Cook, stirring constantly, until mixture comes to a boil and
thickens. Stir in sour cream, but do not boil. Taste for seasoning.

Per serving: Cal 477, Carb 3g, Fib 0g, Pro 43g, Fat 31g, Sod 195mg, Sug 1g

Shopper's Chicken   6 servings

- 6   **chicken breast halves boned, skinned**
- 1   **cup sour cream**
- 2   **tablespoons lemon juice**
- 1   **teaspoon salt**
- 1   **teaspoon paprika**
- ½   **cup butter**

Preheat oven to 350°F. Place chicken, skin-side up, in a sprayed 13x9-inch
baking dish.

Combine remaining ingredients, except butter, and spread over chicken.
Dot with butter. Bake 30 to 40 minutes or until cooked through.

Per serving: Cal 347, Carb 2g, Fib 0g, Pro 26g, Fat 24g, Sod 580mg, Sug 2g

Easy Chicken Stir Fry   4 servings

Cook 1 pound cubed boneless chicken breast in 1 tablespoon oil
until cooked through. Remove and set aside.

If necessary, add more oil, and cook 1 clove garlic, minced with
3 to 4 cups assorted fresh or frozen vegetables, cooking only until
crisp-tender.

Return chicken to skillet and add about ⅓ cup teriyaki or stir-fry
sauce. Cook only until heated through.

Chicken with Artichokes and Cream   4 servings

This is a very delicate flavored dish that calls for a more robust rice, vegetable and salad accompaniment.

- **4 chicken breast halves, skinned and boned**
- **⅓ cup flour**
- **¼ cup butter**
- **1 cup white wine**
- **1½ cups heavy cream**
- **2 cups marinated artichoke hearts, drained and cut up**

Wash chicken and pat dry. Place each chicken breast between plastic wrap and pound to ¼-inch thickness. Cut crosswise into 3 pieces. (If chicken pieces are small, cut into 2 pieces.) Coat lightly with flour.

Heat butter in a large heavy skillet over medium heat. Cook chicken, turning once, until lightly browned and cooked through, about 3 minutes each side.

Pour off butter, but leave any brown pieces in skillet. Add wine and bring to a boil. Reduce heat and simmer 2 to 3 minutes. Add cream and cook over medium heat until slightly thickened. Add artichokes and heat through.

Per serving: Cal 563, Carb 8g, Fib 2g, Pro 37g, Fat 38g, Sod 225mg, Sug 0g

Chicken breast halves come in so many different sizes which can affect the cooking time. Chicken with the bone in takes longer than boneless pieces. Also, bear in mind that frozen boneless chicken breasts are usually quite a bit thinner than the fresh and may take very little time to cook. If your chicken is dry and tough, you may be overcooking it.

Company Chicken   4 servings

For a tropical twist, you can place a sliced pineapple ring between the ham and cheese slices.

- **4 chicken breast halves, skinned, boned**
- **¼ cup flour**
- **2 tablespoons oil**
- **2 slices deli ham, halved**
- **2 slices Monterey Jack cheese, halved**

Dip chicken in flour; shake off excess. Pour oil in medium skillet and heat over medium-high heat. Add chicken and cook until cooked through, turning once.

Top with a slice of ham and then the cheese. Cook until cheese is melted.

Per serving: Cal 299, Carb 2g, Fib 0g, Pro 39g, Fat 15g, Sod 302mg, Sug 0g

Orange Chicken Delight   4 servings

Orange and honey team up to make a very flavorful chicken dish. Serve with Dinner Hash Browns, Broccoli Salad and Poppy Seed French Bread.

- **1   chicken, cut up**
- **1   tablespoon freshly grated orange peel**
- **¼   cup honey**
- **½   cup oil**
- **2   teaspoons ground ginger**

Preheat oven to 350°F. Place chicken, skin-side down, in a sprayed 13x9-inch baking dish. Combine remaining ingredients. Baste chicken with some of the mixture. Bake 30 minutes, turn and bake 30 minutes longer, basting frequently. Watch carefully during last 10 minutes of baking time.

Per serving: Cal 521, Carb 12g, Fib 0g, Pro 42g, Fat 33g, Sod 130mg, Sug 11g

Lemon Chicken   4 servings

- **4   chicken breast halves, skinned and boned**
- **⅓   cup flour**
- **6   tablespoons butter, divided**
- **2   tablespoons finely chopped onion**
- **1   cup chicken broth**
- **3   tablespoons fresh lemon juice**

Slice chicken crosswise into narrow strips. Coat lightly with flour, shaking off excess. Sauté chicken in 3 tablespoons of butter, over medium high heat, until cooked through, stirring frequently. Remove and keep warm.

Remove all but 1 tablespoon butter from skillet; add onion and cook until soft, about 1 to 2 minutes. Add chicken broth and bring to a boil. Add lemon juice and continue to boil until mixture is reduced to about ⅓ cup, about 4 to 5 minutes. Remove from heat and add remaining 3 tablespoons butter. Return chicken to pan and heat through.

Per serving: Cal 352, Carb 3g, Fib 1g, Pro 35g, Fat 21g, Sod 460mg, Sug 1g

Kabob Tips

Kabobs will cook more evenly if you leave a little space between the meat. Grilled vegetables make wonderful accompaniments, but because of the different cooking times, it is best if they are cooked on separate skewers.

Pesto Stuffed Chicken

4 servings

Use your favorite homemade or purchased pesto sauce.

- 4 **large chicken breasts, with skin**
- 4 **tablespoons pesto sauce**
- 1 **tablespoon oil**
- ½ **cup grated Parmesan cheese**

Preheat oven to 350°F. Spread pesto under chicken skin, leaving skin attached. Place in a sprayed 13x9-inch baking dish. Brush with oil and bake 30 minutes.

Brush with drippings and sprinkle with cheese. Bake 10 to 15 minutes or until cooked through.

Per serving: Cal 328, Carb 1g, Fib 1g, Pro 34g, Fat 20g, Sod 274mg, Sug 0g

Chicken & Celery Casserole

4 servings

You'll love how quickly this casserole goes together. The flavorful sauce reminds me a little bit of Stroganoff, only a lot easier to make. I'm not sure why, but this recipe just isn't as good with the lowfat celery soup.

- 4 **chicken breast halves, skinned and boned**
  Salt and pepper (optional)
- 4 **ounces cream cheese, softened**
- 1 **(10¾-oz) can condensed cream of celery soup**
  Parsley, freshly chopped or dried

Preheat oven to 350°F. Rinse chicken and pat dry; sprinkle with salt and pepper. Place, skin-side up, in a sprayed 11x7-inch baking dish. Place cream cheese in mixer bowl and beat until smooth. Gradually add the soup and beat until smooth. Spoon over chicken. Bake 35 to 40 minutes or until chicken is cooked through. Sprinkle lightly with parsley.

Per serving: Cal 344, Carb 7g, Fib 1g, Pro 37g, Fat 18g, Sod 703mg, Sug 1g

menu

Chicken Elegant
Broccoli with Pecan Dressing
Garlic Mashed Potatoes
Almond Spinach Salad
Ice Cream Cake

Chicken Elegant

4 servings

- **4**   **small whole chicken breasts, boned**
- **⅓**   **cup, plus 3 tablespoons butter**
- **1**   **cup chicken broth**
- **¼**   **cup flour**
- **1**   **cup half and half**
-     **Salt and pepper**

Preheat oven to 375°F. Chicken breasts should be left whole with bones removed (do not remove skin). Heat ⅓ cup butter in heavy skillet. Tuck chicken breast ends under, shaping into a nice round mound. Brown bottom side first, turn and brown top side. Place in a sprayed 13x9-inch baking dish. Add chicken broth. Cover with foil and bake 45 to 60 minutes or until cooked through. Remove chicken and keep warm (reserve broth).

Melt the 3 tablespoons butter in a small saucepan; stir in flour until blended. Remove from heat; stir in reserved broth and half and half. Cook, stirring frequently, until mixture boils and thickens. Season to taste with salt and pepper. Place chicken on serving plate; pour sauce over top.

Per serving: Cal 348, Carb 4g, Fib 0g, Pro 38g, Fat 19g, Sod 303mg, Sug 0g

Creamy Chicken Almond

4 servings

Serve with Angel Hair pasta, green peas, a simple green salad and rolls.

- **1**   **chicken, cut up**
- **⅓**   **cup flour**
- **1**   **teaspoon lemon pepper**
- **2**   **tablespoons vegetable oil**
- **1**   **(10¾-oz) can Cream of Chicken soup**
- **⅓**   **cup slivered almonds**

Preheat oven to 350°F. Rinse chicken and pat dry. Combine flour and pepper. Coat chicken with flour, shaking off excess. Heat oil in a large skillet and brown chicken on both sides. Place, skin-side up, in a sprayed 13x9-inch baking dish. Stir soup, then spread over chicken pieces. Sprinkle with almonds. Bake 50 to 60 minutes or until chicken is cooked through and tender.

Per serving: Cal 521, Carb 11g, Fib 1g, Pro 45g, Fat 32g, Sod 182mg, Sug 1g

Panko Chicken Dijon
4 servings

Serve with Dijon Mustard Sauce made by mixing equal parts of Dijon mustard and mayonnaise.

4	chicken breast halves, skinned and boned
4	tablespoons melted butter, divided
1½	tablespoons Dijon mustard
3	tablespoons grated Parmesan cheese
½	cup Panko breading

Preheat oven to 375°F. Wash chicken and pat dry. Combine 3 tablespoons of the butter with the mustard in a small shallow dish. It may look curdled, but that's okay.

Combine Parmesan and Panko in a flat dish. Dip chicken in butter mixture, then in crumb mixture, coating both sides. Place on sprayed shallow baking pan. Brush with remaining tablespoon butter. Bake 30 to 40 minutes or until cooked through and golden.

note: Panko is a crunchy Japanese style breading found in the Asian department of most supermarkets.

Per serving: Cal 269, Carb 5g, Fib 0g, Pro 36g, Fat 10g, Sod 145mg, Sug 0g

Teriyaki Chicken
4 servings

1	chicken, cut up
2	tablespoons oil
½	cup soy sauce
1	teaspoon sugar
⅓	cup finely chopped onion
1	garlic clove, minced

Preheat oven to 350°F. Combine last 5 ingredients. Pour over chicken; marinate at least 2 hours. Place chicken in a sprayed 13x9-inch baking pan. Bake 45 to 60 minutes or until cooked through, basting occasionally.

Per serving: Cal 399, Carb 1g, Fib 0g, Pro 43g, Fat 24g, Sod 304mg, Sug 1g

Chicken Enchiladas   8 servings

- **3**   **whole chicken breasts, cooked**
- **2**   **cups sour cream**
- **1**   **(4-oz) can diced green chilies**
- **3**   **(10¾-oz each) cans condensed cream of chicken soup**
- **4**   **cups (16-oz) Cheddar cheese, shredded**
- **10** **(8-inch) flour tortillas**

Preheat oven to 350°F. Cut chicken into bite-size pieces. Combine chicken with sour cream, chilies, 1 can soup and 1 cup cheese. Spoon a generous amount of filling down center of each tortilla. Roll up and place, seam-side down, in sprayed deep 13x9-inch baking dish.

Combine remaining 2 cans soup and stir to soften. Spread over tortillas. Sprinkle remaining cheese over top. Bake 45 to 60 minutes or until hot and cheese is golden.

Per serving: Cal 687, Carb 34g, Fib 4g, Pro 50g, Fat 38g, Sod 537mg, Sug 4g

Orange Glazed Chicken   4 servings

A great tasting family dish made even better served with Almond Rice Pilaf and fresh green beans. Add ice cream and sliced fruit for dessert.

- **1**   **chicken, cut up**
      Salt and pepper
- **¼**   **cup orange juice**
- **1**   **tablespoon honey**
- **¼**   **teaspoon Worcestershire sauce**
- **¼**   **teaspoon dry mustard**

Preheat oven to 350°F. Place chicken, skin-side up, in sprayed 13x9 baking dish. Sprinkle with salt and pepper. Bake 30 minutes. Combine remaining ingredients and brush some of the sauce over the chicken. Continue baking, brushing occasionally with remaining sauce, 20 to 30 minutes or until cooked through.

Per serving: Cal 409, Carb 4g, Fib 0g, Pro 42g, Fat 24g, Sod 183mg, Sug 4g

Gourmet Baked Chicken Bundles

10 servings

- 10 chicken breast halves, skinned and boned
- 2 cups sour cream
- 1 tablespoon Worcestershire sauce
- 2 teaspoons salt
- 1¼ teaspoons paprika
- 1½ cups fine dry bread crumbs

Preheat oven to 325°F. Place chicken in a 13x9-inch baking dish. Combine sour cream, Worcestershire sauce, salt and paprika; pour over chicken. Turn chicken to coat. Cover and refrigerate overnight.

Drop chicken pieces, one at a time in breadcrumbs, turning to coat. Tuck ends under to make a nice round fillet. Place in sprayed shallow baking pan. Cover and chill at least 1½ hours.

Bake 45 to 60 minutes or until golden and cooked through. (If chicken looks dry, baste with a little melted butter.)

Per serving: Cal 337, Carb 13g, Fib 1g, Pro 38g, Fat 12g, Sod 480mg, Sug 2g

menu

Gourmet Baked Chicken Bundles
Company Rice Casserole
Minted Petite Peas
Strawberry Nut Salad
Sally Lunn Muffins
Rice Chex® Dessert

Basic Chicken Curry

5 servings

- 4 chicken breast, skinned and boned
- 1 tablespoon butter
- 1 small onion, finely chopped
- 1½ teaspoons curry powder
- 1 (14-oz) can coconut milk
- 1 tablespoon finely chopped cilantro

Cut chicken breast into bite size pieces. In a medium saucepan, melt butter. Add chopped onions, sauté until soft. Add chicken, curry powder. Sauté for 1-2 minutes. Add coconut milk and salt and pepper to taste. Simmer uncovered until chicken is done. Garnish with chopped cilantro.

variations: You can use shrimp instead of chicken. Add fresh chopped basil, thinly sliced bell pepper, mushrooms.

Per serving: Cal 382, Carb 5g, Fib 1g, Pro 38g, Fat 23g, Sod 348mg, Sug 1g

Asian Glazed Chicken

4 servings

This recipe imparts a lot of flavor for so few ingredients.

- 4 **chicken breast halves**
- 2 **tablespoons butter, melted**
- 2 **tablespoons Worcestershire sauce**
- 1 **tablespoon soy sauce**

Preheat oven to 350°F. Line a shallow baking pan with foil for easier cleaning. Place chicken on foil, skin-side up.

Combine remaining ingredients. Brush chicken and bake 30 to 40 minutes, basting occasionally.

Per serving: Cal 222, Carb 0g, Fib 0g, Pro 30g, Fat 10g, Sod 142mg, Sug 0g

Chicken & Wine Dish

4 servings

Even after twenty plus years, this is still a family favorite. The sauce is delicious served over rice.

- 4 **chicken breast halves**
- ⅓ **cup butter, thinly sliced**
- ¼ **cup white wine**
- 1 **(10¾-oz) can condensed cream of chicken soup**
- 2 **tablespoons sliced almonds**
- 1 **tablespoon chopped parsley**

Preheat oven to 375°F. Place chicken, skin-side down, in a sprayed 13x9-inch baking dish. Arrange slices of butter over top. Bake 20 minutes. Turn chicken and bake 20 minutes.

Meanwhile, combine wine and soup; spoon over chicken. Sprinkle with almonds and parsley. Bake 10 to 20 minutes. Chicken should be golden and tender.

Per serving: Cal 399, Carb 8g, Fib 1g, Pro 31g, Fat 25g, Sod 184mg, Sug 1g

Mozzarella Chicken Bake

4 servings

What would we do without boneless chicken breasts? You can do so many things with them. They are low in fat, delicious and can be used for almost any occasion.

- 4 **large chicken breast halves, skinned and boned**
- ⅓ **cup flour**
- ¼ **cup butter**
  Salt and pepper
- 4 **large mushrooms, sliced**
- 4 **slices Mozzarella cheese**

Place chicken between waxed paper and pound to ¼-inch thickness, being careful not to tear the meat. Coat chicken with flour and shake off excess.

Heat butter in skillet; add chicken and cook until tender, about 4 to 5 minutes each side. Place chicken on broiler pan; sprinkle with salt and pepper.

Quickly sauté mushrooms in skillet; arrange slices on chicken. Top with a slice of cheese. Place under broiler just long enough to melt cheese.

Per serving: Cal 384, Carb 9g, Fib 1g, Pro 42g, Fat 19g, Sod 370mg, Sug 1g

Company Chicken and Rice

8 servings

This recipe is delicious just as it is, but if want to elaborate just add any of the following: sliced mushrooms, slivered almonds, or water chestnuts.

- 8 **chicken breast halves, skinned and boned**
- 1½ **cups uncooked long-grain rice**
- 1 **(10¾-ounces) can condensed cream of celery soup**
- 1 **(10¾-ounces) can condensed cream of mushroom soup**
- 1 **(10¾-ounces) can condensed cream of chicken soup**
- ½ **cup butter, melted**

Preheat oven to 250°F. Place rice in bottom of large sprayed roasting pan (pan should be at least 2-inches deep). Combine soups in mixing bowl; gradually stir in 1½ soup cans of water, stirring to blend. Pour over rice.

Dip chicken in butter; place skin-side up on rice mixture. Bake, uncovered, at 250°F for 2½ hours or at 350°F for 1½ hours or until liquid is absorbed, and chicken is cooked through.

Per serving: Cal 282, Carb 20g, Fib 1g, Pro 20g, Fat 13g, Sod 357mg, Sug 1g

Quick Chicken Divan
4 servings

Serve with Romaine Artichoke Salad and Quick Focaccia Bread.

- **1   pound fresh broccoli, cooked**
- **4   large slices cooked chicken or turkey**
- **1   (10¾-oz) can cream of chicken soup**
- **⅓   cup milk**
- **½   cup (2-oz) Cheddar cheese, shredded**

Preheat oven to 350°F. Place broccoli in a sprayed 11x7-inch baking dish. Top with chicken.

Combine soup and milk until blended. Pour over chicken. Sprinkle with cheese. Bake 30 minutes or until heated through.

Per serving: Cal 150, Carb 11g, Fib 2g, Pro 15g, Fat 6g, Sod 112mg, Sug 3g

Roquefort Chicken
6 servings

- **6   chicken breast halves, skinned and boned**
- **Salt and pepper**
- **¼   cup butter**
- **4   ounces Roquefort cheese**
- **1   garlic clove, minced**
- **1   cup sour cream.**

Preheat oven to 350°F. Sprinkle chicken with salt and pepper. Heat butter in heavy skillet and lightly brown chicken; remove. Place in a sprayed 13x9-inch baking dish.

Add Roquefort, garlic and sour cream to skillet. Heat, but do not boil. Pour over chicken. Bake 30 to 40 minutes or until cooked through.

Per serving: Cal 400, Carb 2g, Fib 0g, Pro 40g, Fat 24g, Sod 500mg, Sug 1g

Sweet-Sour Chicken
4 servings

A nice sweet-sour sauce flavors this easy chicken recipe. Serve with rice to absorb all the wonderful sauce.

- **1   chicken, cut up**
- **1   cup ketchup**
- **¾   cup white vinegar**
- **1½   teaspoons prepared mustard**
- **1½   cups firmly packed brown sugar**

Preheat oven to 350°F. Rinse chicken and pat dry.

Combine remaining ingredients in a small saucepan. Bring to a boil; reduce heat and simmer 30 minutes.

Place chicken, skin-side down, in a sprayed 13x9-inch baking dish. Brush generously with sauce. Bake 30 minutes; turn and bake 20 to 30 minutes, basting frequently with the sauce.

Per serving: Cal 613, Carb 58g, Fib 0g, Pro 43g, Fat 24g, Sod 591mg, Sug 57g

Chicken Dijon
4 servings

- 4 **chicken breast halves, skinned and boned**
- 3 **tablespoons oil**
- 2 **tablespoons flour**
- ½ **cup half and half**
- 1 **cup chicken broth**
- 2 **tablespoons Dijon mustard**

Rinse chicken pieces and pat dry. Heat oil in a large skillet. Add chicken and cook 10 to 12 minutes or until cooked through, turning once. Remove chicken and keep warm.

Add flour to pan drippings; stir well to blend. Add half and half and chicken broth, stirring until smooth. Add mustard and cook over medium heat until thickened. Return chicken to the pan, coat with sauce and reheat, if necessary.

Per serving: Cal 333, Carb 4g, Fib 0g, Pro 36g, Fat 18g, Sod 442mg, Sug 0g

Quick Chicken Recipes

Brush chicken with mayonnaise or yogurt and roll in crushed cracker crumbs. Bake at 350°F for 30 to 45 minutes.

Brush chicken with Italian dressing; bake at 350°F for 30 to 45 minutes. If cooking for a crowd, I like to do this ahead. Then place on grill over medium coals; brush with barbecue sauce and cook, basting frequently until heated through.

Combine cooked pasta with pesto and cooked cubed chicken. Sprinkle with shredded Parmesan cheese.

Company Swiss Chicken
4 servings

- 4 **chicken breast halves, skinned and boned**
- 2 **tablespoons oil**
- 1 **(6½-oz) jar marinated artichoke hearts, drained**
- 4 **slices Swiss cheese**

Place each chicken breast between plastic wrap and pound to ¼-inch thickness. Heat oil in a large skillet. Add chicken and cook 6 to 8 minutes or until cooked through, turning once.

Arrange artichokes on top of chicken; top with a slice of cheese (trim if too large). Cover skillet and cook until cheese is melted.

variations:
Pineapple slices, cooked broccoli spears, Monterey Jack cheese
Sliced tomatoes, cooked broccoli spears, Mozzarella cheese
Sliced ham, cooked asparagus spears, Swiss cheese

Per serving: Cal 300, Carb 5g, Fib 3g, Pro 42g, Fat 12g, Sod 171mg, Sug 0g

Savory Grilled Chicken

4 servings

1   **chicken, cut up**
     Seasoned salt
     Butter, melted

Place chicken on a large piece of heavy-duty foil. Sprinkle generously with salt. Fold foil over and secure tightly. Place on grill and cook 45 minutes, turning frequently, to avoid burning. Remove chicken from foil and place directly on grill, turning to brown both sides. Baste with butter. Meat is so tender it will literally fall off the bone.

Per serving: Cal 404, Carb 0g, Fib 0g, Pro 42g, Fat 25g, Sod 176mg, Sug 0g

Orange Almond Chicken

6 servings

6   **large chicken breast halves, skinned**
     Salt and pepper
¾   **cup flour**
3   **oranges (you will need ¾ cup orange juice and 1½ teaspoons orange peel)**
6   **tablespoons butter**
6   **tablespoons sliced almonds**

Preheat oven to 350°F. Sprinkle chicken with salt and pepper. Coat with flour. Place in 13x9-inch baking dish, skin-side up. Combine juice and orange peel; pour over chicken. Dot chicken with butter. Sprinkle with almonds. Bake 45 to 60 minutes, basting 2 or 3 times.

note: If using boneless chicken breasts, cooking time will be less.

Per serving: Cal 304, Carb 6g, Fib 1g, Pro 30g, Fat 17g, Sod 200mg, Sug 3g

menu

Orange Almond Chicken,
buttered angel hair pasta
Lemon Broccoli
hot rolls
Almond Angel Food Cake.

Chicken with Sun-Dried Tomatoes 4 servings

4   chicken breast halves, skinned and boned

½   cup chopped oil-packed sun-dried tomatoes (with 2 tablespoons of the oil)

2   large garlic cloves, finely chopped

¼   cup finely chopped onion

1   cup heavy whipping cream

Heat 1 tablespoon of the oil from the tomatoes in a large skillet. Add chicken and cook 4 to 5 minutes per side until cooked through.

Remove and keep warm. Add remaining 1 tablespoon oil, garlic, onion and sun-dried tomatoes to skillet. Sauté until onions are tender, about 3 to 4 minutes. Add cream and simmer 4 to 5 minutes or until sauce has thickened. Spoon over chicken.

Per serving w/2 tbsp of Sauce: Cal 267, Carb 2g, Fib 0g, Pro35g, Fat 12g, Sod 99mg, Sug 0g

Cashew Noodle Casserole 6 servings

This is best served hot from the oven as Chow Mein Noodles tend to soften when reheated.

1½   cups diced cooked chicken or turkey

1   cup finely chopped celery

1   cup cashews, split

2   (10¾-oz each) cans condensed cream of mushroom soup

1   cup chicken broth

1   (5-oz) can Chow Mein Noodles

Preheat oven to 350°F. Combine chicken, celery, and cashews in a mixing bowl.

Combine soup and broth in a small mixing bowl. Pour over chicken mixture; stir to mix.

Layer in sprayed deep 2-quart casserole dish, starting with half of the chicken mixture, then half of the noodles. Repeat, ending with noodles. Bake 45 minutes or until heated through.

variation: add finely chopped onion or sliced mushrooms.

Per serving: Cal 380, Carb 30g, Fib 3g, Pro 16g, Fat 23g, Sod 1247mg,Sug 3g

Chicken & Noodles

4 servings

This recipe is very easy and very fast. If you have some leftover chicken or turkey, this dish can be made in less than 15 minutes.

- **3 cups chicken broth**
- **1½ cups (4-oz) medium egg noodles**
- **2 cups fresh broccoli florets**
- **2 cups cubed cooked chicken (or turkey)**
- **¼ teaspoon lemon pepper**
- **½ cup sour cream**

Heat chicken broth in a 2 quart saucepan; bring to a boil. Add noodles and cook about 4 minutes; stirring occasionally. Add broccoli; cover and continue cooking 4 minutes. Add chicken and lemon pepper; cook about 4 minutes or until heated through and broccoli is just crisp-tender.

At this point you probably have very little liquid left in the pan, but this needs to be drained off. Stir in sour cream and cook, over low heat, until heated through.

Per serving: Cal 263, Carb 21g, Fib 2g, Pro 22g, Fat 9g, Sod 944mg, Sug 2g

Apricot Bread Stuffing

2	tablespoons butter
¼	cup finely chopped onion
¼	cup finely chopped dried apricots
⅓	cup rich chicken broth
¼	cup finely chopped walnuts
1½	cups dry bread cubes, for stuffing

Heat butter in a small skillet. Add remaining ingredients except bread cubes, and cook 3 to 4 minutes or until onion is soft. Pour over bread cubes; toss to coat.

Per ½ cup: Cal 294, Carb 38g, Fib 3g, Pro 7g, Fat 13g, Sod 423mg, Sug 3g

Apple Sausage Stuffing

Makes enough dressing for one large turkey. This recipe has a lot more flavor when cooked in the turkey rather than baked in a casserole. For safety reasons, internal temperature of stuffing, when cooked in the turkey, must reach at least 165°F.

1	pound seasoned bulk sausage
1	cup chopped onion
2	cups chopped apples, peeled
10	cup seasoned bread cubes for stuffing
1	large egg, lightly beaten
½	cup chicken broth

In a large skillet, brown sausage. Remove from skillet. Pour off all but 2 tablespoons fat. Add onion and apples. Cook until tender, about 5 minutes. Combine this mixture with the sausage, bread cubes, egg and broth. Stir until well mixed and bread cubes are coated.

Per ½ cup: Cal 248, Carb 37g, Fib 3g, Pro 11g, Fat 6g, Sod 1048mg, Sug 4g

Spaghetti Carbonara
6 servings

Serve this easy dinner with a crispy hearty salad and a warm baguette.
It is sure to please!

- **2   large eggs**
- **1   cup (4-oz) finely grated Parmesan cheese**
- **6   ounces Prosciutto, finely chopped**
- **1   (16-oz) package spaghetti**
- **3   tablespoons finely chopped parsley**

In a bowl, whisk together eggs and Parmesan cheese; set aside.

In a large skillet (using butter or spray) sauté Prosciutto until crispy. Cook spaghetti according to directions. Drain; reserving 2 cups of the starchy liquid. Do not rinse.

Add hot, drained pasta to saucepan. Add egg mixture, and half of reserved liquid. Toss quickly, otherwise eggs will scramble in chunks and not coat the pasta. Add more liquid if needed to moisten. Add salt and pepper to taste. Garnish with finely chopped parsley and grated Parmesan cheese. Serve immediately.

Per serving: Cal 380, Carb 52g, Fib 3g, Pro 21g, Fat 9g, Sod 681mg, Sug 1g

Pasta with Brie & Shrimp
6 servings

Serve this versatile dish topped with shrimp, crab, or chicken.

- **8   ounces linguine**
- **8   ounces Brie cheese, diced**
- **½   cup whipping cream**
- **2   tablespoons finely chopped parsley**
- **Freshly ground pepper to taste**
- **8   ounces cooked shrimp (should be hot)**

Cook pasta according to package directions. Rinse and drain thoroughly. Return to pot and add Brie, stirring to melt. Add cream, parsley, and pepper.

Place on serving plate and top with shrimp.

note: Crust should be removed from Brie before dicing.

Per serving: Cal 370, Carb 29g, Fib 1g, Prot 21g, Fat 19g, Sod 333mg, Sug 8g

Chicken and Pesto Fettuccine

4 to 6 servings

This pasta dish takes a little more time than some of the recipes, but it is well worth the effort. Serve with toasted bread or rolls, a nice green salad and Apple Raspberry Crisp or ice cream and sliced strawberries for dessert.

4	chicken breast halves, skinned, boned, cubed
½	cup heavy whipping cream
½	cup butter plus 2 tablespoons
1/3	cup freshly grated Parmesan cheese
1	tablespoon pesto, plus ¼ cup
12	ounces fettuccine

Cook pasta according to package directions. If pasta is ready before the rest of the ingredients, drain off the water, return to pan and add about 1 tablespoon butter, tossing to coat. Cover and keep warm.

Meanwhile, in small saucepan, heat the cream. Add ½ cup of the butter and heat until melted. Gradually add the Parmesan cheese, stirring after each addition, until melted. Keep warm until ready to use.

Heat skillet over medium-high heat. Toss chicken with remaining 2 tablespoons butter (melted). Add to skillet and cook, stirring frequently, until chicken is cooked through, being careful not to overcook. Remove chicken and toss with 1 tablespoon pesto.

Add cream sauce and ¼ cup pesto to the pasta, tossing to coat. Place on heated platter and top with the chicken.

note: Most pasta dishes should not be allowed to stand, but should be served immediately. Heated serving dishes will also help to keep the pasta hot as long as possible.

Per serving: Cal 639, Carb 44g, Fib 2g, Pro 34g, Fat 36g, Sod 343mg, Sug 2g

Linguine with Mascarpone

8 servings

These convenient "on hand" ingredients can be thrown together for a quick, yet delectable meal. Does reheat nicely in the microwave.

16	ounces linguine
1	(8-oz) container Mascarpone cheese, softened
¼	cup parsley
½	cup grated Parmesan cheese

Cook pasta according to package directions. Rinse and drain. Return to pot.

Add Mascarpone cheese and parsley. Place on serving plates and sprinkle with Parmesan.

Per serving: Cal 345, Carb 43g, Fib 2g, Prot 11g, Fat 15g, Sod 63mg, Sug 2g

Orzo with Parmesan & Basil 8 servings

Wonderful as a side dish or a hearty one pot dinner!

- 3 **tablespoons butter**
- 1½ **cups orzo pasta**
- 3 **cups chicken broth**
- 1 **cup frozen peas**
- ½ **cup (2-oz) grated Parmesan cheese**
- 5 **tablespoons chopped fresh basil**

In a medium saucepan, melt butter. Add pasta, sauté 2 minutes until lightly brown. Add chicken broth and bring to a boil.

Reduce heat, cover and simmer until pasta is tender and liquid is absorbed, about 20 minutes. Five minutes before pasta is done, in a separate saucepan, heat peas in water just to simmer; drain.

Stir in parmesan cheese, basil and peas. Serve immediately.

note: To make this a main dish, add cooked shrimp, cooked cubed chicken or chunks of smoked salmon the last five minutes.

Per serving: Cal 193, Carb 27g, Fib 2.17g, Pro 7g, Fat 6g, Sod 465mg, Sug 3g

Everyone's Favorite Lasagna 10 to 12 servings

An excellent lasagna recipe that doesn't take all day to make. If desired, make 2 smaller dishes and serve one for dinner and freeze one for later. The lasagna can be prepared and then frozen or baked and frozen and reheated at another time.

- 2 **pounds lean ground beef**
- 1 **tablespoon light brown sugar**
- 1 **(32-oz) jar chunky spaghetti sauce with mushrooms**
- 10 **to 12 lasagna noodles, cooked**
- 2½ **cups (10-oz) Cheddar cheese, shredded**
- 3 **cups (12-oz) Mozzarella cheese, shredded**

Brown ground beef in large skillet; drain off fat. Stir in brown sugar and spaghetti sauce. Bring to a boil; reduce heat and simmer 20 minutes.

Meanwhile, cook noodles according to directions on package. Spread about ½ cup of the meat sauce in sprayed 13x9-inch baking dish. Layer starting with noodles, then sauce, Cheddar cheese and Mozzarella cheese, making 2 layers of everything. Bake 30 minutes or until hot.

Per serving: Cal 420, Carb 25g, Fib 2g, Pro 35g, Fat 20g, Sod 799mg, Sug 7g

Mostaccioli & Sun-Dried Tomatoes

6 servings

8 ounces mostaccioli
¼ cup oil-packed sun-dried tomatoes
1 tablespoon oil from tomatoes
1 (6½-oz) jar marinated artichoke hearts, coarsely chopped

Cook pasta according to directions on package; drain.

Meanwhile, chop tomatoes and place in a large serving bowl. Add the oil (if you don't have enough oil from the tomatoes, add olive oil to make up the difference). Add artichokes and pasta and toss to coat.

Per serving: Cal 184, Carb 33g, Fib 3g, Pro 6g, Fat 4g, Sod 43mg, Sug 2g

Cheese Ravioli

6 servings

Serve with chicken or salmon.

2 (9-oz each) packages cheese-filled ravioli
2 tablespoons butter
1 large garlic clove, minced
1 tablespoon chopped fresh parsley
1 cup heavy whipping cream
¼ cup grated Asiago or Parmesan cheese

In large pot, cook pasta according to directions on package.

Meanwhile, just before pasta is ready, melt butter in a small skillet. Add garlic and parsley and quickly cook over medium-low heat (you don't want the garlic to brown).

Drain pasta and rinse with cold water. Return to pot; add garlic mixture and cream. Cook on low heat until cream is reduced slightly, about 3 to 4 minutes. Place in a sprayed 11 x 7-inch baking dish and sprinkle with cheese. Place under broiler and broil until cheese is melted and lightly browned.

Per serving: Cal 281, Carb 15g, Fib 2g, Pro 6g, Fat 22g, Sod 297mg, Sug 3g

Penne with Gorgonzola　6 servings

Gorgonzola fans will treasure this recipe and those who aren't fans should give it a try. Gorgonzola isn't my favorite cheese, but I love this recipe.

- 8　ounces penne pasta
- 1　cup heavy whipping cream
- 2　ounces Gorgonzola cheese, crumbled
- ⅛　teaspoon freshly ground pepper
- 　Parmesan cheese, freshly grated

Cook pasta according to directions on package.

Meanwhile, in medium saucepan, heat cream to boiling; reduce heat and simmer 2 minutes. Add Gorgonzola and stir until smooth. Add pepper.

Drain pasta and return to pan. Stir in sauce. Spoon onto a serving platter; sprinkle with desired amount of Parmesan.

variation: Add cooked chicken or ham for 4 main dish servings.

Per serving: Cal 308, Carb 30g, Fib 1g, Pro 8g, Fat 18g, Sod 147mg, Sug 2g

Baked Pasta & Cream　6 servings

I could make a whole meal out of this dish. The chewy cheese is a nice contrast to the creamy pasta.

- 8　ounces penne
- 1　cup heavy cream, divided
- 1　cup (4-oz) Mozzarella cheese, softened
- 2　tablespoons grated Parmesan cheese

Preheat oven to 350°F. Cook pasta according to package directions; rinse and drain.

Meanwhile, heat ½ cup of the cream in a large saucepan. Add pasta and cook, stirring frequently until cream is absorbed.

Sprinkle half the Mozzarella cheese in a sprayed 8x8-inch baking dish. Add half the pasta, remaining cheese, then remaining pasta. Pour remaining cream over top. Sprinkle with Parmesan cheese. Bake 25 to 30 minutes or until most of the liquid is absorbed. Let stand 5 minutes.

Per serving: Cal 312, Carb 30g, Fib 1g, Prot 12g, Fat 16.47g, Sod 180mg, Sug 2g

Browned Butter & Myzithra Cheese
4 servings

The Spaghetti Factory restaurants serve this delicious pasta. This is my daughter's version and is equally as good.

- 8 ounces spaghetti
- ⅓ cup butter
- 2 medium garlic cloves, minced
- ½ cup grated Myzithra cheese

Cook pasta according to directions on package; drain.

Meanwhile, in a small skillet, melt butter over medium-low heat. Add garlic and cook until butter turns a light brown. Watch carefully at this point. If it turns too dark, it will have to be discarded. Add to pasta and toss to coat. Place on individual serving dishes and sprinkle with about 2 tablespoons cheese.

Per serving: Cal 394, Carb 44g, Fib 1g, Pro 10g, Fat 19g, Sod 326mg, Sug 2g

Spinach-Tomato Tortellini
4 servings

Serve with Crisp Green Salad and Cheesy Quick Bread.

- 1 tablespoon olive oil
- 1 large garlic clove, minced
- 2 (14.5-oz) cans whole Italian style tomatoes, cut up
- 1 tablespoon sugar
- 1 (8-oz) package spinach tortellini with cheese

Heat oil in a medium saucepan. Add garlic and cook about 2 minutes, but do not brown. Add tomatoes (do not drain); and sugar. Bring to a boil; reduce heat and simmer about 45 minutes or until thickened.

Meanwhile, cook tortellini according to directions on package. Drain and rinse thoroughly. Place tortellini on a large serving platter and top with some of the tomato sauce.

Per serving: Cal 207, Carb 29g, Fib 3g, Pro 7g, Fat 7g, Sod 516mg, Sug 7g

kids corner

Kids Corner

Kids grow up in the Six Ingredients or Less household constantly around food, cooking and enjoying all sorts of food. So, naturally, they have ended up learning to cook and enjoying what they make. Learning to cook has its ups and downs. You will try recipes that you don't like. However, I have put together a group of recipes that are particularly easy and delicious. There are a few things you can do to make sure your cooking is successful:

- If you have very little experience, make sure there is an adult helping you.

- Always read the entire recipes before you begin – no surprises.

- Make sure you have all the ingredients.

- Always wash your hands before cooking.

- Always wash your hands and cooking area after handling raw meat. Make sure no raw meat juices contact anything else.

- Do not use the same cutting board for raw meat, then for raw foods such as salad.

- It helps to have all the ingredients measured before assembling recipe.

- Ask an experienced cook if you don't understand the recipe.

Happy cooking and happy eating!

Peanut Butter Bars
3 dozen bars

1 cup semi-sweet chocolate chips
⅓ cup peanut butter
4 cups Cocoa Krispies®

Melt chocolate chips in top of double boiler. Stir in peanut butter. Remove from heat. Gently stir in Cocoa Krispies®.

Press mixture into a sprayed 8x8-inch baking dish. Let cool and then cut into bars.

Per bar: Cal 54, Carb 7g, Fib 0g, Pro 1g, Fat 3g, Sod 40mg, Sug 4g

Miniature Cherry Cheesecakes
6 servings

My family ate these up fast, and then wanted more.

1 (10-oz) package frozen puff pastry shells
2 (3-oz each) packages cream cheese, room temperature
¼ cup powdered sugar
½ teaspoon lemon or almond extract
1 (21-oz) can cherry pie filling
   Frozen whipped topping, thawed

Preheat oven to 400°F. Place frozen pastry shells on baking sheet. Bake 18 to 20 minutes or until golden brown. Remove from oven and place on baking rack. Using a fork, carefully remove the center top (lid) from the pastry shell. Then remove any soft filling underneath.

In mixer bowl, beat cream cheese until soft. Add sugar and extract and beat until fluffy, 4 to 5 minutes.

Spoon equal amounts of cream cheese mixture into each pastry shell. Place back on baking sheet. Return to oven and bake 5 minutes. Remove from oven and place on rack to cool.

Top each cheesecake with about 1 tablespoon of the cherry pie filling. Top with a dollop of whipped topping.

note: You will have quite a bit of pie filling leftover. You can use this for a topping on ice cream or cheesecake slices.

Per serving: Cal 418, Carb 34g, Fib 1g, Pro 6g, Fat 29g, Sod 206mg, Sug7g

Coconut Chocolate Bars

45 cookies

- **1   (18-oz) package sugar cookie dough, softened**
- **2   cups semi-sweet chocolate chips**
- **2   cups flaked coconut**
- **1   (4-oz) can sweetened condensed milk**

Preheat oven to 350°F. Pat cookie dough evenly into a lightly sprayed
15x10 inch baking pan. Sprinkle with the chocolate chips, coconut and then the
pecans. Pour condensed milk over the top. Bake for 20 to 22 minutes or until
lightly browned and center is set.

Per bar: Cal 133, Carb 16g, Fib 1g, Pro 1g, Fat 8g, Sod 65mg, Sug 10g

Marshmallow Baked Apples

4 servings

A great treat to make while camping.

- **4   medium granny smith apples**
- **½   teaspoon ground cinnamon**
- **40   miniature marshmallows**
- **4   tablespoons brown sugar**

Preheat oven to 350°F or heat grill. Core apples, using a small spoon, being
careful not to cut all the way through. Place apple in center of a square piece of
heavy aluminum foil.

Sprinkle center of each apple with cinnamon; fill with alternating layers of
marshmallows and brown sugar. Wrap foil around each apple to completely
cover apple; crimp to seal.

Place each foil wrapped apple on a baking sheet. Bake for 30 to 35 minutes or
until tender. Unwrap carefully.

If grilling, you may want to use two layers of foil. Place foil-wrapped apples
directly over medium-hot coals for 30 to 35 minutes or until apples are tender.
Unwrap carefully.

Per apple: Cal 120, Carb 33g, Fib 3g, Pro 0g, Fat 0g, Sod 5mg, Sug 29g

Red and White Popcorn Crunch

16 cups

You can serve this to your family and friends on any special occasion. It would also be great for school parties. Just change the color to fit the occasion: Red-Valentine's Day, Green-St. Patrick's Day, Blue-4th of July, Red-Christmas Day

- 4 **quarts popped popcorn**
- ½ **cup butter**
- ¼ **cup light corn syrup**
- 1 **(5-oz) stick peppermint candy, coarsely chopped**
- 1 **to 2 drops of food coloring**

Preheat oven to 250°F. Place popcorn in a very large baking dish or roasting pan. Large enough that you will be able to stir the mixture.

Place butter, corn syrup and chopped candy in a small saucepan. Bring to a boil over medium heat, stirring constantly. Boil 5 minutes, stirring frequently. Add 1 to 2 drops of food coloring (if desired).

Quickly pour over popcorn and toss, using two large spoons or spatulas. Do this carefully because the mixture is very hot and sticky. The popcorn will not be entirely coated.

Place in oven and bake 60 minutes, stirring mixture every 15 minutes. Remove from oven and stir occasionally as it cools. If you do not stir it while cooling, it will form one big clump.

Per cup: Cal 139, Carb 13g, Fib 1g, Pro 1g, Fat 10g, Sod 153mg, Sug 6g

Easy Kid's Cookies

4 dozen

- 1 **cup butter**
- 1 **cup firmly packed light brown sugar**
- 1 **cup flour**
- 1 **teaspoon baking soda**
- 2 **cups quick-cooking oats**

Preheat oven to 350°F. Cream butter and sugar in mixer bowl. Add flour and baking soda and beat until mixed. Stir in oats. Roll into 1-inch balls. Place on an ungreased baking sheet and press slightly. Bake 8 to 10 minutes.

Per cookie: Cal 73, Carb 9g, Fib 1g, Pro 1g, Fat 4g, Sod 29mg, Sug 4g

Chocolate Mousse   9 cups

6   **cups miniature marshmallows**
½   **cup butter**
3½   **cups (18-oz) dark chocolate (70% cocoa solids), chopped**
3   **cups heavy cream**
2   **teaspoons vanilla extract**

Combine marshmallows, butter, chocolate and ¼ cup water in a microware safe bowl and microware for 30 seconds; stir. If chocolate is not melted, microwave additional 30 seconds, stir. Continue until chocolate and marshmallows are melted and smooth. Do not let mixture get too hot or chocolate will harden.

In a mixing bowl, whip cream and vanilla until firm peaks form. Gently fold chocolate mixture into whipped cream. Pour mixture into large serving bowl or individual parfait or wine glasses. Chill until set.

Per ½ cup: Cal 403, Carb 35g, Fib 3g, Pro 3g, Fat 29g, Sod 73mg, Sug 25g

Frozen Fudgesicles   12 to 14 fudgesicles

Believe it or not, these are much better than store bought. Always make more than you think you need. The gown ups like them almost as much as the kids do.

1   **(3.5-oz) package instant chocolate pudding mix**
2   **cups milk**
¼   **cup sugar**
1   **cup canned evaporated milk**

In large mixer bowl, combine pudding and the 2 cups milk. Beat 2 minutes with a mixer and watch carefully, it might splatter on you.

Stir in sugar and canned milk. Pour immediately into popsicle molds (I use Tupperware® molds). Freeze.

Per serving: Cal 79, Carb 13g, Fib 0g, Pro 3g, Fat 2g, Sod 144mg, Sug 11g

Butterscotch Crunchies   3 dozen

- 1   **cup butterscotch chips**
- ½   **cup peanut butter**
- 2   **cups (3-oz can) Chow Mein Noodles**
- 1   **cup miniature marshmallows**

Melt butterscotch chips and peanut butter in top of double boiler; stir to blend. Remove from heat.

Gently stir in noodles and marshmallows. Drop by teaspoon onto waxed paper-lined cookie sheets. Chill until set.

Per cookie: Cal 74, Carb 8g, Fib 0g, Pro 2g, Fat 4g, Sod 40mg, Sug 1g

Quick Cranberry Coconut Bars   36 bars

Keep the ingredients on hand and kids can make these for snacks or treats.

- 1   **(18.25-oz) package white cake mix**
- ⅓   **cup oil**
- 2   **large eggs**
- ½   **cup dried cranberries**
- 1   **cup Angel Flake coconut**

Preheat oven to 350ºF. In mixer bowl, combine first 3 ingredients; mix until blended. Add remaining ingredients and beat just until mixed through.

Place mixture in well greased or sprayed 13x9-inch baking pan. Bake 25 to 30 minutes or until light golden brown. Cool on rack. Cut into squares.

Per cookie: Cal 89, Carb 11g, Fib 0g, Pro 1g, Fat 4g, Sod 99mg, Sug 7g

S'Mores Chow

12 cups

A delightful party snack the kids will love to make and eat!

2	cups semi-sweet chocolate chips
½	cup creamy peanut butter
4	cups miniature marshmallows
6	cups Golden Grahams® cereal
1½	cups powdered sugar

In a large microwave safe bowl, place chocolate chips and peanut butter. Microwave 30 seconds to a minute; stir. Microwave another 30 seconds to a minute. Stir until melted.

Pour in marshmallows and cereal, stir until coated. Sprinkle with powdered sugar; stir until coated.

Store in airtight containers or zipper bags.

Per ½ cup: Cal 204, Carb 36g, Fib 1g, Pro 3g, Fat 7g, Sod 126mg, Sug 26g

Peanut Butter Cupcakes

18 cupcakes

These are quite rich and are equally as good with or without frosting. Have fun and try a different flavor of cake mix.

1	(18.25-oz) package yellow cake mix
1	cup creamy peanut butter
1 ⅓	cups water
3	large eggs
½	cup mini semi-sweet chocolate chips
1	(16-oz) can chocolate frosting

Preheat oven to 350°F. In large mixer bowl, combine first 4 ingredients following mixing directions on package. Stir in chocolate chips.

Spoon batter into sprayed muffin tins, filling 2/3 full. Bake 18 to 20 minutes. Let cool, then spread with frosting.

Per cupcake: Cal 343, Carb 42g, Fib 1g, Pro 7g, Fat 17g, Sod 353mg, Sug 30g

Potato Chip Cookies 4 dozen

Unusual and tasty cookies the kids will love to bake.

- 1 **cup butter**
- ½ **cup sugar, plus 4 tablespoons for rolling**
- 1 **teaspoon vanilla extract**
- 1¾ **cups flour**
- ¾ **cup crushed potato chips**
- ½ **cup finely chopped cashews (optional)**

Preheat oven to 350°F. In a mixer bowl, cream butter and sugar. Add vanilla, flour, potato chips and cashews. Mix until all ingredients are combined.

Form into small balls and roll in granulated sugar. Press flat on ungreased baking sheet with a fork.

Bake for 18-20 minutes or until light golden brown. Cool on rack.

Per serving: Cal 68, Carb 6g, Fib 0g, Pro 1g, Fat 5g, Sod 32mg, Sug 2g

Pretty in Pink Angel Food Cake 12 servings

You'll be impressed by how tall this cake is and how easy it is to make.

- 1 **(16-oz) package angel food cake mix**
- ¼ **cup Kool-Aid® cherry flavored sugar sweetened drink mix**

In mixer bowl, place cake mix and Kool-Aid®. Prepare cake as directed on package using a 10-inch Angel food cake tube pan. Follow directions very carefully. The only other ingredient you have to add is water, as directed on the package. Pour into ungreased pan and bake as directed on package.

To Serve: You can serve the cake by itself or with a serving of fruit or ice cream. A dollop of whipped cream sprinkled with coconut is very good, too.

Per serving: Cal 156, Carb 35g, Fib 0g, Pro 3g, Fat 0g, Sod 328mg, Sug 27g

Lemon Julius Smoothie
7½ cups

1   (6-oz) can frozen lemonade concentrate
1   (6-oz) can frozen orange juice concentrate
2   cups vanilla ice cream

Combine ingredients in blender along with 4 cups water; blend on medium speed until mixed and foamy. If blender is too small to hold all the ingredients, make half the recipe at a time and combine the two mixes.

Per cup: Cal 152, Carb 29g, Fib 0g, Pro 2g, Fat 4g, Sod 31mg, Sug 26g

Raspberry Smoothie
4½ cups

1   (10-oz) package frozen sweetened raspberries, thawed
2   cups orange juice
½   cup milk
6   ice cubes

Place ingredients in blender and process until smooth.

Per cup: Cal 128, Carb 29g, Fib 3g, Pro 2g, Fat 1g, Sod 13mg, Sug 24g

Quick Ham-Broccoli Dish
4 to 6 servings

1½   cups fresh broccoli florettes, chopped
8   ounces process cheese spread, cubed
3   cups cooked small-size penne pasta
¾   cup small cubed ham

In medium saucepan, cook broccoli in a small amount of water, until just tender; drain. Add cheese cubes, pasta and ham and heat until cheese is melted.

Per serving: Cal 261, Carb 25g, Fib 1g, Pro 15g, Fat 11g, Sod 583mg, Sug 4g

Kid's Favorite Flank Steak

4 servings

- 1 **flank steak**
- ¼ **cup soy sauce**

Pour enough soy sauce in a shallow dish to cover bottom. Add flank steak and marinate 60 minutes, turning steak frequently.

Remove from marinade and broil or grill discarding remaining marinade. Do not overcook, as this tends to toughen the meat. Slice crosswise to serve.

Per 4 oz : Cal 179, Carb 1g, Fib 0g, Pro 24g, Fat 8g, Sod 1097mg, Sug 1g

Kid Convincing Soup

8 cups

If you want to, you can make the soup ahead and the reheat it for dinner.

- 1 **(12-oz) package low-fat sausage**
- 1 **cup chopped onion**
- 1 **(14½-oz) can stewed tomatoes with basil**
- 1 **cup frozen mixed vegetables**
- 1 **(14½-oz) can beef broth**
- ¼ **cup Cheddar Cheese, Shredded**

Cook sausage and onion in a 3-quart pot or saucepan; drain off liquid. Add tomatoes, mixed vegetables and broth to soup mixture. Add 1½ cups water. Bring mixture to a boil. Reduce heat and simmer 3 to 5 minutes or until zucchini is just tender.

Per cup: Cal 106, Carb 15g, Fib 2g, Pro 7g, Fat 3g, Sod 710mg, Sug 5g

Easy, Cheesy Mac & Cheese

8 servings

- 1½ **cups pasta (macaroni, bow tie, etc)**
- 1 **(12-oz) can cream of chicken soup**
- 1¼ **cups milk**
- 2½ **cups Cheddar cheese (mild, medium or sharp), shredded**
- 16 **Ritz® crackers**
- 1 **tablespoon butter, melted**

Preheat oven to 350ºF. Spray or grease a 9-inch square baking dish or 1½ quart casserole dish. In a large pot, cook pasta according to directions on box.

Meanwhile, place crackers in a zip-type bag and crush with hands or rolling pin. Pour melted butter into bag and shake.

When pasta is done, drain and put back into pot. Add soup, milk and cheese; stir. Pour into baking dish, top with cracker crumbs and bake about 30 minutes.

note: You may add other ingredients such as black olives, chili peppers or sliced hot dogs. You may also substitute -1 cup of cheddar cheese with pepper jack.

Per serving: Cal 296, Carb 24g, Fib 1g, Pro 13g, Fat 16g, Sod 293mg, Sug 4g

Hotdogs & Breadsticks

12 servings

Have your friends over and impress them with lunch. Serve with Macaroni and Cheese and sliced fresh fruit.

- 1 **(11-oz) package refrigerated breadstick dough**
- 12 **hotdogs**

Preheat oven to 350ºF. Open package and unroll dough. Separate into 12 strips.

Wrap one strip around each hotdog, stretching a little if necessary to wrap around three times with both ends tucked under bottom of the hot dog. Place on a baking sheet. Bake 12 to 15 minutes or until lightly browned.

tip: If desired, use as many hot dogs as needed. If you don't need 12 hotdogs, twist remaining breadstick dough and place on baking sheet. Sprinkle with poppy seeds or garlic salt and bake along with the hotdogs.

Per serving: Cal 211, Carb 24g, Fib 1g, Pro 7g, Fat 9g, Sod 611mg, Sug 4g

Today, you can make the main dish and Mom can make the salad and set the table!

Candied Chicken   6 servings

4   **to 6 chicken breast halves, skinned and boned**
1   **cup maple syrup**
½   **cup ketchup**
¼   **cup white vinegar**
    Salt and pepper

Preheat oven to 425°F. Wash chicken and pat dry. Sprinkle with salt and pepper. Place rounded-side up in a sprayed 13x9-inch baking dish.

Combine remaining ingredients and pour over chicken. Bake 20 minutes. Carefully remove from oven and baste with sauce. Bake 10 minutes and baste again. Bake 10 minutes or until cooked through.

Per serving: Cal 281, Carb 41g, Fib 0g, Pro 23g, Fat 3g, Sod 330mg, Sug 36g

Lemon Dill Sole   4 to 5 servings

1   **to 1¼ pounds fillet of sole**
2   **green onions**
1   **lemon**
2   **tablespoons Dijon mustard**
¼   **cup olive oil**
½   **teaspoon dried dill weed**

Preheat oven to 425°F. Place fish in a sprayed 11x7-inch baking dish. Slice both green and white part of onions and sprinkle over fish.

Squeeze juice from lemon and place in a small bowl. Add mustard, olive oil and dill weed. Beat with a whisk until ingredients are blended and smooth. Pour over fish. Cover dish and marinate in refrigerator at least one hour before baking. Place baking dish in oven. Bake 8 to 10 minutes or until fish flakes easily and a wooden toothpick inserted in center looks dry when removed.

Per serving: Cal 108, Carb 2g, Fib 0g, Pro 19g, Fat 2g, Sod 93mg, Sug 0g

Holiday Sausage Pizza   6 to 8 servings

Pizza is a lot of fun to make. This one is very colorful and I like to make it during the Christmas holidays.

1	(12-oz) package sausage
¾	cup chopped onion
1	12-inch pizza crust (I like Boboli®)
½	cup pizza sauce
12	ounces Mozzarella cheese, shredded
	Sweet peppers, 1 red, 1 yellow and 1 green

Preheat oven to 425°F. Place sausage in a large skillet and break up with spoon or spatula. Add onion and cook over medium heat, stirring often, until sausage is cooked through. Drain off all the fat and set aside.

While sausage is browning, place pizza crust on a baking pan and spread with pizza sauce. Spoon sausage and onion over sauce and sprinkle with cheese.

From the top, cut each pepper into fourths. Remove seeds. Place peppers on cutting board and with small star shaped cookie cutter, cut stars out of the peppers. Place stars over the cheese. Bake 10 to 12 minutes or until cheese is melted and just lightly browned.

Per slice: Cal 317, Carb 32g, Fib 2g, Pro 22g, Fat 11g, Sod 925mg, Sug 4g

Veggie Pesto Pizza   6 servings

1	purchased 12-inch baked pizza crust
½	cup pesto
1½	cups (6-oz) Mozzarella cheese, shredded
¾	cup broccoli florettes, broken into small pieces
¼	cup sliced black olives
1	plum tomato, thinly sliced crosswise

Preheat oven to 425°F. Place pizza crust on large baking sheet. Spread pesto to within 1-inch of edge. Sprinkle with cheese. Sprinkle broccoli and olives over the cheese. Arrange tomato slices in a circle around outer edge of pizza.

Place baking sheet on lower rack in oven and bake 12 to 15 minutes, or until heated through and cheese has melted.

Per slice: Cal 308, Carb 28g, Fib 2g, Pro 17g, Fat 14g, Sod 704mg, Sug 2g

Easy Parmesan Knots   12 roll

- 1   **(11-oz) package refrigerated breadsticks**
- 3   **tablespoons butter**
- 1   **tablespoon grated Parmesan cheese**
- ¼   **teaspoon garlic salt**
- ½   **teaspoon dried parsley**

Preheat oven to 375°F. Unroll breadsticks and separate. Tie each breadstick into a loose knot (remember the bread will get bigger when it bakes) and place on a baking sheet. Bake 10 to 12 minutes or until golden.

While rolls are baking, place butter in a small microwave safe bowl and microwave until melted. Stir in the Parmesan cheese, garlic salt and parsley. Brush butter mixture over each baked roll.

Put rolls in a pretty basket or dish and serve hot.

Per roll: Cal 99, Carb 13g, Fib 0g, Pro 2g, Fat 4g, Sod 238mg, Sug 1g

Yummy Hot Dogs   8 hot dogs

- 1   **(8-oz) package refrigerated Crescent rolls**
- 4   **teaspoons melted butter**
- 4   **teaspoons prepared mustard**
- 8   **hot dog**

Preheat oven to 375°F. Separate crescents into 8 rolls. Brush each with melted butter and spread with mustard. Place hot dog on wide end and roll toward narrow end.

Place on ungreased baking sheet. Brush with melted butter and bake 12 to 14 minutes or until rolls are lightly browned.

Per serving: Cal 265, Carb 22g, Fib 1g, Pro 7g, Fat 16g, Sod 693mg, Sug 4g

menu

Candied Chicken
Rice
Buttered Peas
Easy Parmesan Knots
Banana Pudding or Ice Cream

Fiesta Fold Over   6 servings

This goes fast in my house. We like to top it with salsa, guacamole or sour cream.

- **1   pound ground turkey or ground chicken**
- **1   (8-oz) tube Crescent® seamless dough sheet**
- **½   (1.25-oz) package taco seasoning mix**
- **1   (4-oz) can chili peppers**
- **1   cup (4-oz) shredded Mexican blend cheese**

Preheat oven to 375ºF. In a medium skillet, begin browning meat. Meanwhile, on a sprayed baking sheet roll crescent sheet to 8x13-inches. Once the meat is cooked, add seasoning mix and chilies; stir and drain.

Spoon mixture over one half of dough lengthwise, top with cheese. Fold remaining dough over the mixture and press edges to seal. With a knife or fork poke a few holes across the top to allow steam to escape.

Bake for 18-20 minutes or until golden brown. Slice to serve.

note: Make this even easier by lining baking sheet with parchment paper and roll dough on paper. Top with fillings. Hold edge of paper, fold dough over covered half, press edges and peel back paper.

Per serving: Cal 164, Carb 5g, Fib 1g, Pro 18g, Fat 8g, Sod 475mg, Sug 0g

Beef & Cheese Macaroni   6 servings

- **1   pound lean ground beef**
- **2   cups chunky salsa**
- **2   cups elbow macaroni, uncooked**
- **8   ounces process cheese spread**

Brown meat in a large skillet; drain. Add salsa and 1¾ cups water. Bring to a boil and then add macaroni. Reduce heat to a simmer, cover and cook 8 minutes or until pasta is just tender.

Cut cheese into small cubes. Add to skillet and cook, stirring frequently, until melted.

Per serving: Cal 422, Carb 33g, Fib 1g, Pro 27g, Fat 19g, Sod 1227mg, Sug 6g

Barbecue Chicken Pizza

4   **chicken breast halves, skinned and boned**

2   **large garlic cloves, finely chopped**

1   **tablespoon vegetable oil**

1   **(10-oz) package refrigerated pizza crust**

¾   **cup your favorite barbecue sauce**

1   **package (8-oz) pizza cheese blend**

Preheat oven to 425°F. Wash chicken and pat dry. Cut into small cube-size pieces. Heat oil in a large skillet. Add garlic and about ⅓ of the chicken. Cook over medium-high heat, stirring frequently, until cooked through. Remove and set aside. Cook remaining chicken, adding additional oil, if necessary.

Unroll pizza dough. Press into a 15x10-inch jelly roll pan that has been sprayed with cooking spray, building up the edges slightly. Spread barbecue sauce evenly over pizza dough. Spoon chicken over sauce. Sprinkle with cheese.

Bake 12 to 15 minutes or until crust is lightly browned.

tip: For a crisper crust, pre-bake dough for 6 minutes before adding topping. Even easier: Use a large purchased pizza crust and pre-cooked chicken.

Per serving: Cal 173, Carb 14, Fib 1g, Pro 19g, Fat 4g, Sod 503mg, Sug 1g

slow cooking

Beef & Salsa Dip   5½ cups

This is so good I doubt you'll have leftovers, but if you do, serve over baked potatoes for a quick and easy lunch or dinner.

- **1 pound lean ground beef**
- **16 ounces process cheese spread, cubed**
- **1 (15-oz) can creamed corn**
- **1½ cups salsa**

Brown ground beef; drain and add to slow cooker. Add cheese along with remaining ingredients. Cook on High 1 to 1½ hours or until cheese is melted and mixture is hot. Turn heat to Low, until ready to serve, stirring occasionally. Serve with chips.

Per ¼ cup: Cal 130, Carb 7g, Fib 1g, Pro 8g, Fat 8g, Sod 423mg, Sug 3g

Best-Ever Chili   6 cups

This is very good, easy to make and smells wonderful cooking in the slow cooker.

- **1½ pounds lean ground beef**
- **1½ cups coarsely chopped onion**
- **1 to 2 tablespoons chili powder (or to taste)**
- **1 (19-oz) can dark red kidney beans, drained, rinsed**
- **1 (28-oz) jar pasta sauce (I used Tomato & Basil)**
- **1 (4-oz) can chopped green chilies**

In a large skillet, brown ground beef, onion and chili powder; drain off fat. Spoon into slow cooker and add beans and pasta sauce, and chilies, stirring to mix.

Cover and cook on LOW about 4 hours or on HIGH for 2 hours.

Per cup: Cal 394, Carb 42g, Fib 13g, Pro 29g, Fat 14g, Sod 717mg, Sug 15g

Chili Beef Dish 8 servings

If you can find it in your area, my favorite brand of chili for this recipe is Cattle Drive°. It is a little bit sweet and a little bit spicy and packs a lot of flavor.

- 1½ **pounds lean ground beef**
- 1½ **cups chopped onion**
- 3 **large plum tomatoes, diced**
- 2 **(15-oz) cans chili with beans**

In a large skillet, brown ground beef and onion. Place in slow cooker. Add tomatoes and chili. Cover and cook on Low 4 to 5 hours.

Per serving: Cal 322, Carb 17g, Fib 6g, Pro 27g, Fat 17g, Sod 581mg, Sug 5g

Barbecue Ribs 4 to 5 servings

I don't know anyone who will turn down ribs. They are moist, tender and delicious cooked in a slow cooker. You may want to brush additional sauce on the ribs just before serving or pass extra sauce at the table

- 1½ **racks baby back ribs, about 20 ribs**
- **Choice of barbecue sauce**

Wash and trim ribs of excess fat. Cut into 2-rib sections. Brush both sides of ribs with barbecue sauce. Place as many ribs, meaty side out, as you can, around the pot. Place remaining ribs on the bottom, meaty side up. Cover and cook on Low 6 to 7 hours or until tender.

Per serving: Cal 710, Carb 3g, Fib 0g, Pro 46g, Fat 56g, Sod 392mg, Sug 2g

Chili Roast   8 servings

Serve with steamed vegetables and bread or baked potato.

- **1   (4-lb) beef pot roast**
- **1   (1-oz) package dry onion soup mix**
- **1   (12-oz) jar sweet chili sauce**
- **1   (12-oz) can regular cola flavored soda pop**

Place roast in slow cooker. In a small bowl combine soup mix, chili sauce and cola. Pour over roast, cover and cook on low for 7 to 8 hours or until roast is tender.

Per serving: Cal 514, Carb 18g, Fib 0g, Pro 43g,, Fat 28g, Sod 1526mg, Sug 15g

Lemon Pepper Roast   4 servings

- **1   2½ to 3 pound chuck roast**
- **½   teaspoon seasoned salt**
- **½   teaspoon lemon pepper**
- **¼   teaspoon paprika**
- **1   cup beef broth**

Sprinkle meat with the combined mixture of salt, pepper and paprika. Place in slow cooker. Add beef broth. Cover and cook on High about 4 ½ to 5 hours or until meat is tender.

note: Beef or chicken bouillon cubes are excellent substitutes for canned broth. They are economical to use and often even more flavorful than some of the canned brands we find today. If gravy is desired, thicken liquid with a mixture of about   cup flour dissolved in   cup water. Add enough flour mixture to thicken gravy to desired consistency. To quickly dissolve flour: place water in a small jar, add flour and cover. Shake jar until flour and water are well mixed.

Per serving: Cal 542, Carb 0g, Fib 0g, Pro 68g, Fat 28g, Sod 534mg, Sug 0g

Stroganoff Meatballs

4 to 6 servings

This recipe is only as good as the meatballs you use. There are very good ones you can purchase fresh or frozen and then there are those that aren't so good. Of course, you can always make your own.

- 1 (14½-ounces) can beef broth
- ¼ cup flour
- 1 cup chopped onion
- 2 tablespoons butter, melted
- 30 precooked meatballs, fresh or frozen
- 1 cup sour cream

Combine beef broth and flour in slow cooker, whisking until smooth. Add onion, butter and meatballs. Cover and cook on Low 4 to 5 hours.

Add sour cream and stir until blended. Cook on High 30 minutes. Serve on rice over noodles.

Per serving: Cal 451, Carb 17g, Fib 1g, Pro 27g, Fat 29g, Sod 522mg, Sug 3g

Ground Beef and Beans

10 servings

- 1½ pounds lean ground beef
- 1½ cups chopped onion
- 1 (1.15-lbs) can pork and beans
- 1 (14-oz) can whole tomatoes, drained
- ½ cup firmly packed light brown sugar
- ½ cup ketchup

In a large skillet, brown ground beef and onion; drain. Place in slow cooker.

Cut tomatoes into small pieces and add to pot. Stir in remaining ingredients. Cover and cook on Low 6 to 7 hours.

Per serving: Cal 300, Carb 34g, Fib 5g, Pro 20g, Fat 10g, Sod 647mg, Sug 14g

Beef and Barley Casserole

8 servings

- 1½ **pounds lean ground beef**
- ½ **to 1 cup chopped onion**
- 1½ **cups pearl barley**
- 1 **(10¾-oz) can condensed cream of celery soup**
- 1 **(10¾-oz) can condensed cream of mushroom soup**
- 1 **(5-oz) can water chestnuts, chopped**

In medium skillet, brown ground beef and onions; drain. Place in slow cooker. Add remaining ingredients along with 3 soup cans of water. Cover; cook on low 6 to 7 hours, or until liquid is absorbed and barley is tender.

note: You may wish to add salt & pepper to taste, or top with cheddar cheese when serving.

Per Serving: Cal 398, Carb 43g, Fib 6g, Pro 22g, Fat 16g, Sod 598mg, Sug 3g

Meat Loaf Dijon

6 servings

- 1½ **pounds lean ground beef**
- ⅓ **cup crushed crackers**
- ½ **cup finely chopped onion**
- ⅓ **cup ketchup**
- 1 **tablespoon Dijon mustard**
- 1 **large egg**

In a large bowl, combine all ingredients until well mixed. Place in slow cooker and form into a round about the size of the bottom of the pot. Cook on Low 5 to 6 hours. Temperature should reach no less than 160°F.

Per serving: Cal 285, Carb 7g, Fib 0g, Pro 26g, Fat 17g, Sod 288mg, Sug 4g.

Cuts of beef and pork such as roast, ribs and chops do not need to be browned before slow cooking-although browning will add more flavor and seal in juices.

Ground meats must be cooked before adding to slow cooker. Precooking ensures food safety temperatures, allows you to drain off fat and liquids and prevents clumping. If time is an issue you can precook the ground meat the night before, store in refrigerator overnight and place in slow cooker the next morning along with other ingredients.

Stuffed Green Peppers   4 to 6 servings

- 1½ **pounds lean ground beef**
- 1¼ **cups chopped onion**
- 1 **teaspoon salt**
- ½ **cup cooked long-grain rice**
- 4 **medium green peppers**
- 1 **(8-oz) can tomato sauce**

In large skillet, brown ground beef and onion; drain. Add salt and rice and mix well.

Meanwhile, cut top off the green peppers and remove seeds. Place in slow cooker. Fill with ground beef mixture, spooning remaining meat around the peppers. Pour tomato sauce over top. Cover and cook on Low 4 to 5 hours or until peppers are tender when pierced with a fork.

Per serving: Cal 340, Carb 23g, Fib 3g, Pro 27g, Fat 15g, Sod 658mg, Sug 5g

Broccoli Ham Casserole
4 servings

I have to tell you, this taste a lot better than it looks. But it is a tasty way to use up that last bit of ham and broccoli you may have in the refrigerator.

- 1 (10¾-oz) can condensed cream of mushroom soup
- 1 cup milk
- 1 cup diced ham
- 2 cups broccoli florettes
- 1 cup uncooked instant rice
- 8 ounces process cheese spread, cubed

Place soup in slow cooker and gradually whisk in the milk until smooth. Add remaining ingredients. Cover and cook on Low 3½ to 4 hours. If possible, stir mixture half way through the cooking time.

Per serving: Cal 296, Carb 23g, Fib 1g, Pro 16g, Fat 15g, Sod 967mg, Sug 5g

Pork Chops in Orange Sauce
4 servings

- 4 thick loin cut pork chops
  Lemon pepper
- 1 teaspoon oil
- 1 large orange
- ¼ cup orange marmalade
- ½ cup ketchup

Sprinkle pork chops lightly with lemon pepper. Brown in oil and place in slow cooker.

From the orange you will need ½ cup orange juice and 1 teaspoon orange peel. Then combine with marmalade and ketchup and pour over pork chops. Cover and cook on Low 6 to 8 hours or until meat is tender.

Per chop: Cal 211, Carb 24g, Fib 1g, Pro 13g, Fat 8g, Sod 384mg, Sug 21g

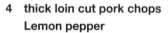

Ham & Pasta Parmesan   6 servings

The most time consuming part of this recipe is cooking the pasta. The rest is easy.

- **12 ounces linguine**
- **¼ cup butter**
- **½ cup heavy cream**
- **⅓ cup sliced green onions, green part**
- **1 cup diced ham**
- **½ cup grated Parmesan cheese**

Cook pasta according to package directions. Rinse and drain. Add pasta and butter to sprayed slow cooker and toss to melt the butter. Add remaining ingredients along with ½ cup water.

Cover. Cook on LOW until heated through but probably no longer than an hour, or it will tend to get a little dry. If this should happen, stir in additional cream.

Per serving: Cal 416, Carb 43g, Fib 2g, Pro 16g, Fat 20g, Sod 138g, Sug 3g

Sausage Rice Casserole   8 to 10 servings

Variations of this recipe have been around for as long as I can remember. Making it in the slow cooker will free you to do other things.

- **1½ pounds sausage**
- **2 cups chopped celery**
- **1 cup chopped onion**
- **¼ cup slivered almonds**
- **2 (4.2-oz) packages chicken noodle soup mix**
- **1 cup uncooked long-grain rice**

In a large skillet, brown sausage until almost cooked through. Add celery and onion and cook until almost soft; drain. Place in slow cooker.

Add remaining ingredients along with 4 cups of water. Cover and cook on Low 4 to 4½ hours or until liquid is absorbed and rice is tender.

Per serving: Cal 280, Carb 28g, Fib 2g, Pro 9g, Fat 15g, Sod 714mg, Sug 3g.

Sherried Chicken
4 servings

- **10**   **chicken legs**
- **1**   **medium onion, sliced**
- **4**   **ounces fresh mushrooms, sliced**
- **½**   **cup dry sherry**
- **1**   **teaspoon Italian seasoning**

Place onion and mushrooms in slow cooker. Top with chicken legs; add sherry and sprinkle with seasoning. Cover and cook on Low 7 to 8 hours or until chicken is tender.

Per serving: Cal 229, Carb 2g, Fib 0g, Pro 31g, Fat 10g, Sod 111mg, Sug 1g

Rosemary Chicken
4 servings

- **1**   **3 to 4 pound chicken**
- **4**   **medium potatoes**
- **1**   **teaspoon olive oil**
- **1**   **teaspoon dried rosemary**

Cut potatoes into 1½-inch chunks, and place in slow cooker. Add ½ cup water. Place chicken over potatoes. Brush with oil and sprinkle with rosemary. Cover and cook on Low 7 to 8 hours or until chicken is cooked through. Watch carefully after 6 hours.

Per serving: Cal 490, Carb 21g, Fib 2g, Pro 44g, Fat 25g, Sod 134mg, Sug 1g

Remember

Slow cookers can vary quite a bit as far as their cooking times. We have found that the newer ones cook at a higher temperature and faster than the older ones. Each time you make a new recipe, note the cooking time and write it down.

Chicken Italian with Rice

4 servings

I prepare this recipe so often in the oven that I decided to try it in the slow cooker. How convenient on days when I am out of the house for just a few hours.

- **4** **large chicken breast halves, skinned and boned**
- **1** **cup uncooked long-grain rice**
- **1** **(.65-oz) package Italian dressing mix**
- **1** **(10¾-oz) can condensed cream of chicken soup**

Place rice in slow cooker. Combine dressing mix and soup. Gradually stir in 1¾ cup water; pour over rice. Place chicken over top. Cover and cook on Low 3½ to 4 hours or until rice is tender.

Per serving: Cal 421, Carb 50g, Fib 1g, Pro 39g, Fat 6g, Sod 673mg, Sug 3g

Cranberry Chicken

4 to 6 servings

Don't omit the coconut. It is that extra touch that really makes the difference.

- **4** **to 6 chicken breast halves, skinned and boned**
- **1** **(16-oz) can whole-berry cranberry sauce**
- **1** **Golden Delicious apple, chopped**
- **1** **teaspoon curry powder**
- **⅓** **cup chopped pecans or walnuts**
- **⅓** **cup Angel Flake coconut**

Place chicken in slow cooker. Combine cranberry sauce, apple and curry; pour over chicken. Cover and cook on Low 3½ to 4 hours. Add nuts. Pass coconut at table.

Per serving: Cal 380, Carb 35g, Fib 3g, Pro 35g, Fat 11g, Sod 118mg, Sug 23g

Cooked Chicken

When you need a lot of cooked chicken for casseroles, salad and soups, it is so easy to just cook it in your slow cooker.

Chicken breasts or parts, with skin
Salt and pepper
2 **stalks celery, cut up**
½ **cup chopped onion**
2 **carrots, cut up**

Place chicken in slow cooker. Sprinkle with salt and pepper. Add remaining ingredients. Add 2 to 4 cups of water to cover the chicken. Cover and cook on Low 4 to 5 hours or until cooked through.

Per 4-oz white meat: Cal 187, Carb 0g, Fib 0g, Pro 35g, Fat 4g, Sod 83mg, Sug 0g
Per 4-oz dark meat: 217, Carb 0g, Fib 0g, Pro 31g, Fat 10g, Sod 103mg, Sug 0g

Garlic Chicken & Potatoes   4 servings

The aroma of this dish cooking will entice everyone into the kitchen.

1 **chicken, cut up**
4 **medium potatoes, peeled and quartered**
8 **large garlic cloves**
¼ **cup butter, melted**
¼ **cup honey**
½ **teaspoon lemon pepper**

Rinse chicken and pat dry. Place potatoes in slow cooker. Arrange chicken over top. Add garlic. Drizzle butter and honey over chicken. Sprinkle with lemon pepper. Cover and cook on Low 5 to 5½ hours or until chicken is tender and potatoes are cooked through.

note: Remove thin, paper-like skin from garlic cloves, but do not peel.

Per serving: Cal 582, Carb 29g, Fib 2g, Pro 43g, Fat 31g, Sod 217mg, Sug 11g

Curried Chicken 4 servings

To Serve: Curries cry out for an accompaniment of something sweet such as a chutney, coconut, peanuts, green onion, raisins, orange pieces, etc. Serve over rice with accompaniments on the side.

- 4 **chicken breast halves, skinned and boned**
- ¼ **cup butter, melted**
- ¼ **cup honey**
- 2 **tablespoons prepared mustard**
- ½ **teaspoon curry powder**
- ½ **teaspoon salt**

Place chicken in slow cooker. Combine remaining ingredients and pour over chicken. Cover and cook on Low 3 to 4 hours or until chicken is cooked through.

Per serving: Cal 351, Carb 17g, Fib 0g, Pro 34g, Fat 15g, Sod 570mg, Sug 16g

Florentine Salmon 4 servings

Serve with Garlic Mashed Potatoes, sautéed yellow squash and a Caesar Salad and you have an easy and delicious company meal.

- 4 **(6-oz) salmon fillets**
- 2 **tablespoons butter**
- ¾ **cup sliced small mushrooms**
- ⅓ **cup sliced green onions**
- ½ **bunch fresh spinach**
- ⅓ **cup dry white wine**

In a large skillet, quickly sauté mushrooms and onions in the butter. Add spinach and toss to mix. Cook mixture until spinach is just slightly wilted.

Cut a long slit in top of each fillet and spread slightly. Fill pockets with spinach mixture. Place in a sprayed slow cooker and add the wine. Cover and cook on Low 1½ to 2 hours or until salmon tests done.

Per serving: Cal 413, Carb 3g, Fib 1g, Pro 39g, Fat 25g, Sod 166mg, Sug 0g

Easy Barley Casserole

6 servings

I really should cook barley more often. This recipe is easy to prepare, quite delicious and inexpensive. You can serve it with just about anything in place of rice or potatoes.

- **1 cup pearl barley**
- **2 tablespoons butter**
- **¾ cup chopped onion**
- **⅓ cup slivered almonds**
- **3 cups chicken broth**

Rinse barley and drain. Melt butter in medium skillet. Add barley, onion and almonds. Cook until lightly browned. Place in slow cooker, add chicken broth, cover and cook on Low 4½ to 5 hours or until barley is tender and most of the liquid is absorbed.

Per serving: Cal 153, Carb 22g, Fib 3g, Pro 3g, Fat 6g, Sod 399mg, Sug 2g

Ground Beef and Cheese Soup

7 cups

Everyone in my family was amazed by this delicious soup. They didn't think they liked process cheese, but they loved this recipe.

- **1 pound ground beef**
- **⅔ cup chopped onion**
- **2 cups cubed potatoes**
- **1 cup peas**
- **1 cup corn**
- **16 ounces process cheese spread, cubed**

Brown ground beef and onion in a large skillet; drain. Place in slow cooker. Add potatoes and 2 cups water. Cook on Low 8 to 10 hours.

Add corn and peas and cook about 20 minutes, or until heated through.

Add cheese cubes, and cook 5 to 10 minutes or until melted. Stir to blend.

note: The soup may be quite thick when reheated. You can thin with milk or broth. Potatoes take a long time to cook in a slow cooker. To shorten the cooking time, you can partially cook the potatoes before adding to the slow cooker.

Per cup: Cal 413, Carb 24g, Fib 3g, Pro 27g, Fat 23g, Sod 1031mg, Sug 8g

Potato-Corn Chowder 7 cups

1 pound frozen O'Brien hash browns, thawed
¼ cup chopped onion
1 (15-oz) can whole corn, undrained
1 (15-oz) can creamed corn
1 (12-oz) can evaporated milk
½ teaspoon salt

Combine ingredients in slow cooker, cover and cook on Low 7 to 8 hours.

Per cup: Cal 218, Carb 36g, Fib 3g, Pro 7g, Fat 7g, Sod 513mg, Sug 11g

Veggie Cheese Soup 12 cups

1 (15-oz) can creamed corn
4 cups potatoes, cubed
1½ cups carrots, cubed
¾ cup finely chopped onion
2 (14.5oz each) cans chicken broth
16 ounces process cheese spread, cubed

Place first 5 ingredients in slow cooker. Cover and cook on Low 8 to 10 hours or until vegetables are tender. Add cheese, cover and cook until melted.

Per cup: Cal 212, Carb 24g, Fib 2g, Pro 9g, Fat 11g, Sod 931mg, Sug 7g

Who would have thought?

Entertaining and short on oven space or time?

Make mashed potatoes ahead of time and keep hot in your slow cooker. Set slow cooker on LOW, top with a tablespoon or two of butter and cover until ready to serve.

Wild Rice and Cheese Casserole   8 to 10 servings

A lot of flavor is packed into these six ingredients. It can also be turned into a main dish with the addition of cooked cubed chicken or ground beef.

2	(6-oz each) packages white and wild rice with seasoning packet
1½	cups chopped onion
1	cup chopped celery
½	cup butter, melted
8	ounces process cheese spread, cubed
1	(10¾-oz) can condensed cream of mushroom soup

Place first 5 ingredients in slow cooker.

Place soup in a medium mixing bowl and gradually add 1 cup water, whisking until smooth. Add to rice mixture along with 2 cups water. Cover and cook on Low 4 to 5 hours or until onion is soft and liquid is absorbed. Mixture will still be quite moist. If rice starts to brown around the edges, stir once or twice during cooking time.

Per serving: Cal 308, Carb 34g, Fib 1g, Pro 7g, Fat 16g, Sod 1141mg, Sug 4g

Acorn Squash   4 servings

This is what I do if acorn squash is hard to cut: with a strong knife, pierce squash deeply in 2 or 3 places. Place in microwave and heat for 1 minute. The squash should feel slightly warm. Then cut in half. It works every time.

2	small acorn squash
	Salt and pepper
	Butter

Cut squash in half lengthwise; remove seeds. Rinse with water (don't dry) and place, cut side up in slow cooker. Sprinkle lightly with salt and pepper. Cover and cook on Low 2 to 3 hours, depending on size. Remove and place a thin slice of butter in each center.

Additions after cooking:
Dot with butter and brown sugar and cook until melted.
Fill with cooked apples and pears. Sprinkle lightly with nutmeg.
Fill with hot buttered peas.

Per serving: Cal 111, Carb 22g, Fib 3g, Pro 2g, Fat 3g, Sod 100mg, Sug 5g

Company Carrots

12 servings

The slow cooker is a great way to cook carrots for a crowd. It frees up your oven, stove and warming tray. Just make sure you allow enough time for them to cook.

- 3 **pounds carrots, sliced diagonally into ½-inch slices**
- ¼ **cup packed light brown sugar**
- 1 **teaspoon salt**
- ½ **teaspoon cracked black pepper**
- ½ **cup butter**

Place carrots in slow cooker. Sprinkle with brown sugar, salt and pepper. Distribute butter slices over top. Cover and cook on High 4 to 5 hours. Stir carrots half way through cooking time. .Watch carefully the last hour of cooking time to ensure that the carrots aren't overcooked.

Per serving: Cal 128, Carb 15g, Fib 3g, Pro 1g, Fat 8g, Sod 329mg, Sug 9g

Baked Beans & Bacon

8 to 10 servings

I think Baked Beans were made to be cooked in a slow cooker. It is ideal for cooking in quantities and for keepimg the beans warm.

- 2 **(31-oz each) cans pork and beans**
- ½ **cup packed light brown sugar**
- 2 **teaspoons dry mustard**
- ½ **cup ketchup**
- 8 **slices bacon, cooked and crumbled**

Drain off most of the liquid from the top of the beans. Place in slow cooker along with the next three ingredients. Cover and cook on Low 5 to 6 hours. If beans are more liquid than you like, cook on High for an additional hour. Add bacon the last 30 minutes of cooking time.

Per serving: Cal 258, Carb 48g, Fib 10g, Pro 11g, Fat 5g, Sod 975mg, Sug 12g

Au Gratin Potatoes   6 servings

Potatoes take a long time to cook in a slow cooker. You may want to cook on High for the last few hours. If desired, add cooked cubed chicken or ham and serve as a main dish.

I haven't had a lot of success cooking sliced potatoes on Low in a slow cooker. They tend to take so long to cook that by the time they are tender, they often turn an ugly brown. If you have the same problem, cook your recipes on High, but watch carefully the last hour of cooking time.

8   medium potatoes, peeled (8 cups sliced)
1   (10¾-oz) can condensed cream of chicken soup
⅓   cup milk
1   teaspoon salt
¼   teaspoon pepper
1   cup (4-oz) Cheddar cheese, shredded

Place potato slices in slow cooker. Combine soup, milk, salt and pepper. Pour over potatoes. Add cheese and stir until mixed. Cover and cook on Low, 9 to 10 hours or until potatoes are tender. Stir, if possible, about half way through cooking time.

Per serving: Cal 291, Carb 47g, Fib 4g, Pro 10g, Fat 8g, Sod 521mg, Sug 3g

Baked Potatoes   4 servings

If you layer and cook more than 4 potatoes, you will need to rotate them once or twice as the bottom layer will cook faster than the top layer.

4   medium baking potatoes
    Choice of toppings

Wash potatoes, but do not dry. Place in slow cooker in one layer. (If using more potatoes, stand them on end, so each one is touching the bottom.) Cover and cook on Low 7 to 8 hours or until cooked through.

Per potato: Cal 161, Carb 37g, Fib 4g, Pro 4g, Fat 0g, Sod 17mg, Sug 2g

Baked Apples   1½ cups

You can use other baking apples than Golden Delicious, but I have found some take a little longer to bake, such as the Granny Smiths.

- **4   Golden Delicious apples**
- **1   cup apple cider**
- **¼   cup butter**
- **1   (14-oz) can sweetened condensed milk**
- **⅓   cup chopped pecans**
- **1   teaspoon rum extract**

Core apples (do not peel) and place in slow cooker. Add apple cider. Cook on Low 3½ to 4 hours or until apples are tender. Test for doneness with the thin blade of a sharp knife.

Meanwhile, melt butter in a small saucepan. Add remaining ingredients and cook over medium heat, stirring constantly, until mixture is smooth and creamy, about 8 to 10 minutes. Sauce will thicken as it cools. Reheat the sauce when ready to serve with the apples.

Per apple: Cal 67, Carb 19g, Fib 2g, Pro 0g, Fat 0g, Sod 4mg, Sug 16g,
Per 2 tbsp sauce: Cal 170, Carb 20g, Fib 0g, Pro 3g, Fat 9g, Sod 68mg, Sug 19g

Classic Rice Pudding   14 servings

For about $3 you get a large batch of delicious homemade rice pudding - and its super simple.

- **1   cup jasmine rice**
- **8   cups whole milk**
- **¼   cup butter**
- **1   cup sugar**
- **1   teaspoon vanilla**

Place rice, milk and butter in slow cooker and set on low. Cook stirring occasionally for 5-5½ hours, or until rice is soft and mixture has thickened. When done, stir in sugar and vanilla. Turn off slow cooker and stir occasionally while cooling to prevent skin from forming. When cool enough, transfer to bowl and cover with plastic wrap laying wrap on surface of pudding.

note: If desired, sprinkle with nutmeg or cardamom and/or add nuts and raisins when serving.

Per Serving: Cal 203, Carb 29g, Fib 0g, Pro 6g, Fat 8g, Sod 96mg, Sug 17g

salads, dressings & sauces

Ice Cold Salad Greens

A nice cold crisp salad is hard to beat, but sometimes hard to achieve. My favorite method for chilling salad greens works every time, but you do have to allow some chilling time in the refrigerator. Line a large bowl with several layers of paper towels. Place clean dry greens in bowl. Cover greens with 3 to 4 layers of paper towels. Cover paper towels with one layer of ice cubes. Chill at least 8 hours or overnight. Before serving, if paper towels get too wet, replace with new ones and add additional ice cubes

Romaine Artichoke Salad   8 servings

A perfect salad with almost any meal.

8	**cups romaine**
1	**(6.5-oz) jar marinated artichoke hearts, drained**
6	**tablespoons oil**
2	**tablespoons garlic red wine vinegar**
¼	**cup grated Parmesan cheese, divided**
8	**cherry tomatoes, halved**

Place romaine in a large salad bowl. Cut artichokes into smaller pieces and add to bowl.

Combine oil, vinegar and 2 tablespoons of the Parmesan. Toss salad with just enough dressing to lightly coat. Serve on salad plates. Sprinkle with remaining Parmesan and garnish with tomatoes.

Salad only: Cal 48, Carb 8g, Fib 3g, Pro 2g, Fat 2g, Sod 123mg, Sug 2g
Per 2 tbsp of dressing: Cal 134, Carb 0g, Fib 0g, Pro 1g, Fat 14g, Sod 28mg, Sug 0g

Caesar Salad 6 servings

You can't beat a really good Caesar salad. You can use purchased dressing, but if you have the time, make my Caesar Salad Dressing recipe. It can be made a day ahead and is well worth the small effort involved.

- **2 bunches romaine lettuce, torn into bite-size pieces, chilled**
  Croutons, desired amount
  Purchased Caesar salad dressing or see dressing on page 297.
  Freshly grated or shredded Parmesan cheese.

Combine romaine and croutons in a large salad bowl. Toss with just enough dressing to lightly coat. Sprinkle with Parmesan.

Nutritional analysis will vary depending on amount of dressing, croutons and cheese.

Croutons 2 cups

This is a great way to use leftover breads and is so easy I don't know why we don't make them more often. You can make them ahead and they can also be frozen.

- **2 cups (½ to 1-inch cubes) French bread**
- **1½ tablespoons olive oil**
- **3 tablespoons freshly grated Parmesan cheese**

Place bread cubes in a mixing bowl. Add olive oil as needed to lightly coat the bread - it may take more or less oil according to the type of bread used. Spread in a single layer on a baking sheet and bake 8 to 10 minutes or until crisp and lightly browned. Remove from oven and place in a mixing bowl. Toss with Parmesan cheese.

Per ½ cup: Cal 116, Carb 11g, Fib 0g, Pro 3g, Fat 6g, Sod 175mg, Sug 0g

Company Spinach Salad 6 servings

A nice touch of color for a special company dinner.

8	**cups fresh spinach**
½	**cup toasted pecan halves**
¾	**cup strawberries, sliced**
½	**cup Poppy Seed Dressing, page 299**

Combine first 3 ingredients in a large salad bowl. Toss with just enough dressing to lightly coat.

variation: Substitute ¼ cup pomegranate seeds for the strawberries.

Salad only: Cal 84, Carb 4g, Fib 2g, Pro 2g, Fat 7g, Sod 32mg, Sug 2g

Sweet-Sour Spinach Salad 4 servings

You may not be able to entice your children to eat cooked spinach, but you can serve them a salad. Just don't tell them it is spinach and they'll never know.

1	**bunch fresh spinach**
1	**tablespoon white vinegar**
1	**tablespoon sugar**
¼	**cup mayonnaise**
1	**very small red onion, thinly sliced, separated into rings**
8	**slices bacon, cooked, crumbled**

Wash spinach thoroughly and dry. Remove long stems and tear into bite-size pieces; chill. Combine vinegar, sugar and mayonnaise; chill.

When ready to serve, combine spinach, onion and bacon. Toss with just enough dressing to lightly coat. Serve immediately; greens have a tendency to get limp if allowed to sit very long.

Salad only: Cal 87, Carb 5g, Fib 2g, Pro 6g, Fat 5g, Sod 316mg, Sug 1g
2 tbsp of dressing: Cal 143, Carb 3g, Fib 0g, Pro 0g, Fat 15g, Sod 120mg, Sug 3g

Mushroom Spinach Salad

6 servings

- **1 pound spinach**
- **½ cup sliced raw mushrooms**
- **6 slices cooked bacon, crumbled**
- **1 small onion, thinly sliced and separated into rings**
- **1 hard boiled egg, chopped**
- **Vinaigrette dressing**

Combine first 4 ingredients in large salad bowl. Toss with just enough dressing to lightly coat.

Salad only: Cal 67, Carb 4g, Fib 2g, Pro 5g, Fat 4g, Sod 195mg, Sug 1g

Spinach Salad with Jicama

6 servings

Jicama is a delightful vegetable. It is crisp, slightly sweet and tastes wonderful in a salad or as a vegetable with dips. It's also great when dieting.

- **1 large bunch spinach**
- **2 medium oranges**
- **½ cup jicama, julienned**
- **⅓ cup toasted sliced almonds or pecan halves**
- **2 teaspoons dried cranberries**
- **Poppy seed dressing**

Wash spinach, remove stems and let dry. Peel oranges, slice and cut into small segments. Place in large salad bowl along with the jicama, almonds and onion. Toss with just enough dressing to lightly coat.

note: Can substitute fresh pomegranate seeds for dried cranberries.

Salad only: Cal 71, Carb 10g, Fib 3g, Pro 3g, Fat 3g, Sod 46mg, Sug 5g

Spinach Salad with Sugared Almonds

6 servings

You will love the crunch of the sliced almonds. They add that extra special touch to a salad. If you prefer a mild vinegar taste, make dressing ahead to blend flavors and to mellow somewhat

- ½ **cup sliced almonds**
- 3 **tablespoons sugar**
- ½ **cup olive oil**
- 3 **tablespoons balsamic vinegar**
- 1 **(11-oz) can mandarin oranges, well drained; save juice**
- 1 **(10-oz) package fresh spinach; remove stems**

Place almonds and sugar in small nonstick skillet over medium-low heat. Cook, stirring frequently, until sugar has melted and almonds are glazed. Watch carefully the last few minutes to prevent burning.

Combine the oil and balsamic vinegar with 2 tablespoons of the mandarin orange juice. Place oranges and spinach in a large salad bowl. Toss with dressing to lightly coat. Top with almonds.

Salad only: Cal 91, Carb 13g, Fib 3g, Pro 3g, Fat 4g, Sod 40mg, Sug 9g
2 tbsp of dressing: Cal 151, Carb 2g, Fib 0g, Pro 0g, Fat 16g, Sod 2mg, Sug 2g

Waldorf Coleslaw

8 servings

Needless to say, there are many versions of coleslaw. Everyone has their own idea of what a coleslaw should be, but the one constant is that you must use raw cabbage. You can then add your favorite combination of ingredients and your choice of dressings.

- 5 **to 6 cups shredded cabbage**
- ½ **cup dried cranberries or raisins**
- ⅓ **cup pecans**
- 1 **Golden Delicious apple, cubed**
- ¾ **cup mayonnaise**
- 2 **tablespoons sugar**

Combine first 4 ingredients in a large mixing bowl.

Combine mayonnaise and sugar until well mixed. Add to cabbage mixture and toss to coat. Cover and chill at least 30 minutes before serving.

Per serving: Cal 231, Carb 14g, Fib 2g, Pro 1g, Fat 20g, Sod 145mg, Sug 11g

Family Coleslaw 6 servings

- 4 **cups shredded cabbage**
- ½ **cup raisins**
- ½ **cup mayonnaise**
- 1 **tablespoon milk**
- 1 **tablespoon sugar**
   Salt and pepper to taste

Combine cabbage and raisins. In small mixing bowl, combine remaining ingredients and pour over cabbage; mix well. Cover and chill at least 30 minutes before serving.

Per Serving: Cal 193, Carb 15g, Fib 2g, Pro 1g, Fat 15g, Sod 180mg, Sug 13g

Honey Mustard Salad 4 servings

- ¼ **cup mild-flavored honey**
- ¼ **cup oil**
- 1 **tablespoon red wine vinegar**
- ¼ **teaspoon dry mustard**
- ⅓ **cup coarsely chopped walnuts**
- 6 **cups assorted greens**

Combine first 4 ingredients. Cover and chill. When ready to serve, combine walnuts and salad greens. Drizzle with just enough dressing to lightly coat.

Salad only: Cal 78, Carb 4g, Fib 3g, Pro 3g, Fat 7g, Sod 21mg, Sug 1g
Per 2 tbsp of dressing : Cal 167, Carb 15g, Fib 0g, Pro 0g, Fat 12g, Sod 4mg, Sug 14g

We could make a different salad everyday and still not exhaust the possibilities. Unfortunately, it is easy to get into a rut and make the same tossed green salad with perhaps a few assorted vegetables thrown in. We are also purchasing a lot of salad dressings at the store.

Commit yourself to making one new salad and one new salad dressing recipe a week. Then choose your favorites that you'll want to make again and again.

Pear & Gorgonzola Cheese Salad 6 servings

- **8**   **cups assorted salad greens**
- **1**   **small red onion, thinly sliced**
- **½**   **cup pecan halves**
-     **Purchased dressing or Raspberry Vinaigrette on page 299**
- **1**   **pear, thinly sliced**
- **6**   **tablespoons crumbled Gorgonzola cheese**

Combine salad greens, onion and pecans in a large mixing bowl. Toss with just enough dressing to lightly coat. Spoon onto plates. Arrange 2 to 3 pear slices on each salad, then sprinkle with 1 tablespoon Gorgonzola cheese.

Salad only: Cal 120, Carb 9g, Fib 4g, Pro 4g, Fat 9g, Sod 114mg, Sug 4g

Ham Salad 2 cups

Serve on a bed of lettuce as a salad or on toasted bread for a sandwich.
To make the salad go a little further, add 1 to 2 hard-boiled eggs, chopped.

- **2**   **cups (8-oz) cooked ham, ground**
- **1**   **teaspoon prepared mustard**
- **3**   **tablespoons sweet pickle relish**
- **½**   **cup diced Cheddar cheese**
- **½**   **cup mayonnaise (approximately)**

In a small mixing bowl, combine first 4 ingredients. Add enough of the mayonnaise to moisten.

Per ½ cup: Cal 340, Carb 4g, Fib 0g, Pro 20g, Fat 27g, Sod 347mg, Sug 1g

Broccoli Bean Salad   8 servings

The dressing makes the salad, so choose a brand you really enjoy, or better yet, make your own.

- **4   cups broccoli florettes**
- **4   plum tomatoes, chopped**
- **1   (8¾-oz) can garbanzo beans, drained**
- **1   small red onion, sliced**
- **1   cup (4-oz) Monterey Jack cheese, cubed**
- **¾   cup Italian style dressing**

Combine first five ingredients in a large bowl. Toss with just enough dressing to lightly coat. Cover and chill at least 2 hours.

Salad only: Cal 109, Carb 10g, Fib 3g, Pro 6g, Fat 5g, Sod 190mg, Sug 4g

Broccoli Pasta Salad   8 servings

For a main course salad, add leftover cooked roast beef, ham or chicken.

- **2   cups small shell macaroni, cooked, cooled**
- **2½   cups fresh broccoli, cooked until just tender**
- **1   cup cherry tomatoes, halved**
- **½   cup (2-oz) Swiss cheese, cubed**
- **½   cup Italian dressing**

Combine ingredients in a large bowl, using just enough dressing to lightly coat. Cover and chill.

Salad only: Cal 97, Carb 14g, Fib 3g, Pro 5g, Fat 3g, Sod 34mg, Sug 1g

Best Ever Broccoli Salad

6 servings

There are so many variations of this colorful, delicious and nutritious salad. Any of the following are delicious additions: sliced red onion, raisins, sunflower seeds, Cheddar cheese, sliced water chestnuts, almonds, dried cranberries, etc.

- 1 **large bunch broccoli (about 5 cups florettes)**
- 1 **cup (4-oz) Monterey Jack cheese, cubed**
- ½ **cup sugar**
- 1 **cup mayonnaise**
- 2 **tablespoons white vinegar**
- 8 **slices bacon, cooked and crumbled**

Place broccoli and cheese in a large bowl. Combine sugar, mayonnaise and vinegar, stirring until smooth. Pour over broccoli and mix well. Cover and chill at least 2 hours before serving, stirring occasionally. When ready to serve, add bacon and toss.

Per serving: Cal 437, Carb 15g, Fib 2g, Pro 8g, Fat 39g, Sod 548mg, Sug 12g

Carlean's Favorite Potato Salad

8 servings

For additional color, add 2 tablespoons finely chopped pimiento. If desired, decorate top of salad with egg slices and tomato wedges; sprinkle with cracked pepper.

- 6 **medium red potatoes (about 5 cups diced)**
  Salt and pepper
- 2 **tablespoons chopped green onion**
- 3 **hard-boiled eggs, chopped**
- ¼ **cup finely chopped celery**
- 1¼ **cups mayonnaise (approximately)**

Cook potatoes in boiling water just until tender. Cool slightly; peel. While still warm, dice potatoes and sprinkle with salt and pepper. Add remaining ingredients; toss gently to mix. Cover and chill several hours or overnight.

Per serving: Cal 346, Carb 26g, Fib 2g, Pro 5g, Fat 24g, Sod 253mg, Sug 2g

Waldorf Salad   4 servings

Still a favorite salad with almost everyone. For a main course salad add 2 cups cooked cubed chicken.

- 2   Golden Delicious apples cut into cubes
- 1   cup sliced celery
- ⅓   cup coarsely chopped walnuts
- ½   cup raisins
- 2   tablespoons lemon juice
- ¾   cup mayonnaise

Combine first 5 ingredients in mixing bowl. Add mayonnaise and gently toss to coat. Chill until ready to serve.

Per serving: Cal 464, Carb 27g, Fib 3g, Pro 3g, Fat 40g, Sod 298mg, Sug 22g

Taco Salad   4 servings

- 1   pound lean ground beef
- 1   (1¼-oz) package Taco seasoning mix
-      Shredded lettuce
-      Shredded Cheddar cheese
-      Chopped tomatoes
-      Salsa (or Thousand Island Dressing)

In medium skillet brown ground beef; drain. Add seasoning mix and amount of water called for on package. Bring to a boil; reduce heat and simmer uncovered, 15 to 20 minutes, stirring occasionally, until liquid is absorbed.

Place shredded lettuce in salad bowl; top with ground beef, cheese, tomatoes and salsa. Toss lightly and serve.

variation: For a unique twist add chopped jicama, corn and a drizzle of barbeque sauce

Per serving of taco meat only: Cal 42, Carb 5g, Fib 0g, Pro 2g, Fat 1g, Sod 536mg, Sug 0g

Pecan Chicken Salad 2 servings

This recipe works wonderfully as a salad, a sandwich or to fill cream puffs, croissants and cantaloupe halves.

- **2** **cups cubed cooked chicken**
- **½** **cup pecan halves, broken in half**
- **⅓** **cup chopped celery**
- **½** **cup mayonnaise**

Combine ingredients, adding just enough mayonnaise to moisten. Cover and chill until ready to serve.

variation: Add ⅓ cup dried cranberries.

Per serving: Cal 278, Carb 2g, Fib 1g, Pro 17g, Fat 23g, Sod 135mg, Sug 1g

Hawaiian Chicken Salad 4 servings

I have found that men enjoy chicken salad as much as women do and this recipe is quite popular. One of our local deli's uses cooked rice as an extender, and it is quite good paired with the taste of curry.

- **4** **cups diced cooked chicken**
- **½** **cup thinly sliced celery**
- **¾** **cup crushed pineapple, drained**
- **⅓** **cup Angel Flake coconut**
- **¼** **teaspoon curry powder (or to taste)**
- **1** **cup mayonnaise**

In large mixing bowl, combine first 4 ingredients. Combine curry powder and mayonnaise. Add enough mayonnaise to chicken mixture to lightly coat. Cover and chill.

Per serving: Cal 292, Carb 7g, Fib 1g, Pro 22g, Fat 19g, Sod 198mg, Sug 6g

Pasta Herb Chicken Salad   6 servings

One of our local restaurants serves a delicious pasta salad with chicken. This recipe comes very close to the one they make.

1½   **cups cubed, cooked chicken**
2½   **cups cooked rotini pasta**
1   **head lettuce, torn into bite-size pieces**
¼   **cup grated carrots**
½   **cup sliced almonds**
   Bernstein's® Creamy Herb & Garlic Italian Dressing

Combine first 5 ingredients in a large mixing bowl. Toss with just enough dressing to lightly coat.

Per serving: Cal 345, Carb 22g, Fib 2g, Pro 17g, Fat 21g, Sod 368mg, Sug 4g

Linda's Pesto Pasta Salad   8 servings

This is a delicious combination. For a complete meal just add cooked chicken or shrimp. If desired, you may moisten with a little milk before serving.

3   **cups penne**
1   **(9-oz) can artichokes hearts, diced**
1   **cup frozen peas, thawed**
¾   **cup pesto**
¼   **cup mayonnaise**
½   **to 1 cup shredded Parmesan cheese**

Cook pasta according to directions on package. Rinse until cool and drain thoroughly. Place in a large mixing bowl and stir in remaining ingredients. Cover and chill at least 2 hours before serving.

Per Serving: Cal 356, Carb 35g, Fib 5g, Pro 13g, Fat 18g, Sod 352mg, Sug 2g

Jicama Chicken Salad   6 servings

Jicama is a very good substitute for the apples traditionally found in Waldorf Salads.

3   **cups cubed, cooked chicken**
⅓   **cup chopped celery**
¾   **cup chopped jicama**
⅓   **cup chopped walnuts**
½   **cup mayonnaise**

Combine first 4 ingredients with just enough mayonnaise to moisten. Cover and chill before serving.

Per Serving: Cal 269, Carb 3g, Fib 1g, Pro 17g, Fat 21g, Sod 163mg, Sug 2g

Broccoli-Cranberry Pasta Salad   8 servings

This salad has become another of my new favorite salads. If desired, omit the cranberries and add   cup of split cashews, just before serving.

1   **(12-oz) package rotini**
4   **cups small broccoli florets**
⅓   **cup dried cranberries**
2   **cups mayonnaise**
⅔   **cup sugar**
⅓   **cup white vinegar**

Cook pasta according to directions on package. Rinse until cool and drain thoroughly. Place in a large mixing bowl and stir in the broccoli and cranberries.

Combine remaining ingredients and stir to dissolve the sugar. Add half the dressing to the pasta mixture. Cover and chill at least 2 hours before serving.

When ready to serve, add additional dressing, if needed. Save remaining dressing for any leftover salad the next day.

note: The dressing may seem like a lot and it would be with just the broccoli, but the pasta quickly absorbs a lot of dressing.

Per Serving: Cal 612, Carb 48g, Fib 2g, Pro 6g, Fat 45g, Sod 365mg, Sug 17g

Pistachio Fruit Salad 8 servings

This delicious recipe has stood the test of time. It is the perfect accompaniment to a summer's barbecue.

- 1 **(12-oz) container frozen whipped topping, thawed**
- 1 **(3.4-oz) box pistachio instant pudding mix**
- 1 **(11-oz) can Mandarin oranges, save 3 table spoons juice**
- 1 **(17-oz) can chunky mixed fruits, drained**
- 2 **cups miniature marshmallows**

In large bowl, combine whipped topping and pudding mix with the reserved juice. Gently fold in remaining ingredients. Cover and chill.

Per serving: Cal 289, Carb 47g, Fib 1g, Pro 2g, Fat 11g, Sod 196mg, Sug 38g

Pineapple-Strawberry Salad 4 servings

With fresh fruits on hand, this salad takes just minutes to prepare.

- 1 **cup fresh pineapple chunks**
- 1 **pint strawberries**
  Lettuce leaves
- 2 **tablespoons oil**
- 2 **tablespoons lime juice**
- 1 **tablespoon honey**

Combine pineapple and strawberries; place on lettuce leaves on salad plates. Combine remaining ingredients and drizzle over fruit.

Per Serving Cal 129, Carb 17g, Fib 2g, Pro 1g, Fat 7g, Sod 5mg, Sug 13g

Strawberries & Cream Salad 6 servings

Make sure your sour cream is at room temperature. If you have a little difficulty blending in the sour cream, use a rotary beater or a mixer at low speed.

- **1 (3-oz) box strawberry gelatin**
- **1 cup boiling water**
- **1 cup sour cream, room temperature**
- **1 (10-oz) package frozen strawberries, thawed**

Combine gelatin and water; stir to dissolve. Stir in sour cream until blended. Add strawberries. Pour into serving dish or mold and chill until set.

Per serving: Cal 148, Carb 18g, Fib 1g, Pro 3g, Fat 7g, Sod 53mg, Sug 16g

Strawberry Nut Salad 8 servings

A simple version of a very old recipe. Don't plan on having any left-over's.

- **1 (3-oz) box strawberry gelatin**
- **½ cup boiling water**
- **1 (10-oz) package frozen strawberries, thawed**
- **1 (13-oz) can crushed pineapple (and juice)**
- **2 medium bananas, mashed**
- **½ cup chopped walnuts**

Combine gelatin and water, stirring to dissolve. Add remaining ingredients. Pour into a 5 cup mold or 11x7-inch glass dish. Chill until set.

Per serving: Cal 154, Carb 27g, Fib 2g, Pro 3g, Fat 5g, Sod 26mg, Sug 21g

Lemon Fruit Salad   8 servings

The celery adds a nice crunch, but can be omitted.

- **1 (6-oz) box lemon gelatin**
- **1 cup boiling water**
- **2 cups lemon-lime soda**
- **½ cup raspberries**
- **½ cup sliced strawberries**
- **⅓ cup thinly sliced celery**

Thoroughly dissolve gelatin in boiling water. Add soda. Chill until consistency of unbeaten egg white.

Fold in fruit and celery. Pour into an 11x7-inch glass baking dish. Chill until set.

Per Serving: Cal 110, Carb 27g, Fib 1g, Pro 2g, Fat 0g, Sod 86mg, Sug 25g

All Seasons Fruit Bowl   6 servings

- **6 canned pear halves, chilled**
- **3 medium bananas, sliced**
- **2 small apples, cubed**
- **2 (11-oz) cans Mandarin oranges, chilled**
- **1½ cups sliced strawberries**
- **1 (4-oz) container frozen whipped topping, thawed**

When ready to serve, drain fruit. Slice pears. Combine with remaining ingredients and toss gently to coat.

variation: Sour cream can be substituted for the whipped topping, if desired.

Per serving: Cal 225, Carb 46g, Fib 6g, Pro 2g, Fat 5g, Sod 14mg, Sug 35g

Peachy Fruit Salad   8 servings

You shouldn't have a problem getting your children to eat this delicious "fruity" salad.

- **1 (6-oz) box strawberry gelatin**
- **4 cups boiling water, divided**
- **1 cup thinly sliced peaches**
- **½ cup thinly sliced bananas**
- **½ cup thinly sliced strawberries**

Combine gelatin and 2 cups water. Stir until dissolved. Add remaining 2 cups water. Chill until consistency of unbeaten egg white. Gently fold in fruit. Pour into 13x9-inch glass dish; chill until firm.

Per serving: Cal 97, Carb 23g, Fib 1g, Pro 2g, Fat 0g, Sod 49mg, Sug 22g

Orange Sherbet Salad 8 servings

We serve this at many family gatherings. Often we make the Pudding Fruit Salad (below), do not freeze, and place it in the center of this salad after unmolding.

1   (6-oz) box orange gelatin
1   pint orange sherbet, softened
2   (11-oz) cans Mandarin oranges save juice
1   (8-oz) can crushed pineapple, save juice
1   cup whipping cream, whipped

Pour juice in measuring cup; add water to make 2 cups. Heat to boiling in saucepan. Remove from heat; add gelatin and stir until dissolved. Add sherbet; stir until melted. Chill until just slightly thickened.

Add Mandarin oranges and pineapple; fold in whipped cream. Pour into a ring mold or 11x7-inch glass dish. Chill until set.

Per serving: Cal 279, Carb 42g, Fib 2g, Pro 4g, Fat 12g, Sod 81mg, Sug 38g

Pudding & Fruit Salad 8 servings

This fruit salad is a hit with children (adults too). If you choose not to freeze the salad (my favorite), it is best served same day made.

1   (3.4-oz) box instant vanilla pudding mix
2   cups milk
1   (4-oz) container frozen whipped topping, thawed
1   (11-oz) can Mandarin oranges, drained
1   (16-oz) can fruit cocktail, drained
3   bananas, sliced

Prepare pudding mix with milk as directed on package. Stir in whipped topping. Add the remaining ingredients. Pour into an 11x7-inch glass dish. Cover and freeze. Remove from freezer 1 hour before serving. Or, instead of freezing, place in refrigerator and chill at least 2 hours before serving.

Per serving: Cal 213, Carb 42g, Fib 3g, Pro 3g, Fat 5g, Sod 203mg, Sug 33g

Creamy Caesar Dressing 1½ cups

- 1 **medium garlic clove**
- ¼ **cup fresh lemon juice**
- 1 **tablespoon Dijon mustard**
- 1 **teaspoon Worcestershire sauce**
- ½ **cup freshly grated Parmesan cheese**
- 1 **cup mayonnaise**

Combine first 4 ingredients in a blender or small food processor and process until mixed. (You can do this by hand if you mince the garlic first.) Add cheese and mayonnaise and process just until blended. Cover and chill at least one hour to allow flavors to blend.

note: If you are in a hurry, use the minced garlic that comes in a jar. ½ teaspoon = 1 clove

Per 2 tbsp: Cal 144, Carb 1g. Fib 0g, Pro 1g, Fat 15g, Sod 170mg, Sug 0g

Red Wine Garlic Dressing ¾ cup

A sweet-sour type dressing that makes a delicious salad mixed with Romaine, red onion, mandarin oranges and toasted walnuts or pecans. This is the dressing I use most often for company. The Poppy Seed Dressing is a close second.

- ¼ **cup sugar**
- 1 **garlic clove, thinly sliced**
- ⅓ **cup red wine vinegar**
- ⅓ **cup olive or vegetable oil**

Combine ingredients and chill at least two hours to blend flavors. Remove garlic slices before tossing dressing with the salad.

Per 2 tbsp: Cal 126, Carb 6g, Fib 0g, Pro 0g, Fat 12g, Sod 0mg, Sug 6g

Dijon Vinaigrette   1¾ cup

This dressing is convenient to make ahead and chill.

- **1¼   cups vegetable oil**
- **⅓   cup Dijon mustard**
- **⅓   cup garlic red wine vinegar**
- **¼   teaspoon freshly ground black pepper**

Place ingredients in a 2 cup jar or plastic container. Cover tightly and shake until blended. Will keep about one week.

Per 2 tbsp: Cal 173, Carb 0g, Fib 0g, Pro 0g, Fat 20g, Sod 74mg, Sug 0g

Caesar Salad Dressing   1¼ cup

This is my favorite Caesar salad dressing. You can make it several hours ahead. If desired, add anchovies to taste or toss the salad with anchovies.

- **2   large garlic cloves**
- **1   tablespoon stone ground or Dijon mustard**
- **1   teaspoon Worcestershire sauce**
- **¼   cup fresh lemon juice**
- **½   cup olive oil**
- **½   cup freshly grated Parmesan cheese**

Combine first 4 ingredients in a blender or small food processor and mix until smooth. Slowly add olive oil until blended. Add cheese and blend 2 to 3 seconds. Chill, covered, at least two hours to blend flavors.

Per 2 tbsp: Cal 114, Carb 1g, Fib 0g, Pro 1g, Fat 12g, Sod 60mg, Sug 0g

Honey Mustard Dressing   1 cup

This dressing is very good on a tossed salad or a salad with pasta, chicken, lettuce and artichoke hearts. Dressing can be thinned with 1 to 2 teaspoons of milk, if necessary.

- 1 **cup mayonnaise**
- 1 **tablespoon sugar**
- 1 **tablespoon prepared mustard**
- 1 **tablespoon honey**
- 1 **teaspoon fresh lemon juice**
  Dash of salt and pepper or to taste

Combine all ingredients and beat with a whisk until well mixed. Cover and chill until ready to serve.

Per 2 tbsp: Cal 212, Carb 3g, Fib 0g, Pro 0g, Fat 22g, Sod 245mg, Sug 3g

French Dressing   ¾ cup

This dressing is good on almost any green salad.

- ⅓ **cup vegetable oil**
- 2 **tablespoons red wine vinegar**
- 2 **tablespoons ketchup**
- ¼ **cup sugar**
- ¼ **teaspoon salt**

Combine ingredients in a jar or small container with a tight fitting lid. Shake well to blend and dissolve sugar. Chill until ready to serve.

Per 2 tbsp: Cal 131, Carb 7g, Fib 0g, Pro 0g, Fat 12g, Sod 152mg, Sug 7g

Raspberry Vinaigrette   ½ cup

A sweet-tart type of dressing. Can be made in just minutes and chilled until ready to use.

- 2   tablespoons sugar
- ¼   teaspoon salt
- 1   teaspoon Dijon mustard
- 3   tablespoons raspberry wine vinegar
- ⅓   cup olive oil

Combine all ingredients and mix thoroughly.

Per 2 tbsp: Cal 185, Carb 6g, Fib 0g, Pro 0g, Fat 19g, Sod 162mg, Sug 5g

Asian Dressing   1 cup

My favorite dressing to serve on a salad of shredded lettuce, cooked cubed chicken or bacon, and toasted almonds.

- ¼   cup sugar
- 1   teaspoon salt
- ½   teaspoon freshly ground black pepper
- 6   tablespoons rice wine vinegar
- ½   cup vegetable oil

Combine ingredients in a jar and shake to mix thoroughly. Let stand to dissolve the sugar.

Per 2 tbsp: Cal 141, Carb 6g, Fib 0g, Pro 0g, Fat 14g, Sod 291mg, Sug 5g

Poppy Seed Dressing   1¼ cup

This popular recipe seems to be a hit with children as well as adults. The flavor is wonderful teamed with a spinach or romaine salad combined with some fruit, toasted nuts and pomegranate seeds.

- 1   tablespoon finely chopped onion
- 6   tablespoons sugar
- ½   teaspoon dry mustard
- 3   tablespoons white vinegar
- ½   cup vegetable oil
- ½   teaspoon poppy seeds

Combine ingredients in a small bowl or jar and mix thoroughly. Cover and chill at least one hour to blend flavors. Let stand at room temperature 30 minutes before using.

Per 2 tbsp: Cal 146, Carb 7g, Fib 0g, Pro 0g, Fat 14g, Sod 5g, Sug 7g

Thousand Island Dressing ¾ cup

Do try this recipe. It is so much better than any purchased dressing I have tried.

- ½ cup mayonnaise
- ¼ cup whipping cream
- 2 tablespoons finely chopped pimiento
- ¼ cup chopped sweet pickles or pickle relish
- 1 tablespoon finely chopped onion
- ⅓ cup chili sauce

Combine ingredients and chill to blend flavors.

Per 2 tbsp: Cal 195, Carb 7g, Fib 0g, Pro 0g, Fat 18g, Sod 609mg, Sug 4g

Roquefort Dressing 4 cups

This is a large recipe, but will keep several weeks in the refrigerator. May also be used as a dip with fresh vegetables or chips.

- 8 ounces Roquefort cheese
- 1 (12-oz) can evaporated milk
- 1 quart mayonnaise
- 2 small garlic cloves, minced

Combine Roquefort and milk in top of double boiler. Cook over low heat until cheese is melted, stirring until blended and smooth. Add mayonnaise and garlic. Cover and chill overnight to blend flavors.

Per 2 tbsp: Cal 240, Carb 1g, Fib 0g, Pro 2g, Fat 25g, Sod 318mg, Sug 1g

Spinach Salad Dressing ⅓ cup

A delicious dressing when combined with 1 bunch fresh spinach, thinly sliced red onion rings and cooked crumbled bacon or sliced mushrooms. If using spinach, add to salad and serve immediately.

- 1 tablespoon sugar
- 1 tablespoon white vinegar
- ¼ cup mayonnaise

Combine ingredients and mix well. Chill to mix flavors and dissolve sugar. Add dressing to salad just before serving.

Per 2 tbsp: Cal 163, Carb 3g, Fib 0g, Pro 0g, Fat 17g, Sod 136mg, Sug 3g

Creamy Mustard Dressing   1½ cup

This is a wonderful dressing for anyone who is on a low-carb diet. Just one carbohydrage gram per 2 tablespoons of dressing.

- ¼ **cup Dijon mustard**
- ¾ **teaspoon dried dill weed**
- ¼ **cup tarragon wine vinegar**
- 1 **cup oil**
- 1 **tablespoon Half & Half**
- 1 **tablespoon grated Parmesan cheese**

Combine mustard, dill weed and vinegar. Gradually add oil, whisking after each addition until blended. Stir in Half & Half and Parmesan.

Per 2 tbsp: Cal 164, Carb 0g, Fib 0g, Pro 0g, Fat 19g, Sod 69mg, Sug 0g

Sweet Onion Dressing   1 cup

This dressing is especially good on spinach salads and has an added bonus of keeping several days in the refrigerator.

- ½ **cup olive oil**
- ¼ **cup cider vinegar**
- ¼ **cup finely chopped onion**
- ½ **teaspoon prepared mustard**
- ½ **teaspoon salt**
- 1 **tablespoon sugar**

Combine ingredients, mixing well to blend. Chill until ready to use.

Per 2 tbsp: Cal 137, Carb 3g, Fib 0g, Pro 0g, Fat 14g, Sod 78mg, Sug 3g

Chicken Salad Dressing   1 cup

This makes a wonderful dressing for almost any chunky style chicken salad.

- ⅔ **cup mayonnaise**
- ⅓ **cup sour cream**
- 1 **teaspoon lemon juice**
- ½ **teaspoon salt**
- ¼ **teaspoon pepper**

Combine ingredients and mix well.

Per 2 tbsp: Cal 152, Carb 0g, Fib 0g, Pro 0g, Fat 16g, Sod 269mg, Sug 0g

White Sauce (Béchamel) 2 cups

Sauce	Butter	Flour	Salt	Pepper	Milk
Thin	2 tbsp.	2 tbsp.	1 tsp.	1/4 tsp.	2 cups
Medium	4 tbsp.	4 tbsp.	1 tsp.	1/4 tsp.	2 cups
Thick	8 tbsp.	8 tbsp.	1 tsp.	1/4 tsp.	2 cups

Melt butter in a heavy saucepan over low heat. Stir in flour, salt, and pepper until well blended. Remove from heat. Add milk all at once and stir until blended. Return to heat and cook, stirring constantly, until thickened and smooth.

Clarified Butter 1½ cups

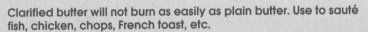

Clarified butter will not burn as easily as plain butter. Use to sauté fish, chicken, chops, French toast, etc.

    1 pound butter

Melt butter in a small saucepan. Pour melted butter into a glass measuring cup; let stand. Skim off foam. Carefully pour off butter and discard the milky sediment that accumulates on the bottom. Refrigerate and use as needed.

Crème Fraîche 2 cups

Cream Fraiche is good served over fresh fruit, especially strawberries, and over fruit desserts and molded salads. It can be sweetened and flavored with vanilla. In some recipes, it can also be substituted for sour cream, and will not curdle if brought to a boil

    1 cup heavy whipping cream
    1 cup sour cream

Combine heavy cream and sour cream in a small bowl. Cover loosely with plastic wrap and let stand at room temperature, overnight or until thickened. Bowl should be placed in a warm area of the kitchen.

Cover and refrigerate until well-chilled before serving.

Per 2 tbsp: Cal 81, Carb 1g, Fib 0g, Pro 1g, Fat 8g, Sod 13mg, Sug 1g

Chocolate Sauce Supreme 2½ cups

Keep this sauce on hand during the cold winter months when hot chocolate and snow are a match made in heaven. You can also use this recipe for delicious chocolate milk and of course as an ice cream topping.

- **2 cups heavy cream**
- **2 cups semisweet chocolate chips**

Pour cream into a heavy medium saucepan. Over medium heat, bring to a boil. Remove from heat; add chocolate chips and stir quickly until chocolate is melted and sauce is smooth.

Pour into a container; cover and store in refrigerator. Mixture will thicken as it cools.

Hot Chocolate: Spoon about 4 tablespoons chocolate sauce (or to taste) in a 12-ounce mug. Fill with milk and microwave about 1½ minutes or until desired temperature.

tip: For best results use a good brand of chocolate chips. Do not use ultra-pasteurized cream or milk chocolate chips.

Per 2 tbsp: Cal 163, Carb 11g, Fib 1g, Pro 1g, Fat 14g, Sod 11mg, Sug 9g

Caramel Sauce 3¼ cups

Yum! This is so good and also makes a wonderful fondue sauce.

- **½ cup butter**
- **¾ cup light corn syrup**
- **1 (14-oz) can sweetened condensed milk**
- **1½ cups packed brown sugar**

Combine ingredients in a heavy medium saucepan. Cook over medium heat, stirring frequently, until sugar is dissolved. This should take about 8 to 10 minutes.

Per 2 tbsp: Cal 152, Carb 27g, Fib 0g, Pro 1g, Fat 5g, Sod 56mg, Sug 28g

Orange Cream Cheese   1¼ cups

Serve with crackers, muffins, French toast or pancakes. Also good with fruit.

- 1 (8-oz) package cream cheese, softened
- ¾ cup sifted powdered sugar
- 1 tablespoon frozen orange juice concentrate
- 1 tablespoon grated orange peel
- 1 tablespoon Grand Marnier Liqueur

In a mixer bowl, beat the cream cheese until smooth. Add remaining ingredients and mix until blended. Cover and chill.

Per 2 tbsp: Cal 130, Carb 13g, Fib 0g, Pro 2g, Fat 8g, Sod 67mg, Sug 12g

Honey Butter   ¾ cup

To substitute, use fresh lemon peel for the orange peel. Serve on breads and French toast.

- ½ cup butter
- ¼ cup honey
- 2 teaspoons freshly grated orange peel

Whip butter until fluffy. Gradually add honey and orange peel; mix until blended.

Per 2 tbsp: Cal 179, Carb 12g, Fib 0g, Pro 0g, Fat 15g, Sod 113mg, Sug 11g

Peanut Dipping Sauce   1½ cups

Serve with chicken kabobs.

- 1 (14-oz) can coconut milk
- ¼ cup creamy peanut butter
- 1 tablespoon brown sugar
- Juice of 1 lime

In a small saucepan, combine all ingredients. Simmer over medium heat stirring frequently about 20 minutes or until sauce thickens.

Per 2 tbsp: Cal 128., Carb 5g,. Fib 1g, Pro 2g, Fat 12g, Sod 34mg, Sug 3g

Orange-Cranberry Relish   2 cups

This relish makes a wonderful gift during the holidays. Spoon into small decorative jars and tie with raffia or ribbon.

1¾   cups (6-oz) fresh cranberries, coarsely chopped
1   (18-oz) jar orange marmalade
2   tablespoons Grand Marnier

Combine ingredients in a medium saucepan. Cook on medium heat, stirring occasionally until cranberries are soft, about 10 to 15 minutes.

Per 2 tbsp: Cal 91, Carb 23g, Fib 1g, Pro 0g, Fat 0g, Sod 18mg, Sug 21g

Chunky Applesauce   5 cups

You'll never want to buy applesauce again. See Slow Cooking section to make it in your slow cooker.

5   large Golden Delicious apples, about 12 cups
5   large Rome apples
¾   cup sugar
½   teaspoon cinnamon
    Dash ginger
5   large strips orange peel

Peel, core and slice apples into ¼ to ½-inch slices. Put apples and remaining ingredients in a large heavy stockpot. Add ½ cup water. Cover and simmer 45 to 60 minutes or until apples are just tender. Don't let the apples get too soft, unless you prefer them that way. Remove from heat and discard orange peel. Let cool. Store in refrigerator.

Per cup: Cal 244, Carb 69g, Fib 8g, Pro 1g, Fat 0g, Sod 5mg, Sug 58g

Family Favorite Barbecue Sauce 1¾ cups

- ½ cup firmly packed brown sugar
- 1 cup ketchup
- 2 tablespoons Worcestershire sauce
- 1 tablespoon prepared mustard
- ¼ cup fresh lemon juice

Combine ingredients and let stand at least an hour to blend flavors. Serve at room temperature.

note: If making the recipe ahead, cover and store in the refrigerator.

Per 2 tbsp: Cal 46, Carb 12g, Fib 0g, Pro 0g, Fat 0g, Sod 232mg, Sug 11g

Cheese Sauce 2 cups

This sauce is absolutely delicious served over baked potatoes. Pass the sauce and let everyone pour their own.

- 3 tablespoons butter
- 3 tablespoons flour
- 1 cup milk or half and half
- ½ cup (2-oz) Cheddar cheese, shredded
- ½ cup (2-oz) American cheese, shredded
- 1 to 2 tablespoons Sherry

Melt butter in saucepan; stir in flour and cook 2 minutes, but do not allow to brown. Remove from heat and add milk; stir until smooth. Cook over low heat, stirring constantly, until thickened.

Add cheese and sherry; stir until cheese is melted and sauce is hot, but do not allow to boil.

Per 2 tbsp: Cal 66, Carb 2g, Fib 0g, Pro 2g, Fat 5g, Sod 106mg, Sug 0g,

Tartar Sauce 1 cup

Some people like tartar sauce with their French Fries. Personally, I think I'll stick with ketchup.

- ¾ **cup mayonnaise**
- 1 **teaspoon finely chopped or grated onion**
- 1 **tablespoon finely chopped fresh parsley**
- 1 **tablespoon finely chopped sweet pickle**

Combine ingredients; cover and chill at least 1 hour to blend flavors.

Per 2 tbsp: Cal 152, Carb 1g, Fib 0g, Pro 0g, Fat 17g, Sod 147mg, Sug 0g

Mustard Sauce 1¼ cups

Serve with ham. Can make day ahead and store in refrigerator until ready to use.

- 1 **cup whipping cream, whipped**
- ½ **cup mayonnaise**
- ¼ **cup prepared mustard**

Combine ingredients; cover and chill at least 2 hours to blend flavors.

Per 2 tbsp: Cal 162, Carb 1g, Fib 0g, Pro 1g, Fat 18g, Sod 171mg, Sug 0g

Whole Berry Cranberry Sauce
4 cups

Fresh cranberry sauce is so much better than any sauce purchased in a can. Do try it and I think you will agree with me. Leftover sauce can be frozen. We make this every Thanksgiving.

- **1 pound fresh whole cranberries**
- **2 cups sugar**
- **½ cup apricot jam or preserves**
- **¼ cup fresh lemon juice**

Wash cranberries; discard the not so good ones. In a large saucepan, combine sugar and ¾ cup water. Bring to a boil and cook 3 to 4 minutes. Add cranberries and cook 6 to 8 minutes. Cranberries will burst, cause a popping sound and will become transparent.

Remove from heat and stir in apricot jam and lemon juice. Cover and chill before serving. Mixture will be a little thin but will thicken as it cools.

Per 2 tbsp: Cal 51, Carb 14g, Fib 1g, Pro 0g, Fat 0g, Sod 0g, Sug 13g

Snappy Horseradish Sauce
¾ cup

For that special dinner, fill large mushroom caps with sauce; garnish with finely chopped chives or green onions and bake at 325°F for 10 to 15 minutes. Serve on dinner plate with prime rib, roast beef, etc.

- **½ cup sour cream**
- **¼ cup mayonnaise**
- **1½ teaspoons prepared horseradish**
- **¼ teaspoon onion salt**
- **¼ teaspoon garlic salt**

Combine ingredients and mix thoroughly. Cover and chill at least 1 hour to blend flavors.

Per 2 tbsp: Cal 107, Carb 1g, Fib 0g, Pro 1g, Fat 11g, Sod 142mg, Sug 1g

Pizza Sauce   1 cup

If you run out of pizza sauce and don't want to make a special trip to the store, this makes a very good substitute.

- ¼ **teaspoon garlic powder**
- ¼ **teaspoon oregano**
- ½ **teaspoon basail**
- ½ **cup grated Parmesan cheese**
- 1 **(8-oz) can tomato sauce**

In a small mixing bowl, combine all the ingredients and mix well.

Per 2 tbsp: Cal 22, Carb 2g, Fib 1g, Pro 1g, Fat 1g, Sod 191mg, Sug 1g

Portobello Steak Sauce   4 servings

This is just one of several ways that you can prepare portobello mushrooms. They take on an almost meaty texture and can be purchased in your local supermarkets. Serve this recipe over flank steak, grilled steaks or ground beef patties.

- 2 **tablespoons vegetable oil or butter**
- 2 **large portobello mushrooms**
- 1 **bunch green onions**
- ½ **cup beef broth**
- 2 **tablespoons Sherry**

Heat oil in a large skillet. Meanwhile, cut portobellos in half, then in slices. Cut green onions into 1-inch slices. Cook mushrooms and onions in oil, over medium heat, until just tender, 5 to 6 minutes. Add broth and Sherry and bring to a boil.

variation: Substitute a variety of mushrooms for the portobellos.

Per serving: Cal 91, Carb 5g, Fib 1g, Pro 2g, Fat 7g, Sod 164mg, Sug 1g

Mock Hollandaise Sauce 1 cup

So easy. Serve warm over cooked asparagus, broccoli, or green beans. Can be made ahead and reheated.

- ½ **cup sour cream**
- ½ **cup mayonnaise**
- 2 **teaspoons fresh lemon juice**
- 1 **teaspoon prepared mustard**

In a small saucepan, combine all the ingredients and cook over very low heat until heated through.

Per 2 tbsp: Cal 130, Carb 1g, Fib 0g, Pro 1g, Fat 14g, Sod 107mg, Sug 1g

Easy Bordelaise Sauce about 2 cups

Excellent served with steaks or beef fondue. Especially nice with beef tenderloin.

- 4 **tablespoons minced shallots (or onion)**
- 4 **tablespoons butter, divided**
- 2 **bay leaves, finely crumbled**
- 1 **cup Burgundy wine**
- 5 **teaspoons cornstarch**
- 1½ **cups canned condensed beef broth or bouillon (undiluted)**

In saucepan, sauté shallots in 2 tablespoons of the butter until tender but not browned. Add crumbled bay leaves and wine; simmer over medium heat until reduced to about one-third its original volume.

Combine cornstarch and about ¼ cup beef broth, mixing to form a smooth paste. Stir into wine mixture along with remaining beef broth. Cook, stirring frequently, until sauce thickens. Add remaining 2 tablespoons butter.

Per 2 tbsp: Cal 41, Carb 3g, Fib 0g, Pro 0g, Fat 3g, Sod 275mg, Sug 2g

Marinades

Easy Beef Marinade

Use to marinate sirloin, chuck and flank steak.

Combine ingredients; pour over meat and marinate, in refrigerator, several hours or overnight, turning occasionally.

- ¼ **cup soy sauce**
- ¼ **cup oil**
- 2 **tablespoons fresh lemon juice**
- 1 **tablespoon sugar**
- ¼ **teaspoon garlic salt**
- ⅔ **teaspoon oregano**

Ginger Marinade

A good marinade for beef, pork or chicken.

Combine ingredients; pour over meat and marinate, in refrigerator, several hours or overnight, turning occasionally.

- ⅓ **cup soy sauce**
- ⅓ **cup packed brown sugar**
- 2 **tablespoons white vinegar**
- 1½ **tablespoons Worcestershire sauce**
- 1 **tablespoon olive oil**
- 3 **slices fresh ginger**

Herb Marinade

A good marinade for fish, chicken and meats.

Combine ingredients; pour over meat and marinate, in refrigerator, several hours or overnight, turning occasionally.

- ¼ **cup oil**
- 2 **tablespoons lemon juice**
- 1½ **tablespoons dry red wine**
- 1 **teaspoon dried thyme**
- 1 **medium garlic clove, minced**
- ¼ **teaspoon pepper**

Sweet and Sour Sauce ¾ cup

Serve with chicken nuggets, chicken wings, egg rolls, etc.

- 1 (6-oz) can pineapple juice
- ¼ cup apple cider vinegar
- ¼ cup finely packed brown sugar
- 1 tablespoon cornstarch

Combine ingredients in a small pan. Mix well to dissolve the sugar and cornstarch.

Cook over medium heat until mixture thickens, stirring frequently with a whisk.

Per 2 tbsp: Cal 53, Carb 14g, Fib 0g, Pro 0g, Fat 0g, Sod 2mg, Sug 8g

Stir-Fry Sauce ¼ cup

- 1 teaspoon cornstarch
- ¾ teaspoon sugar
- 1½ teaspoons wine vinegar
- 2 teaspoons water
- 2½ tablespoons soy sauce
  Dash Tabasco

Combine ingredients and mix well. Use as a stir-fry sauce for: beef, pork, chicken, vegetables, etc.

Per 1 tbsp: Cal 100, Carb 29g, Fib 0g, Pro 1g, Fat 0g, Sod 823mg, Sug 28g

Brown Gravy

1 cup

Use this recipe to make a gravy when you haven't cooked a roast. Additional seasonings such as minced onion, garlic powder, celery salt, etc. can be added. If a darker gravy is desired, stir in a few drops of Kitchen Bouquet.

- 2 **tablespoons butter**
- ½ **teaspoon sugar (for browning)**
- 2 **tablespoons flour**
- 1 **cup beef broth**
  Salt and pepper

Melt butter in saucepan over low heat. Add sugar; cook 2 minutes, stirring occasionally. Add flour; cook about 3 minutes or until flour is lightly browned. Add broth, stirring until smooth. Add salt and pepper to taste. Cook over low heat 5 minutes, stirring frequently until thickened.

Per 2 tbsp: Cal 36, Carb 2g, Fib 0g, Pro 1g, Fat 3g, Sod 170mg, Sug 0g

Orange-Raisin Ham Sauce

2 cups

A delicious relish-jam recipe to serve on breads or with pork or ham. When in season, freeze fresh cranberries and you can prepare the relish year 'round.

- ⅔ **cup orange juice**
- 2 **tablespoons cornstarch**
- ⅛ **teaspoon ground allspice**
- ½ **cup orange marmalade**
- 1 **cup raisins**

In small saucepan, combine first 3 ingredients along with 1 cup water. Heat, stirring constantly, until mixture thickens. Stir in marmalade and raisins and heat through.

Per 2 tbsp: Cal 65, Carb 17g, Fib 1g, Pro 0g, Fat 0g, Sod 7mg, Sug 14g

Turkey Gravy   4 cups

If you don't have 4 cups turkey stock, add chicken broth or water to make up the difference. If gravy is too thin, stir in additional flour mixed with a small amount of water or stock. Add diced cooked turkey to leftover gravy. Reheat and serve over mashed potatoes, rice or noodles.

- ½ **cup fat drippings**
- ½ **cup flour**
- 4 **cups turkey stock (from turkey or from cooking giblets)**
- **Salt and pepper**

Remove turkey from oven and pour meat juices into a large measuring cup. Fat will rise to the top. Pour off ½ cup fat into a medium saucepan. Discard remaining fat, but save the turkey stock.

Reheat the drippings over medium heat. Stir in flour and cook until lightly browned. Add 4 cups turkey stock. Cook over medium heat, stirring frequently, until thickened and smooth. Season with salt and pepper.

Per 2 tbsp: Cal 37, Carb 2g, Fib 0g, Pro 0g, Fat 3g, Sod 93mg, Sug 0g

Roast Pan Gravy   2 cups

- ¼ **cup fat from roast**
- ¼ **cup flour**
- 2 **cups liquid (meat juices plus water or broth)**
- **Salt and pepper**

Remove roast and keep warm. Pour meat juices into a large measuring cup, leaving crusty bits in pan. Skim off fat, reserving 4 tablespoons. Return reserved fat to pan and heat until bubbly. Stir in flour. Cook over low heat, stirring frequently, until mixture is thickened.

Remove pan from heat. Add 2 cups liquid all at once; stir to mix well. Return to heat and bring to a boil. Reduce heat and simmer 3 to 4 minutes, stirring frequently until thickened. Add salt and pepper to taste.

Per 2 tbsp: Cal 34, Carb 2g, Fib 0g, Pro 1g, Fat 3g, Sod 132mg, Sug 0g

vegetables

Stir Fry Asparagus   4 servings

This recipe is delicious with broccoli as well.

- **1   pound fresh asparagus**
- **2   tablespoons oil**
- **⅛   inch slice fresh ginger**
- **2   teaspoons soy sauce**
- **¼   cup chicken broth or bouillon**
- **½   teaspoon cornstarch**

Wash asparagus and break end off where it snaps easily. Cut diagonally into 1-inch pieces. Place in rapidly boiling water; remove from heat and let stand 4 minutes. Drain.

Heat oil in a large skillet or wok. Add ginger and sauté about 1 minute; remove. Add asparagus to skillet and heat through.

Meanwhile, combine remaining ingredients in a small bowl, stirring to dissolve the cornstarch. Add to asparagus and simmer 2 to 3 minutes or until asparagus is just crisp tender.

Per serving: Cal 96, Carb 6g, Fib 3g, Pro 3g, Fat 7g, Sod 282mg, Sug 3g

Hazelnut Asparagus   4 servings

- **1   pound asparagus, trimmed**
- **1   tablespoon butter**
- **2   tablespoons chopped hazelnuts**
- **¼   teaspoon dried basil**
- **⅛   teaspoon ground pepper**
- **2   tablespoons grated Parmesan cheese**

Heat ¼ cup water in a medium skillet. Add asparagus and cook on medium-high heat 4 to 6 minutes or until just crisp-tender. Drain. Remove and set aside.

Add butter to skillet and sauté hazelnuts until lightly toasted. Return asparagus to skillet; season with basil and pepper and heat through. Place on serving plate and sprinkle with Parmesan.

Per serving: Cal 85, Carb 6g, Fib 3g, Pro 3g, Fat 5g, sod 43mf, Sug 3g

Asparagus with Butter Sauce
4 servings

A colorful green vegetable is the perfect side dish for your favorite family or company meal.

- **1 pound fresh asparagus**
- **1 cup chicken broth**
- **3 tablespoons butter**
- **3 tablespoons sliced almonds**

Wash asparagus; break off where it snaps easily. Place in medium skillet. Add chicken broth and bring to a boil. Reduce heat, cover and cook 6 to 8 minutes or until just crisp tender.

Meanwhile, lightly toast almonds in butter. Remove asparagus from skillet and drain. Place in serving dish and cover with butter sauce.

Per serving: Cal 139, Carb 6g, Fib 3g, Pro 4g, Fat 11g, Sod 314mg, Sug 3g

Tender Asparagus Insurance

Take fresh asparagus and trim 1 to 2-inches from ends. Place upright in a pitcher or bowl and add about 3-inches of water. Let stand in refrigerator for a minimum of 1 hour or until ready to use (can be kept for several days). Stems will soak up water and become tender.

Asparagus & Red Peppers
4 servings

This is a colorful dish to serve for the holidays, but equally as good year 'round.

- **1¼ pounds fresh asparagus**
- **½ small red peppers cut into narrow strips**
- **1 tablespoon butter**
- **Dash of freshly ground black pepper**
- **1 teaspoon freshly grated**
- **Parmesan cheese**

Wash asparagus; snap off ends where they break easily. Place asparagus and pepper strips in steamer basket. Cover; steam over hot water, 5 to 7 minutes or until just crisp tender.

Place in serving dish. Gently toss with butter. Sprinkle with pepper and Parmesan.

Per serving: Cal 67, Carb 7g, Fib 3g, Pro 3g, Fat 3g, Sod 25mg, Sug 3g

Snappy Company Beans
4 servings

- **1 pound cooked green beans or 2 cans (14.5-oz) drained**
- **⅓ cup chopped onion**
- **3 tablespoons butter**
- **1 tablespoon prepared horseradish**
- **1 tablespoon prepared mustard**

In medium skillet, cook onion in butter until soft. Add horseradish and mustard. Add green beans and toss to coat. Cook until heated through.

variation: Add sliced mushrooms or water chestnuts.

Per serving: Cal 99, Carb 5g, Fib 2g, Pro 1g, Fat 8g, Sod 463mg, Sug 3g

Green Beans with Almonds
4 servings

- **1 pound cooked green beans or 2 (14.5 oz) cans drained**
- **⅓ cup thinly sliced celery**
- **¼ cup slivered almonds**
- **2 tablespoons butter**
- **Salt and pepper**

In medium skillet, sauté celery and almonds in butter until celery is tender and almonds are toasted.

Add beans and heat through. Add salt and pepper to taste.

Per serving: Cal 108, Carb 5g, Fib 3g, Pro 2g, Fat 9g, Sod 454mg, Sug 2g

German Style Green Beans

4 servings

- 4 slices bacon
- 1 tablespoon finely chopped onion
- 2 tablespoons red wine vinegar
- 1 tablespoon sugar
- 1 pound cooked green beans or 2 (14.5-oz) cans drained

In a small skillet, cook bacon until crisp. Drain, leaving 1 tablespoon of drippings in pan. Add onion and cook until tender.

Stir in vinegar and sugar. Crumble bacon and add along with the green beans. Cook until heated through.

Per serving: Cal 84, Carb 6g, Fib 2g, Pro 3g, Fat 6g, Sod 460mg, Sug 4g

Fresh green beans are usually preferred over canned, that is, if you can find some that are fresh. Unfortunately, by the time most of us find them at the supermarket, they may be several days old. Check out your local farmer's market and produce stands.

Easy Baked Beans

6 servings

An addition of an 8-oz can of crushed pineapple is good. If you have the time, cook and crumble bacon ahead and add to the beans.

- 2 (16-oz) cans pork and beans
- ½ cup firmly packed light brown sugar
- 1 teaspoon dry mustard
- ½ cup ketchup
- 6 slices bacon, diced

Preheat oven to 325°F. Combine beans, brown sugar, mustard and ketchup. Pour into a sprayed 1½-quart casserole. Top with bacon. Bake 1 to 1½ hours.

Per serving: Cal 270, Carb 51g, Fib 9g, Pro 10g, Fat 5g, Sod 984mg, Sug 20g

Broccoli with Pecan Dressing

8 servings

I love to serve this recipe with ham, mashed potatoes, a favorite jello salad and homemade rolls. A real company pleaser.

- 7 **cups broccoli florettes**
- ½ **cup, plus ⅓ cup butter**
- ¼ **cup flour**
- 2 **cups milk**
- ¾ **cup pecans**
- 3 **cups herb bread stuffing mix**

Preheat oven to 400°F. Steam broccoli until it starts to turn a bright green (do not cook until tender). Place in a sprayed 11x7-inch baking dish.

Heat the ½ cup butter in medium saucepan. Add flour and mix well. Cook about one minute. Add milk and stir to blend. Cook over low heat, stirring frequently, until thickened. Pour over broccoli.

Melt remaining ⅓ cup butter. Combine butter with ⅓ cup water, pecans and stuffing mix; spoon over broccoli. Bake 30 minutes or until heated through and top is golden.

Per serving: Cal 383, Carb 27g, Fib 4g, Pro 8g, Fat 28g, Sod 483mg, Sug 4g

Broccoli is Amazing

Amongst all of the commonly consumed cruciferous vegetables, broccoli stands out as the most concentrated source of a premiere antioxidant nutrient-vitamin C. Considered as a group, the vitamins, minerals, flavonoids, and carotenoids contained in broccoli work to lower risk of oxidative stress in the body.

Broccoli Can Enhance Detoxification

Broccoli Stir-Fry

4 servings

During the Christmas holidays, add one tablespoon chopped pimiento.

- 4 **cups cut broccoli, florettes and stems**
- 1 **tablespoon oil**
- 6 **thin slices fresh ginger**
- 1 **garlic clove, minced**
- 1 **teaspoon sugar**
- ½ **teaspoon salt**

Steam broccoli until tender. Heat oil in a large skillet or wok. Add ginger and garlic. Cook, stirring frequently, about a minute. Add broccoli, sugar, salt and one tablespoon water. Cook, stirring frequently, until heated through.

Per serving: Cal 60, Carb 6g, Fib 2g, Pro 2g, Fat 4g, Sod 315mg, Sug 2g

Broccoli Meringue   8 servings

This is one recipe where the broccoli needs to be cooked beyond crisp-tender. It should be somewhat on the soft side.

- 5   cups broccoli florets
- 2   large egg whites, room temperature
- ¼   teaspoon salt
- ½   cup (2-oz) Edam, Cheddar, or Swiss cheese, shredded
- ½   cup mayonnaise

Microwave or steam broccoli; drain thoroughly. Place in a sprayed 8x8-inch baking dish.

Beat egg whites and salt until stiff peaks form. Fold in the cheese and mayonnaise. Spread evenly over broccoli. Broil 5 to 6 inches from heat 2 to 3 minutes or until golden brown.

Per serving: Cal 145, Carb 3g, Fib 1g, Pro 4g, Fat 14g, Sod 232mg, Sug 0g

Broccoli and vitamin D

When large supplemental doses of vitamin D are needed to offset deficiency, ample supplies of vitamin K and vitamin A help keep our vitamin D metabolism in balance. Broccoli has an unusually strong combination of both vitamin A (in the form of beta-carotene) and vitamin K. For people faced with the need to rebuild vitamin D stores through vitamin D supplements, broccoli may be an ideal food to include in the diet.

Brussels Sprouts Sauté   4 servings

This was a taste tester favorite. Not as good reheated.

- 1   pound Brussels sprouts
- ¼   cup butter
- ½   teaspoon basil
-       Salt and pepper to taste

Trim Brussels sprouts and remove outer leaves. Cut each, crosswise, into 3 or 4 slices.

Heat butter in medium skillet. Add Brussels sprouts and remaining ingredients and toss to coat. Cook 8 to 10 minutes or until just crisp-tender.

Per serving: Cal 150, Carb 10g, Fib 4g, Pro 4g, Fat 11g, Sod 186mg, Sug 3g

Red Cabbage with Balsamic Vinegar   7 servings

Adds a lot of color and flavor to your meal.

- **3 tablespoons butter**
- **¼ teaspoon caraway seeds**
- **8 cups thinly sliced red cabbage**
- **⅓ cup balsamic vinegar**

In a large skillet, melt butter and add caraway seeds and briefly stir on medium heat. Add cabbage and vinegar; stir to mix.

Sauté until half of the cabbage is slightly wilted and half is crisp. Season with salt and pepper.

variation: Substitute ¼ teaspoon whole cloves for caraway. Remove cloves before serving.

note: If desired, you may cook longer until all cabbage is soft. The flavor will be different.

Per ½ cup: Cal 71, Carb 7g, Fib 2g, Pro 1g, Fat 5g, Sod 86mg, Sug 4g

Basil Carrots   4 servings

Asparagus, broccoli or brussels sprouts can be substituted for the carrots.

- **1 pound carrots, cut diagonally into ½-inch slices**
- **2 tablespoons butter, melted**
- **2 tablespoons sliced almonds**
- **¼ teaspoon salt**
- **⅛ teaspoon pepper**
- **1 tablespoon fresh basil, chopped**

Steam carrots until tender, but still crisp.

Combine remaining ingredients. Pour over carrots, tossing to coat.

Per serving: Cal 119, Carb 12g, Fib 3g, Pro 2g, Fat 7g, Sod 246mg, Sug 7g

Carlean's Baked Carrots

4 servings

A favorite entertaining recipe

- 1 **pound carrots, sliced into ½-inch slices**
- 3 **tablespoons butter, sliced thin**
- 1 **tablespoon packed light brown sugar**
- ½ **teaspoon salt**
- ¼ **teaspoon cracked pepper**

Preheat oven to 350°F. Place carrots in a sprayed 1½-quart casserole. Distribute butter pieces over top. Sprinkle with brown sugar, salt and cracked pepper. Cover and bake 45 to 60 minutes or until carrots are tender.

Per serving: Cal 138, Carb 15g, Fib 3g, Pro 2g, Fat 8g, Sod 413mg, Sug 10g

Judy's Cauliflower Dish

6 servings

Some of our best recipes come from our friends.

- 1 **(20-oz) package frozen cauliflower, thawed**
  Salt and pepper
- 1 **cup mayonnaise**
- 1 **tablespoon prepared mustard**
- 1 **cup (4-oz) Cheddar cheese, shredded**

Preheat oven to 350°F. Place cauliflower in a sprayed 8x8-inch baking dish. Bake 8 minutes. Sprinkle with salt and pepper.

Combine mayonnaise and mustard. Spread over cauliflower. Bake 8 minutes.

Sprinkle with cheese and bake 8 to 10 minutes or until cauliflower is tender.

Per serving: Cal 367, Carb 5g, Fib 2g, Pro 7g, Fat 36g, Sod 472mg, Sug 2g

Corn Pudding 6 to 8 servings

Impressive and easy. Can be doubled for large parties.

- ¼ **cup sugar**
- 3 **tablespoons butter, softened**
- 3 **large eggs, lightly beaten**
- 3½ **cups cut fresh corn or frozen corn, thawed**
- 1½ **cup half and half**
- ½ **teaspoon salt**

Preheat oven to 350°F. In mixer bowl, cream the butter and sugar. Add eggs and mix until blended. Stir in the corn, half and half and salt. Pour into a sprayed 1½-quart casserole. Bake 40 to 45 minutes or until firm.

Per serving: Cal 198, Carb 21g, Fib 2g, Pro 6g, Fat 12g, Sod 229mg, Sug 7g

Eggplant Parmesan

For added color, top with a little marinara or spaghetti sauce.

- 1 **eggplant, about ¾-pound**
- ½ **cup dry white bread crumbs**
- 3 **tablespoons grated Parmesan cheese**
- 1 **large egg, lightly beaten**
- ½ **cup (2-oz) Mozzarella cheese, shredded**

Preheat oven to 375°F. Cut eggplant into ¼-inch slices (do not peel).

Combine bread crumbs and Parmesan. Dip eggplant in egg, then in crumb mixture. Place on sprayed baking sheet. Bake 20 to 25 minutes or until lightly browned and cooked through. Sprinkle cheese on slices and bake just until cheese is melted.

Per serving: Cal 74, Carb 7g, Fib 1g, Pro 2g, Fat 2g, Sod 176mg, Sug 1g

Sautéed Kale 4 servings

There are many reasons to include kale in our diet. It has several disease fighting components and is high in vitamin A, as well as calcium and potassium.

1	**large bunch kale, about 10 ounces**
1½	**tablespoons oil**
	Salt and pepper
2	**teaspoons fresh lemon juice**

Strip kale leaves from stems. Rinse and drain well.

Heat oil in large nonstick skillet. Add kale and cook covered for 1 minute. Uncover. Cook 1 minute or until just wilted, stirring frequently. Sprinkle lightly with salt, pepper and lemon juice.

Per serving: Cal 81, Carb 7g, Fib 2g, Pro 2g, Fat 6g, Sod 103mg, Sug 0g

Kale - another Super Food

Researchers can now identify over 45 different flavonoids in kale. With kaempferol and quercetin heading the list, kale's flavonoids combine both antioxidant and anti-inflammatory benefits in way that gives kale a leading dietary role with respect to avoidance of chronic inflammation and oxidative stress.

Okra with Onions & Tomatoes 6 servings

If you've never cooked okra before, try this recipe- it's easy and tasty!

½	**medium onion, sliced**
1	**tablespoon thinly sliced ginger**
1	**medium tomato, thinly sliced**
1	**(12-oz) package frozen okra**
2	**teaspoons paprika**

In a medium saucepan (using butter, oil or spray) sauté onions and ginger until onion begins to soften. Add remaining ingredients; stir until okra is tender. Season with salt and pepper to taste.

Per serving: Cal 57, Carb 5g, Fib 2g, Pro 2g, Fat 4g, Sod 82mg, Sug 2g

Caramelized Onions　about 2 cups

- **3　large onions (about 48-oz)**
- **1　tablespoon vegetable oil**
- **1　tablespoon butter**

Thinly slice the onions and separate into rings. In large skillet or Dutch oven, heat oil and butter and cook onions over medium heat 30 to 45 minutes, stirring frequently, especially the last 10 minutes.

note: I have found that the cooking time can vary considerably, depending on intensity of heat, size and thickness of pan used and the amount and thickness of onion slices. The time may vary to 1 hours. I prefer a medium golden color, but some prefer a dark brown color. You be the judge as to how long you want to cook them.

Per cup: Cal 396, Carb 69g, Fib 10g, Pro 6g, Fat 13g, Sod 63mg, Sug 29g

Baked Onion Blossoms　4 servings

These delicious little gems look attractive served on a plate with grilled chicken, steaks or fish. They look rather unattractive in the pan, but look nice on a dinner plate.

- **4　small sweet onions**
- **2　tablespoons butter, melted**
- **2　teaspoons Dijon mustard**
- **2　tablespoons packed brown sugar**
- **　Coarsely ground black pepper**
- **1　tablespoon chopped parsley**

Preheat oven to 350°F. Peel onions and trim, but don't cut off the root end, as this is the only thing that will hold the onion together. Cut onion almost to the root, cutting into 8 wedges. Place in a sprayed 8x8-inch baking dish.

Combine butter, mustard, and brown sugar. Pour over onions. Sprinkle lightly with pepper. Cover dish with foil and bake 30 minutes. Remove foil; baste onions with liquid. Bake 10 to 15 minutes or until tender. Remove from oven and sprinkle with parsley. Carefully lift a blossom and place on each serving plate.

Per serving: Cal 119, Carb 17g, Fib 2g, Pro 1g, Fat 6g, Sod 79mg, Sug 11g

Standard Measurements

Pinch	Less than 1/8 teaspoon
1 tablespoon	3 teaspoons
¼ cup	4 tablespoons
⅓ cup	5 tablespoons + 1 teaspoon
½ cup	8 tablespoons
1 cup	16 tablespoons
2 cups	1 pint
2 pints	1 quart
4 quarts	1 gallon

Sautéed Mushrooms   4 servings

Wonderful with steak, chicken or burgers

- 3 **tablespoons butter**
- ¼ **cup chopped onion**
- 8 **ounces mushrooms, whole or sliced**
- 1 **garlic clove, minced**
- 2 **tablespoons Worcestershire sauce**
- ¼ **cup red wine**

Heat butter in medium skillet. Add onion, garlic, Worcestershire sauce and red wine. Cook 1-2 minutes. Add mushrooms and cook until tender.

Per serving: Cal 110, Carb 5g, Fib 1g, Pro 2g, Fat 9g, Sod 158mg, Sug 3g

Scalloped Potatoes Deluxe
6 servings

This recipe is almost too easy to be so good, but it does come at a price. It is quite expensive to make and high in fat. I usually save it for special occasions. This is also an easy recipe to make for any number of servings. Just layer the dish with the desired amount of potatoes and seasonings. Add cream to almost cover. You shouldn't fill the dish too full or you will have quite a mess in your oven. If desired, you can layer the potatoes with sliced onion, separated into rings. Increase or decrease the cooking time as needed.

- 7 **medium potatoes, about 8 cups sliced**
- 2 **cups whipping cream**
  Salt and Pepper
- ¼ **cup freshly grated Parmesan cheese, divided**

Preheat oven to 450°F. Peel and slice potatoes about ¼-inch thick. Place half the potatoes in a sprayed 13x9-inch baking dish. Pour half the cream over the potatoes. Sprinkle with salt, pepper and 2 tablespoons Parmesan cheese. Layer with remaining potatoes, cream, salt, pepper and cheese. Bake about 45 minutes or until golden and potatoes are tender. Watch closely the last 15 minutes and if too brown, cover with foil.

Per serving: Cal 469, Carb 45g, Fib 4g, Pro 7g, Fat 30g, Sod 127mg, Sug 3g

Oven Roasted New Potatoes
8 servings

Serve with steaks, chicken or fish.

- 18 **small new red potatoes**
- ¼ **cup oil**
- 4 **medium garlic cloves, minced**
- 1 **tablespoon chopped fresh rosemary**

Preheat oven to 350°F. Place potatoes in a large bowl. Add remaining ingredients and toss well to mix.

Spoon into a shallow baking pan and bake 30 to 40 minutes or until potatoes are tender.

Per serving: Cal 340, Carb 62g, Fib 6g, Pro 7g, Fat 8g, Sod 25mg, Sug 5g

New Potatoes with Butter Sauce

4 servings

- **2 pounds small new potatoes, peeled**
- **¼ cup butter**
- **1½ teaspoons lemon juice**
- **Salt and pepper**
- **1 teaspoon dried parsley**

Cook whole potatoes in boiling salted water until tender, about 25 to 30 minutes.

Meanwhile, melt butter with remaining ingredients. Drain potatoes; place in serving bowl. Pour butter mixture over top.

Per serving: Cal 284, Carb 43g, Fib 4g, Pro 7g, Fat 11g, Sod 169mg, Sug 2g

Two Cheese Potatoes

6 servings

This is one of those stand-by recipes you'll want to make often. It's quick and easy to make and looks beautiful – a nice golden color.

- **4 to 5 large russet potatoes (8 cups sliced)**
- **¼ cup butter**
- **¼ cup flour**
- **2 cups milk**
- **1 cup (4-oz) Cheddar cheese, shredded**
- **½ cup grated Parmesan cheese, divided**

Preheat oven to 350°F. In a medium saucepan, melt the butter; stir in flour with a whisk. Add milk and stir until smooth. Bring to a boil over medium heat and cook, stirring frequently, until thickened. This should be about the consistency of a medium white sauce or gravy. Remove from heat. Add Cheddar cheese and ¼ cup Parmesan cheese. Stir until cheese is melted.

Layer half the potatoes and half the sauce in a sprayed 11x7-inch baking dish. Repeat with remaining potatoes and sauce. Sprinkle remaining ¼ cup Parmesan cheese over the top. Cover with foil and bake 1 hour. Remove foil and bake 30 to 40 minutes or until potatoes are tender.

Per serving: Cal 397, Carb 49g, Fib 4g, Pro 13g, Fat 16g, Sod 274mg, Sug 6g

Dinner Hash Browns   8 servings

Rich, creamy, great for family and guests.

1	(24-oz) package frozen hash browns, partially thawed
2	cups half and half
¼	cup butter
¾	teaspoon salt
⅛	teaspoon white pepper
½	cup grated Asiago cheese

Preheat oven to 325°F. Arrange potatoes in a sprayed 13x9-inch baking dish. Combine half and half, butter, salt and pepper; heat in microwave or on top of the stove until hot. Pour over potatoes. Sprinkle with the cheese. Bake 40 to 50 minutes or until golden brown.

Per serving: Cal 225, Carb 18g, Fib 1g, Pro 5g, Fat 15g, Sod 371mg, Sug 0g

Criss-Cross Potatoes   4 servings

Faster than a baked potato; savory and a kid pleaser.

2	large baking potatoes, halved lengthwise
¼	cup butter, melted
	Salt and pepper
	Paprika

Preheat oven to 450°F. Score potatoes in crisscross pattern, making cuts about 1-inch deep, without cutting through skins.

Brush with butter. Sprinkle with salt, pepper and paprika. Place on baking sheet and bake 35 minutes or until done, basting occasionally with butter.

Per serving: Cal 158, Carb 13g, Fib 2g, Pro 1g, Fat 11g, Sod 164mg, Sug 0g

Fried Rice   6 servings

This is a great dish for using leftovers such as diced pork, ham or sausage. For variety, add 1 cup bean sprouts and/or 1 can sliced water chestnuts.

1	cup uncooked long-grain rice, cooked and chilled
5	slices bacon, cut into ½-inch pieces
1	cup peas and carrots
¼	cup soy sauce
1	large egg, beaten
2	green onions, sliced

Heat large skillet or wok; add bacon and cook until partially browned. Add onion and cook, stirring occasionally, until tender but not browned. Stir in soy sauce and rice.

Push the rice to the sides; pour the egg into the middle. Cook until egg is cooked through, stirring to scramble. Stir egg into the rice along with the green onions. Cook until heated through.

Per serving: Cal 217, Carb 30g, Fib 1g, Pro 7g, Fat 8g, Sod 1018mg, Sug 2g

Cheesy New Potato Casserole   6 servings

I think garlic improves almost any dish, especially this one.

1¼	cups whipping cream
4	small garlic cloves, peeled, halved
1	pound new red potatoes, unpeeled, thinly sliced
2	tablespoons butter, diced
1½	cups (6-oz) Gruyère cheese

In a medium saucepan, heat the whipping cream and garlic and bring just to a boil. Remove and discard garlic.

Spread the potatoes evenly in a sprayed 11x7-inch baking dish. Pour cream over top. Sprinkle butter over potatoes. Sprinkle with the cheese. Bake 30 to 40 minutes or until potatoes are tender. Cover with foil if cheese is getting too brown.

tip: New red potatoes are the very small red potatoes.

variation: Add leftover ham and serve with a green vegetable and tossed salad.

Per serving: Cal 392, Carb 17g, Fib 1g, Pro 11g, Fat 31g, Sod 149mg, Sug 1g

Family Favorite Rice Dish

6 servings

Whether being served to family or friends, this flavorful rice dish never fails to please. Our family has enjoyed it for almost forty years. My daughter likes to add pecans or water chestnuts, and for a main dish she adds 12 ounces of cooked sausage.

- 1 **tablespoon vegetable oil**
- 2 **cups instant rice (do not substitute)**
- 1 **(2-oz) can sliced mushrooms**
- 1 **(10¾-oz) can condensed French onion soup**
  Dash of salt and pepper
- 1 **(8-oz) can slice water chestnuts, drained (optional)**

Preheat oven to 350°F. Heat oil in a small skillet. Add rice and cook until lightly browned, stirring frequently.

Place rice in a sprayed 1½-quart casserole dish. Add remaining ingredients along with ½ soup can of water. Bake, covered, 45 to 60 minutes or until liquid is absorbed and rice is tender.

Per serving: Cal 150, Carb 27g, Fib 1g, Pro 3g, Fat 3g, Sod 436mg, Sug 2g

Almond Rice Pilaf

6 servings

For such a simple recipe, this version of Rice Pilaf using instant rice has become one of my favorite and most often used recipes.

- 2 **tablespoons butter**
- ½ **cup finely chopped onion**
- ⅓ **cup sliced almonds**
- 2 **cups chicken broth**
- 1 **tablespoon chopped fresh parsley or 1 teaspoon dried**
- 2 **cups uncooked instant rice**

Melt butter in a medium saucepan; add onion and almonds and cook until onion is soft and almonds are just lightly browned. Add broth and parsley and bring to a boil. Stir in rice. Cover; remove from heat and let stand 6 to 7 minutes or until liquid is absorbed.

Per serving: Cal 188, Carb 26g, Fib 2g, Pro 4g, Fat 7g, Sod 366mg, Sug 1g

Almonds

A high-fat food that's good for your health? That's not an oxymoron, its almonds. Almonds are high in monounsaturated fats, the same type of health-promoting fats as are found in olive oil, which have been associated with reduced risk of heart disease.

Minted Petite Peas 4 servings

When in season, use fresh cooked peas and add a small amount of butter along with the apple-mint jelly.

- **1 (10-oz) package frozen baby peas in butter sauce**
- **¼ cup apple-mint jelly**

Cook peas according to directions. Add jelly and stir until melted

Per serving: Cal 113, Carb 23g, Fib 3g, Pro 3g, Fat 1g, Sod 232mg, Sug 15g

Spinach Stir-Fry 4 servings

Don't skimp on the spinach. I am always amazed at how much it cooks down.

- **3 bunches fresh spinach**
- **4½ tablespoons olive oil**
- **⅓ cup slivered almonds**
- **2 tablespoons soy sauce**
- **1 teaspoon sesame seeds (optional)**

Remove stems from spinach, rinse, and spin dry.

Heat oil in a large wok or Dutch oven. Add spinach and cook, stirring frequently, until leaves just start to wilt. This doesn't take long, so don't walk away from it.

Add almonds and soy sauce. Spoon into serving bowl and sprinkle with sesame seeds.

Per serving: Cal 261, Carb 12g, Fib 7g, Pro 10g, Fat 22g, Sod 861mg, Sug 2g

Crumb Baked Tomatoes

6 servings

Try to purchase the best-tasting tomatoes you can find. Of course, garden fresh tomatoes are always best.

- **6 medium tomatoes**
- **2 tablespoons honey**
- **2 slices white bread**
- **1½ teaspoons salt**
- **½ teaspoon pepper**
- **4 teaspoons butter, melted**

Preheat oven to 350°F. Remove just the core area from bottom of tomatoes. Turn over and slice off just the top of the tomatoes at the point where you will have a flat surface across. Place in a 13x9-inch baking dish. Drizzle honey over the surface of the tomatoes.

Crumble bread into very small pieces, about ¼-inch. Place in a bowl and combine with the salt, pepper and butter. Sprinkle evenly over the tomatoes.

Bake 10 to 15 minutes or until just heated through. If the bread isn't quite browned enough, place under the broiler until golden.

Per serving: Cal 88, Carb 14g, Fib 1g, Pro 2g, Fat 3g, Sod 650mg, Sug 8g

Spaghetti Squash

Serve as a substitute for pasta.

- **1 spaghetti squash**
- **2 tablespoons butter**

Preheat oven to 350°F. Cut squash in half lengthwise. Remove seeds and place, cut-side down, in a shallow pan. Add a small amount of water, about ½ cup, and bake 40 to 50 minutes or until cooked through.

With a fork, pull into strands and toss with just enough butter to lightly coat. Servings depend on the size of the squash.

Yam and Apple Casserole 12 servings

This is a large recipe, and is delicious served with turkey or ham.

- 6 **yams or sweet potatoes cooked and peeled (or use canned)**
- 6 **tart apples, peeled (such as Rome)**
- ½ **cup butter**
- 1 **cup sugar**
- 3 **tablespoons cornstarch**

Preheat oven to 350°F. Cut yams and apples into ½-inch slices. Layer in a sprayed 3-quart casserole dish, starting with apples and ending with yams.

Meanwhile, combine butter and 2 cups water in a medium saucepan and bring to a boil. Mix sugar with cornstarch; add just enough cold water to make a paste. Add to boiling water mixture, stirring constantly. Return to a boil and remove from heat. Pour over yams and bake 50 to 60 minutes or until apples are tender.

Per serving: Cal 199, Carb 45g, Fib 4g, Pro 2g, Fat 4g, Sod 292mg, Sug 25g

Zucchini Tomato Casserole 6 servings

This is an attractive dish to serve with almost anything. If you want the vegetables crisp tender, watch baking time carefully; if you prefer the vegetables soft and juicy, cook a few minutes longer.

- 2 **medium zucchini, sliced**
  Salt and pepper
- 1 **medium onion, thinly sliced**
- 1 **green pepper, thinly sliced**
- 2 **tomatoes, sliced**
- 1½ **cups (6-oz) Cheddar cheese, shredded**

Preheat oven to 350°F. Place zucchini slices in a sprayed 2-quart deep casserole dish; sprinkle with salt and pepper. Separate onion slices into rings and spread on top of zucchini. Top with green pepper rings and tomato slices. Sprinkle with cheese. Bake, uncovered 60 minutes.

Per serving: Cal 132, Carb 5g, Fib 1g, Pro 8g, Fat 10g, Sod 227mg, Sug 2g

Sweet potatoes are not low carb, but may improve the rate at which your body converts calories into energy. They contain complex carbohydrates and contribute to the creation of fat-burning muscle. Sweet potatoes are high in vitamin A, which assists your body in metabolizing carbohydrates. Experiment with them.

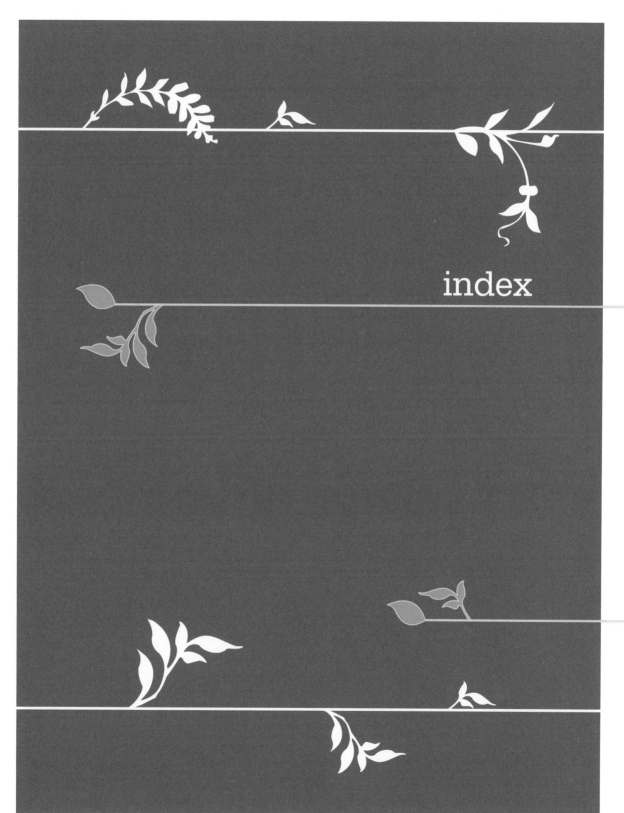

index

Chicken

S